TRACING EISENMAN

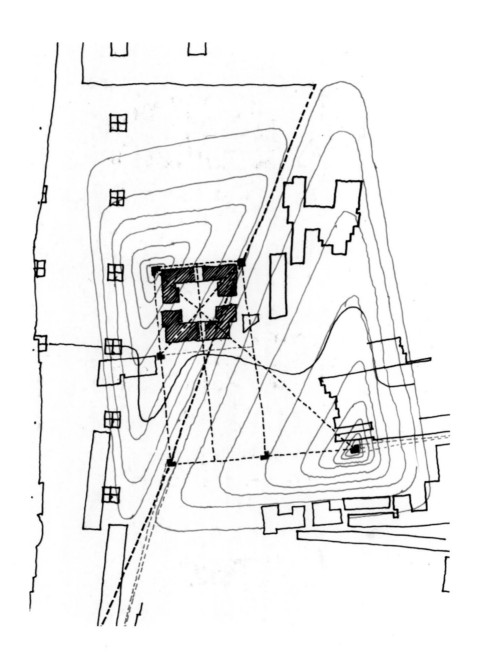

TRACING EISENMAN

PETER EISENMAN
COMPLETE WORKS

with essays by

STAN ALLEN

CYNTHIA DAVIDSON

GREG LYNN

SARAH WHITING

GUIDO ZULIANI

edited by

CYNTHIA DAVIDSON

RIZZOLI
NEW YORK

Acknowledgments

Four years in the making, *Tracing Eisenman* is the product of many contributors, not only of the architects who have worked with Peter Eisenman in the course of his long career, but also of the authors whose essays appear here, of the designers Juliette Cezzar and Michael Bierut, who developed the original design concept for the book, of Larissa Babij and Mathew Ford, who worked tirelessly to assemble the images collected here, and of Cat Green and Lucas Dietrich at Thames & Hudson, whose perseverance helped us all. – C.D.

First published in the United States of America
in 2006 by Rizzoli International Publications, Inc.
300 Park Avenue South
New York, NY 10010
www.rizzoliusa.com

Originally published in the United Kingdom in 2006
by Thames & Hudson Ltd
181A High Holborn
London WC1V 7QX

ISBN-10: 0-8478-2889-1
ISBN-13: 978-0-8478-2889-0

Library of Congress Control Number 2006925127

2006 2007 2008 2009 / 10 9 8 7 6 5 4 3 2 1

Printed and bound in China by C&C Offset Printing Co Ltd

Photo Credits

Collection Centre Canadien d'Architecture/Canadian Centre for Architecture, Montréal @ CCA: 2, 8, 20, 22, 32, 41, 44, 45, 74, 76–77, 78, 79, 113, 140, 141, 142, 143, 204, 298, 299, 300, 301, 302–303

dbox: 271, 273, 314, 376–377, 380, 381, 389, 390–391

Ben Elfrink: 354, 355

Ron Forth: 109, 159

Dick Frank Studio: 11, 16, 26, 27, 31, 34, 35, 44, 47, 53, 56, 59, 60, 62–63, 64–65, 69, 70, 73, 74, 75, 76, 79, 84, 85, 86, 99, 100, 103, 107, 121, 134, 143, 145, 146, 147, 150-151, 152, 153, 168, 169, 170, 171, 172, 173, 174, 175, 190, 192, 193, 196, 202, 203, 205, 213, 214, 215, 216, 217, 218, 219, 221, 224, 228–229, 230, 236–237, 238, 240, 241, 245, 247, 248, 249, 251, 252, 253, 281, 304, 305

Roberto Gennari: 122

Jeff Goldberg/Esto: 17, 18–19, 29, 109, 113, 114, 138, 139, 154–155, 159, 160, 161, 182, 183, 189, 195, 206, 207, 208–209

Reingard Gorner: 81, 82, 83

Roland Halbe: 7, 293, 294, 296–297, 349

Hedrich-Blessing: 263

Wolfgang Hoyt/Esto: 86–87, 88, 89

Hunt Construction: 274, 275, 276

Hertha Hurnaus: 242, 243

Dakota Jackson: 306, 307

Courtesy JC Decaux: 254, 255

Edward Keller: 222

Hermann E. Kiessling: 256

Gunter Lepkowski: 295

Jöchen Littkemann: 226, 227

Greg Lynn: 176, 177, 180–181

Norman McGrath: 37, 38–39, 43

Miller-Hare: 367

Michael Moran: 128, 129, 303

Courtesy Museo di Castelvecchio, Verona, Italy: 23, 392, 393, 395

Shigeo Ogawa/Shinkenchiku: 6, 30, 200, 202, 203

The Ohio State University Photo Archive: 112

D.G. Olshavsky/ARTOG: 10, 113, 114, 115, 116, 117, 207, 209

Paisajes Españoles S.A.: 313, 314, 317

Jack Pottle/Esto: 381

Peter Rigaud: 66–67, 71

Mark C. Schwartz: 127

Masao Ueda: 9, 162, 163, 164, 166, 167

Van der Vlugt & Claus: 198, 199

Courtesy Wexner Center for the Visual Arts, Columbus, Ohio: 114

Contents

Projects

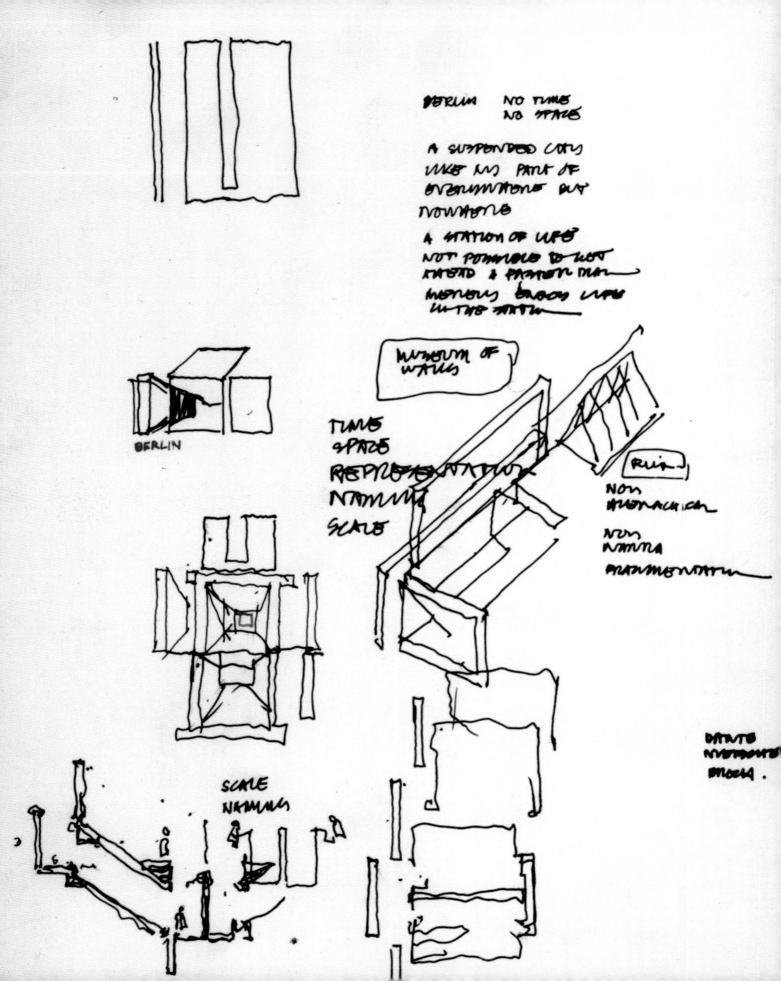

BERLIN   NO TIME
          NO SPACE

A SUSPENDED CITY
LIKE NO PART OF
EVERYWHERE BUT
NOWHERE

A STATION OF LIFE
NOT POSSIBLE TO NOT
illegible & *illegible*
illegible
illegible

MUSEUM OF
WALLS

TIME
SPACE
REPRESENTATION
NAMING
SCALE

BERLIN

RUIN

NON
illegible

NON
NAMING

illegible

SCALE
NAMING

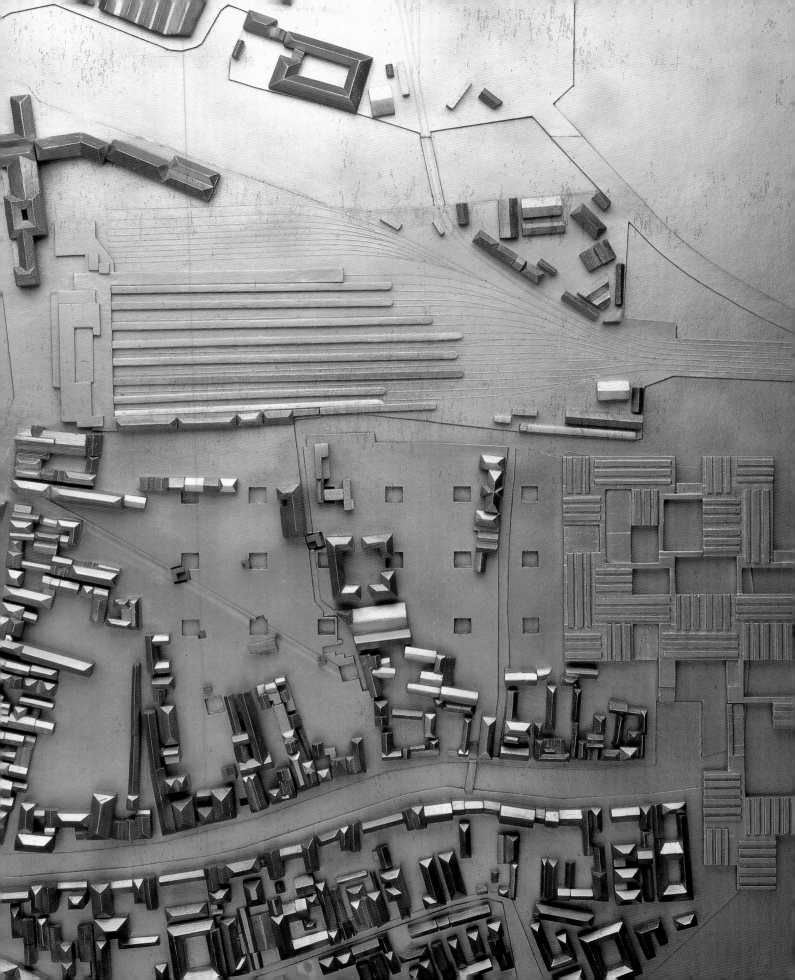

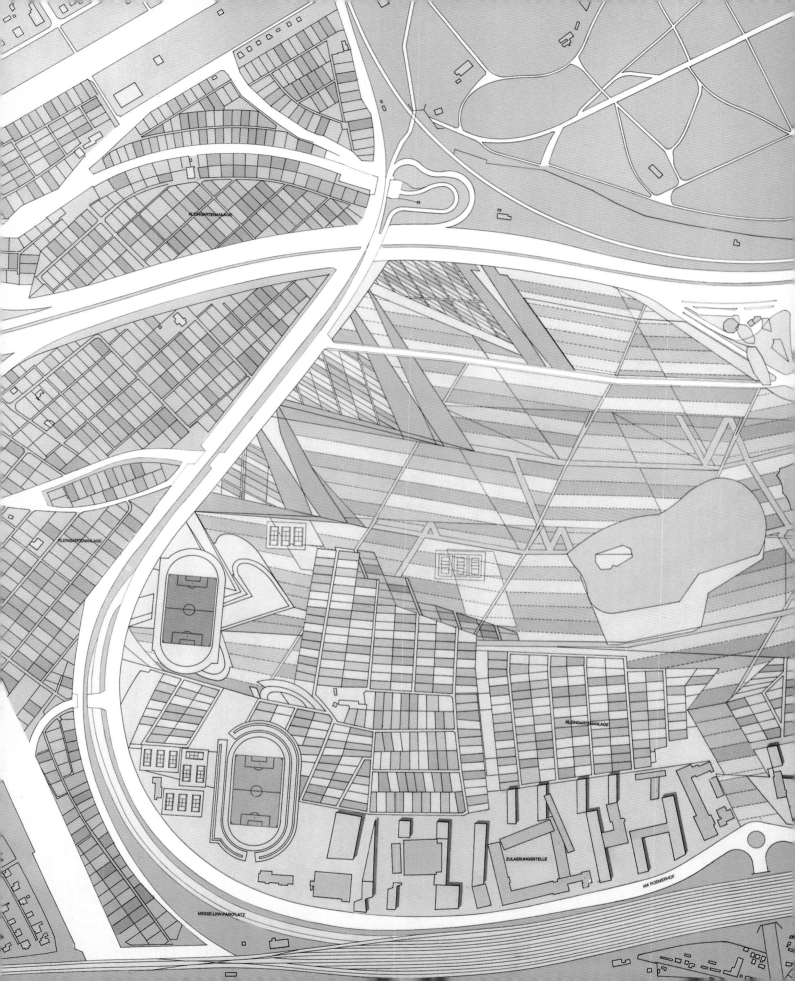

KLEINGARTENANLAGE

KLEINGARTENANLAGE

KLEINGARTENANLAGE

ZULASSUNGSSTELLE

AM ROEMERHOF

MESSE-LKW-PARKPLATZ

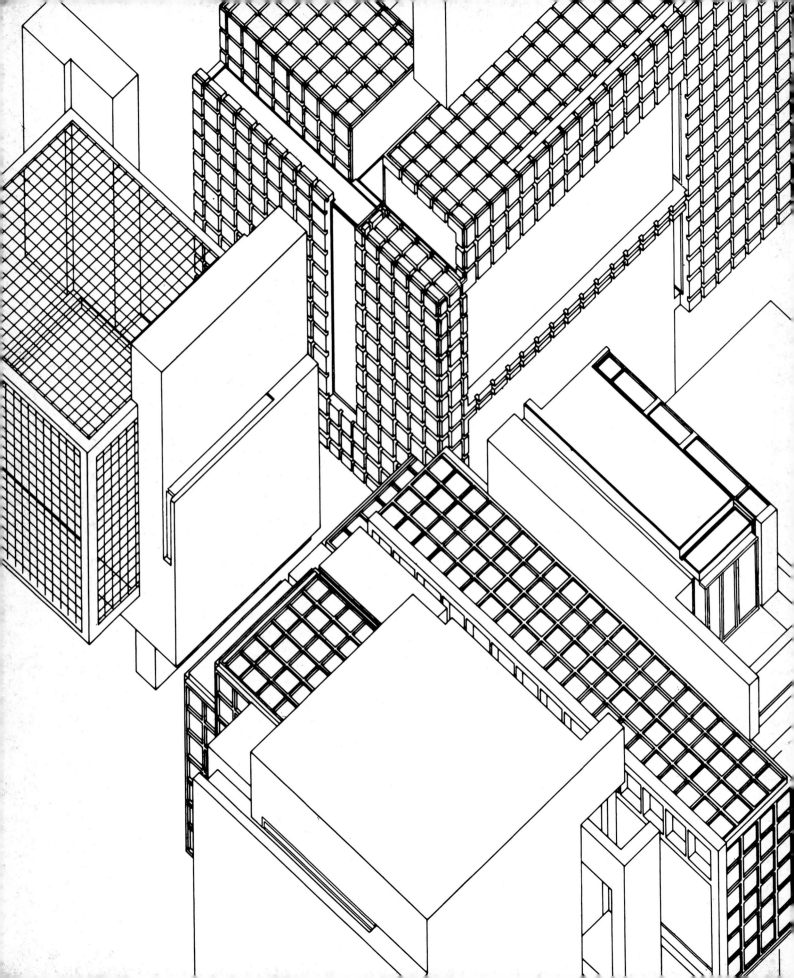

THE QUESTION AS TO THE NATURE OF
THE SECOND DIAGRAM IS CRUCIAL.
DOES THE PROCESSES OF THAT
DIAGRAM NEED TO BE IMMANENT
IN THE PROGRAM, SITE OR
ARCHITECTURE OF THE FIRST,
WHILE ON FIRST THOUGHT IT
WOULD SEEM THAT THERE
SHOULD BE SOME IMMANENCE
IT IS PRECISELY SUCH AN
IMMANENCE WHICH COULD BE
SAID TO RESITUATE IN THE
SAME ATTITUDE OF LEGITIMATION
THAT SUCH A DIAGRAM IS
TRYING TO ESCAPE FROM.
PERHAPS IT IS PRECISELY
THE SEEMINGLY ARBITRARY
NATURE OF THE SECOND DIAGRAM
WHICH WOULD HELP OPEN UP
AND REVEAL THE NEW
POSSIBILITIES WHICH PREVIOUS
MODES OF LEGITIMATION HAVE
OBSCURED.
IT IS PRECISELY THE POTENTIALLY
ARBITRARY NATURE OF THE
SECOND DIAGRAM WHICH INTRODUCES
THE MACHINIC INTO WHAT MIGHT
APPEAR TO BE AN ORGANIC OR
MECHANICAL PROCESS.

and that, in the last instance, the difference between signified and signifier *is nothing*. This proposition of transgression, not yet integrated into a careful discourse, runs the risk of formulating regression itself. One must therefore *go by way of* the question of being as it is directed by Heidegger and by him alone, at and beyond onto-theology, in order to reach the rigorous thought of that strange nondifference and in order to determine it correctly. Heidegger occasionally reminds us that "being," as it is fixed in its general syntactic and lexicological forms within linguistics and Western philosophy, is not a primary and absolutely irreducible signified, that it is still rooted in a system of languages and an historically determined "significance," although strangely privileged as the virtue of disclosure and dissimulation; particularly when he invites us to meditate on the "privilege" of the "third person singular of the present indicative" and the "infinitive." Western metaphysics, as the limitation of the sense of being within the field of presence, is produced as the domination of a linguistic form.[13] To question the origin of that domination does not amount to hypostatizing a transcendental signified, but to a questioning of what constitutes our history and what produced transcendentality itself. Heidegger brings it up also when in *Zur Seinsfrage*, for the same reason, he lets the word "being" be read only if it is crossed out (*kreuzweise Durchstreichung*). That mark of deletion is not, however, a "merely negative symbol" (p. 31) [p. 83]. That deletion is the final writing of an epoch. Under its strokes the presence of a transcendental signified is effaced while still remaining legible. Is effaced while still remaining legible, is destroyed while making visible the very idea of the sign. In as much as it de-limits onto-theology, the methaphysics of presence and logocentrism, this last writing is also the first writing.

To come to recognize, not within but on the horizon of the Heideggerian paths, and yet in them, that the sense of being is not a transcendental or trans-epochal signified (even if it was always dissimulated within the epoch) but already, in a truly *unheard of* sense, a determined signifying trace, is to affirm that within the decisive concept of ontico-ontological difference, *all is not to be thought at one go*; entity and being, ontic and ontological, "ontico-ontological," are, in an original style, *derivative* with regard to difference; and with respect to what I shall later call *differance*, an economic concept designating the production of differing/deferring. The ontico-ontological difference and its ground (*Grund*) in the "transcendence of Dasein" (*Vom Wesen des Grundes* [Frankfurt am Main, 1955], p. 16 [p. 29]) are not absolutely originary. Differance by itself would be more "originary," but one would no longer be able to call it "origin" or "ground," those notions belonging essentially to the history of onto-theology, to the system functioning as the effacing of difference. It can, however, be thought of in the closest proximity to itself only on

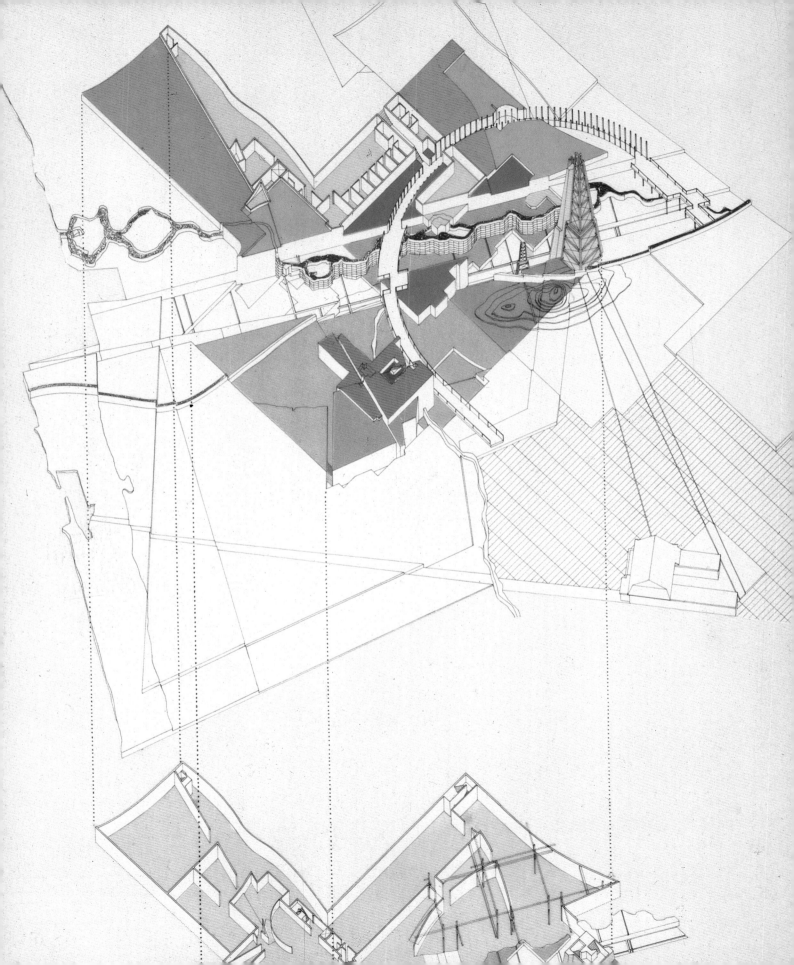

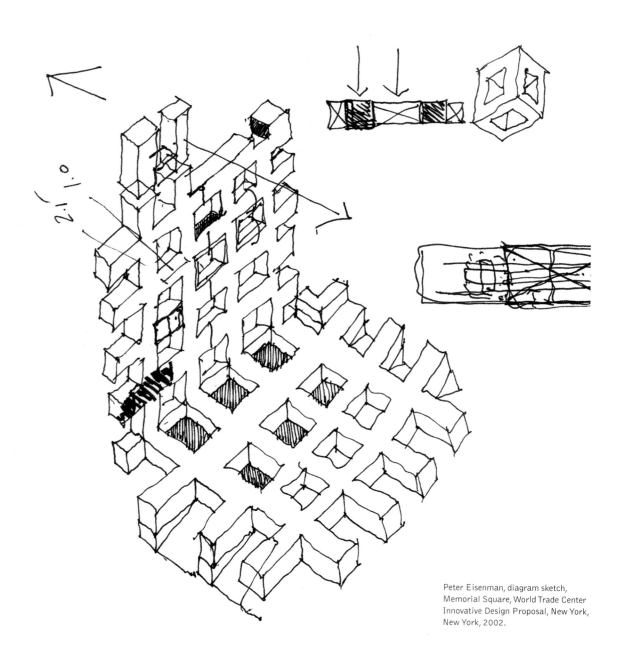

Peter Eisenman, diagram sketch,
Memorial Square, World Trade Center
Innovative Design Proposal, New York,
New York, 2002.

THE ABSENCE OF PRESENCE;
OR, THE VOID

Cynthia Davidson

Following the trail, the career, and the "productivity" of a certain perpetrator whose crimes are bloodless acts of architecture: this is our assignment here. To trace the path of an architect who himself traces, digs, investigates, analyzes, writes, builds, and, most potent of all, teaches – for some 40 years now. To attempt to understand this project, one must go back to go forward, must trace absence to find presence.[1]

Years ago, before Google Image, tell-all blogs, and instant messaging, Peter Eisenman took a plane to a faraway city, to a place where his face was not well known, and proceeded to disappear. At the lecture he was scheduled to give, he arrived and claimed to his host (or so the story goes) that Peter Eisenman had been unable to make the trip, but that "he," this stranger, would give the lecture in "his" place. And so it proceeded, the architect referring to himself in the third person, in perhaps the most bizarre displacement of presence with "absence" that an individual might enact. In its retelling, the story seems reduced to a game, the kind that Eisenman enjoys playing so much. Double entendres, doubled presence, a mirrored absence. Tracing, too, is doubling, doubling back, going over to find a new truth, another history. To find the presence of something thought to be absent.

1. Peter Eisenman resisted the idea of a monograph of "complete works" until this editor conceived it as a detective novel in which "detectives" would trace, or retrace, his steps, looking for clues to the motivations for his work. As to the framing conceit of a detective novel, the noir writer Raymond Chandler says, "An effect of movement, intrigue, cross-purposes, and the gradual elucidation of character . . . is all the detective story has any right to be about." Raymond Chandler, "The Simple Art of Murder: An Essay," in *The Simple Art of Murder* (New York: Vintage, 1988), 17.

25

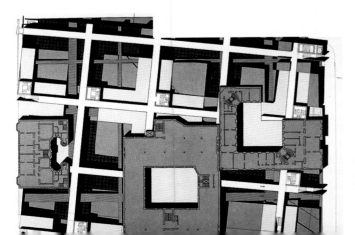

Presentation plan of the IBA Social Housing at Checkpoint Charlie, Berlin, West Germany.

House II, Hardwick, Vermont.

What was absent in Eisenman's early career was a deep sense of self. Not until he entered Jungian psychoanalysis in 1978 did his buildings begin to "enter" the ground, both literally and conceptually, rather than simply see the ground as a necessary inconvenience. The analogy is obvious: dig into oneself, and the self-examination leads to a change in one's overt work. However, absence, or the void, was present in Eisenman's work long before he began analysis. In his "Notes on Conceptual Architecture," published in 1970, only footnotes appeared for an "absent" text.[2] In House II [37], the second in his series of numbered houses, I to 11a, which he began in 1967 as a supposed study of the column and the non-load-bearing wall, the northeast corner is simply a frame of columns and beams, some so thick they read as walls. It is as if something solid had been eaten out of the architectural proposal, perhaps for a cost saving. Then again, this was Eisenman's "cardboard" period, when his houses were intended to look like models, thereby causing some confusion on the landscape as to their substance, or presence. The axonometric drawings for House II, however, show that the framed void is the result of the careful control of highly rational transformations of a cube in space, which includes the possibility of excavation, or carving out. Something indeed is missing, and not just literally. While anyone can read it as an absence, the careful observer can see it as a clue to the idea of the house.

"Such a logical structure of space aims not to comment on the country house as a cultural symbol but to be neutral with respect to its existing social meanings," Eisenman

2. See Peter Eisenman, "Notes on Conceptual Architecture: Towards a Definition," *Design Quarterly* 78/79 (1970): 1–5.

Plan view of Virtual House model.

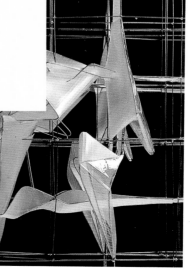

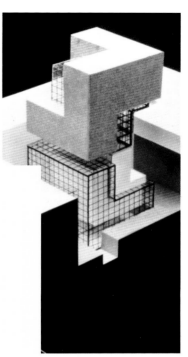

House 11a model.

3. Peter Eisenman, "Cardboard Architecture: House II," in *Five Architects* (New York: Oxford University Press, 1975 [first published in 1972 by Wittenborn & Company, New York]), 27.

4. According to Jaquelin Robertson, then dean of the School of Architecture at Virginia, the letters of invitation were signed by Eisenman, Michael Graves, Charles Gwathmey, Robert Siegel, and himself, but the "mysterious imprimatur P3" under which the letters were sent was a mystery, "one probably better left uninvestigated." See Jaquelin Robertson, "Introduction," in *The Charlottesville Tapes* (New York: Rizzoli International, 1985), 6.

writes of House II in *Five Architects*.[3] But something has happened since 1972 to make House II, a purely formal exercise that still sits pristinely on a remote Vermont hilltop, now appear as settled and settling as a traditional New England white clapboard colonial; that is, it has acquired a symbolic value.

* * *

We live in a "futureless present" in which buildings have lost their meaning, Eisenman said in 1982. The occasion was a meeting to which he, with several New York colleagues, had cryptically (again, as a hidden protagonist) invited twenty-two architects to each present a current project for peer review.[4] The site was the University of Virginia at Charlottesville, the masterpiece of America's "first" architect, Thomas Jefferson. Eisenman showed his IBA Social Housing project for Checkpoint Charlie, a site close to the Berlin Wall [80] and, in the then divided city, loaded with meaning. The project was an early "artificial excavation," in which layers of mappings – what he called superpositions – led to a building the meaning of which "stems from its own internal process," and not from its context or the hand of its author. Rem Koolhaas critiqued Eisenman's intent, arguing that there is "no built-in assurance that [IBA] will be perceived as anything more than a private neurosis." Rafael Moneo said: "The grid is his artificial context . . . his own syntax. . . . He is speaking a language in which words have lost their meaning." Eisenman replied: "If it is possible to make words empty of meaning, I'd like to try."[5]

5. *The Charlottesville Tapes*, 143–45.

CYNTHIA DAVIDSON 27

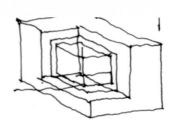

Were Eisenman able to succeed in emptying words of meaning, architecture would of necessity have to assume greater cultural meaning if some sort of standard of social communication were to be maintained. But, instead, Eisenman empties architecture of traditionally accepted meaning, questioning the column as a sign of itself, a sign of structure; questioning the "truths" of architecture that derive from a dominance of vision – architecture's need to "stand up" conflated with "looking like" it stands up – and opening "chasms" in its own history. At the same time, he insists on another temporal history.

The architects who came to Charlottesville recorded their conversation, which was published in 1985 in *The Charlottesville Tapes*. For Eisenman, the book and the building are intertwined, having learned from Palladio and Le Corbusier that recording one's buildings can be as effective in books as in stone or plasterboard. Witness the volumes, beginning with *Five Architects* in 1972, in which Eisenman is directly involved.[6] Clearly, there is no void of information; if anything, these books are shields against a "memory-void," the voids between one "run" of history and the next. These literal containers of memory are in sharp contrast to the conceptual memory voids that appear in his projects soon after Eisenman begins probing his own memory and being through analysis. Two projects in particular, House 11a and the Cannaregio proposal for Venice [76], posed the different idea of the void as conceptual absence.

In House 11a, Eisenman for the first time drills his work into the ground, almost literally, with a torqued, spatial form

6. As of 2004, Eisenman's bibliography ran to over 125 typed pages of single-spaced entries. Among these were approximately forty-three books entirely devoted to his writing, his architecture, or to a single Eisenman building or project.

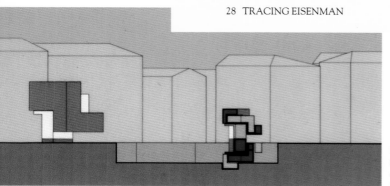

Partial transverse and longitudinal sections of Cannaregio, Venice, Italy. Above: Nesting els of proposed Cannaregio houses.

The Aronoff Center for Design and Art, Cincinnati, Ohio, includes a snakelike addition that generates a void between its form and the original building, creating a skylit gathering place.

7. Rationality, and the point at which it spins out of control, is another theme in Eisenman's work. Its ultimate conceptual realization to date is in the Memorial to the Murdered Jews of Europe in Berlin (1998–2005).

8. Phyllis Lambert, "Director's Note," in *Cities of Artificial Excavation: The Work of Peter Eisenman, 1978–1988*, Jean-François Bédard, ed. (New York: Rizzoli International and the Canadian Centre for Architecture, 1994), 7.

composed of colliding, three-dimensional L-shaped volumes. At the moment at which the house descends below grade, there is an inaccessible void, a space framed and trapped by the colliding els; a volumetric trace that is a mute recall of the process of creating its form. For the Cannaregio project, Eisenman articulates Le Corbusier's grid for the Venice hospital as a series of voids – a grid of holes in the ground that is a virtual ghost of Le Corbusier's project. These holes, Eisenman writes, "embody the emptiness of rationality."[7] Though the voids are possibly the sites of houses at three scales, each a variation on House 11a, they contain nothing. Rather, they are simply traces, marking what Le Corbusier would call some "ineffable logic."

Whether moving backward or forward in time, the void, the presence of absence, appears repeatedly in Eisenman's work. In a continuing confrontation with meaning and signification, in a struggle to overcome the truths of vision that dominate how architecture is perceived and experienced, Eisenman relies again and again on process as a way to "free architecture of its own traditional language and concerns,"[8] that is, from presence as a manifestation of truth. With the rise of philosophical deconstruction in the early 1980s, Bernard Tschumi introduced Eisenman to the philosopher Jacques Derrida and asked them to design a garden for the Parc de la Villette [140]. In this joining of minds, Derrida's reading of Plato's idea of *chora* gave new meaning to Eisenman's grid of holes and castle wall, forms imported to the Paris site from Cannaregio and his Moving Arrows, Eros, and Other Errors project [118].

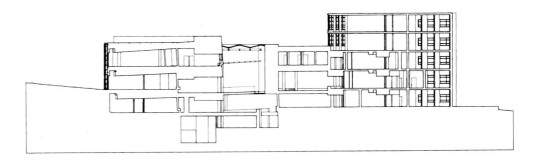

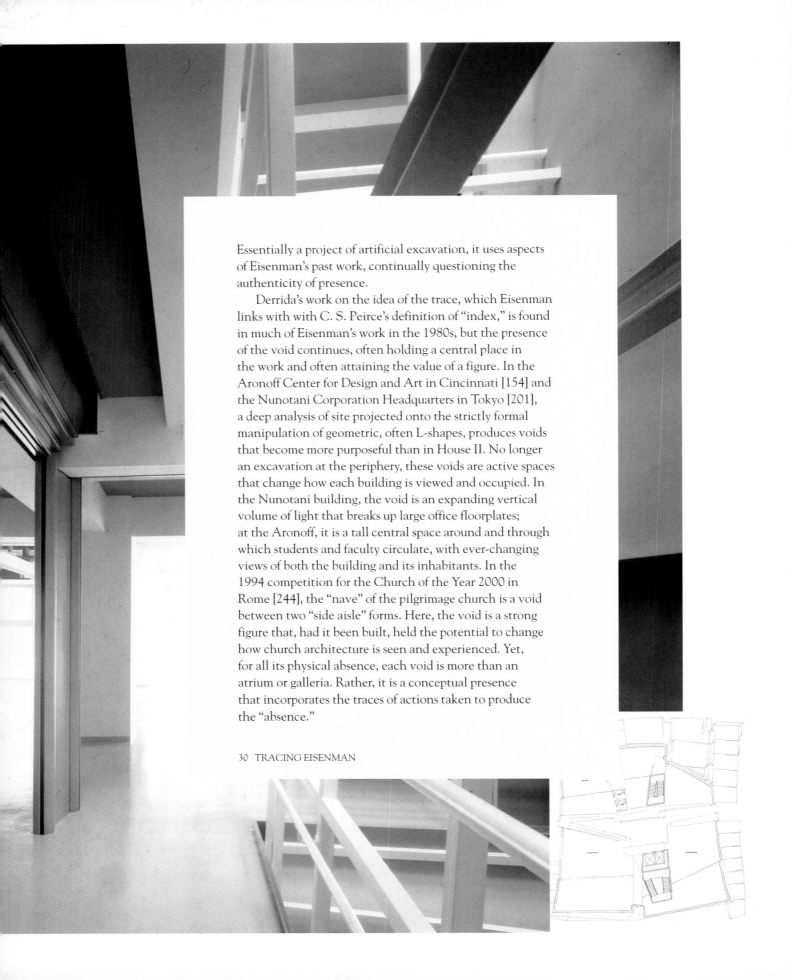

Essentially a project of artificial excavation, it uses aspects of Eisenman's past work, continually questioning the authenticity of presence.

Derrida's work on the idea of the trace, which Eisenman links with with C. S. Peirce's definition of "index," is found in much of Eisenman's work in the 1980s, but the presence of the void continues, often holding a central place in the work and often attaining the value of a figure. In the Aronoff Center for Design and Art in Cincinnati [154] and the Nunotani Corporation Headquarters in Tokyo [201], a deep analysis of site projected onto the strictly formal manipulation of geometric, often L-shapes, produces voids that become more purposeful than in House II. No longer an excavation at the periphery, these voids are active spaces that change how each building is viewed and occupied. In the Nunotani building, the void is an expanding vertical volume of light that breaks up large office floorplates; at the Aronoff, it is a tall central space around and through which students and faculty circulate, with ever-changing views of both the building and its inhabitants. In the 1994 competition for the Church of the Year 2000 in Rome [244], the "nave" of the pilgrimage church is a void between two "side aisle" forms. Here, the void is a strong figure that, had it been built, held the potential to change how church architecture is seen and experienced. Yet, for all its physical absence, each void is more than an atrium or galleria. Rather, it is a conceptual presence that incorporates the traces of actions taken to produce the "absence."

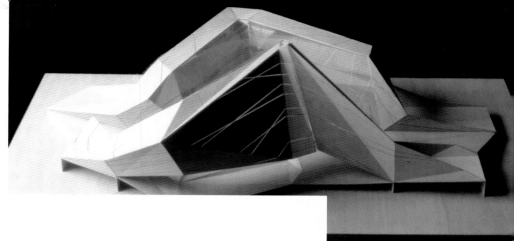

When in 2002 Eisenman joined with Richard Meier, Charles Gwathmey, and Steven Holl to propose a design for the World Trade Center site in New York [377], the team discussed ways to acknowledge through architecture the absence of the Twin Towers and the lives lost on 9/11. Holl recalled the formal void of House II, and Eisenman's gridded sketch for a new tower is a powerful emblem of that idea. The team agreed to develop towers that signified absence with presence, ironically loading meaning onto an abstract vertical grid. The very abstraction of it, however, did not satisfy a broad public looking for instantly recognizable symbolism. House II in itself may have acquired symbolic value as a "modern house" in rural Vermont, but framed absence, voids seen against the New York sky, could not find acceptance in the fullness of the city.

Across a span of forty years, the purely formal process that carved out the void in House II has led not only to an idea of conceptual absence in presence and the void as trace, but also, Eisenman claims, to the disappearance of the author. Yet Eisenman the author wants to be caught, as Manfredo Tafuri writes, in the web of his own weaving,[9] for the traces he leaves pose a mystery not for solution today but as questions for tomorrow.

9. See Manfredo Tafuri, "Meditations of Icarus," in *Houses of Cards* (New York: Oxford University Press, 1987).

CYNTHIA DAVIDSON 31

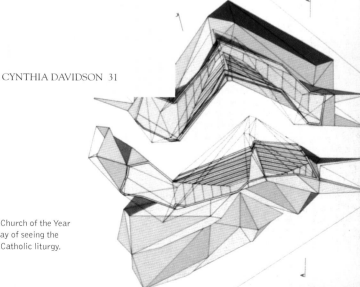

Opposite: A central void divides floors in the Nunotani advertising agency Corporation Headquarters in Tokyo, Japan.

The nave as void in the Church of the Year 2000 suggests a new way of seeing the church and the Roman Catholic liturgy.

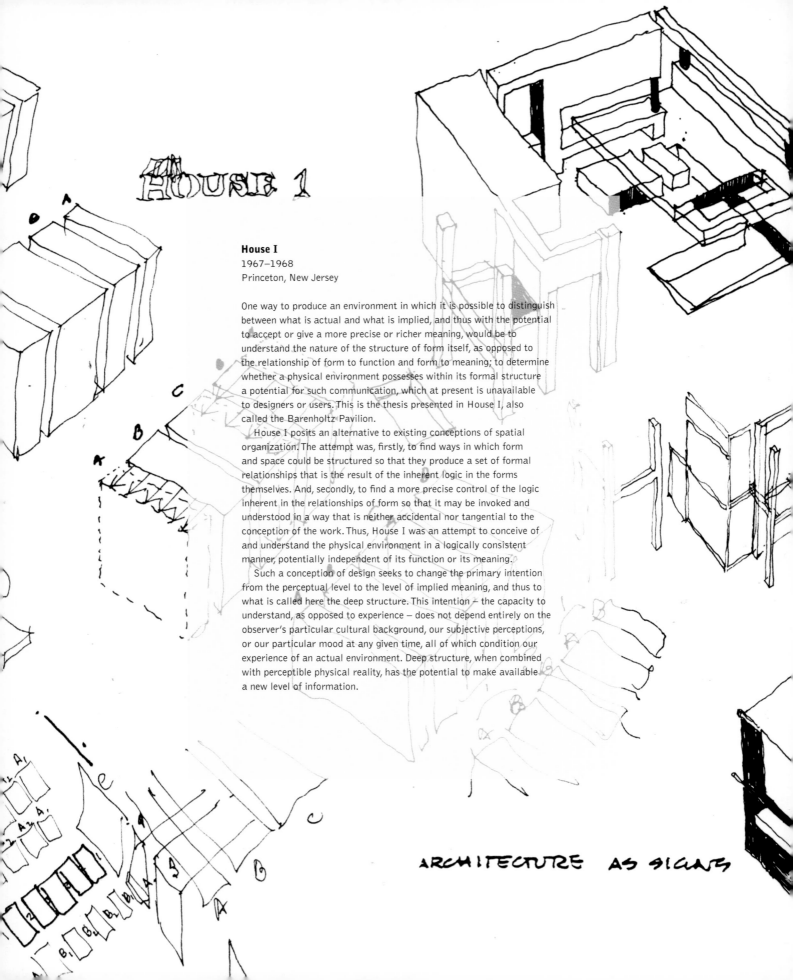

HOUSE 1

House I
1967–1968
Princeton, New Jersey

One way to produce an environment in which it is possible to distinguish between what is actual and what is implied, and thus with the potential to accept or give a more precise or richer meaning, would be to understand the nature of the structure of form itself, as opposed to the relationship of form to function and form to meaning; to determine whether a physical environment possesses within its formal structure a potential for such communication, which at present is unavailable to designers or users. This is the thesis presented in House I, also called the Barenholtz Pavilion.

House I posits an alternative to existing conceptions of spatial organization. The attempt was, firstly, to find ways in which form and space could be structured so that they produce a set of formal relationships that is the result of the inherent logic in the forms themselves. And, secondly, to find a more precise control of the logic inherent in the relationships of form so that it may be invoked and understood in a way that is neither accidental nor tangential to the conception of the work. Thus, House I was an attempt to conceive of and understand the physical environment in a logically consistent manner, potentially independent of its function or its meaning.

Such a conception of design seeks to change the primary intention from the perceptual level to the level of implied meaning, and thus to what is called here the deep structure. This intention – the capacity to understand, as opposed to experience – does not depend entirely on the observer's particular cultural background, our subjective perceptions, or our particular mood at any given time, all of which condition our experience of an actual environment. Deep structure, when combined with perceptible physical reality, has the potential to make available a new level of information.

ARCHITECTURE AS SIGNS

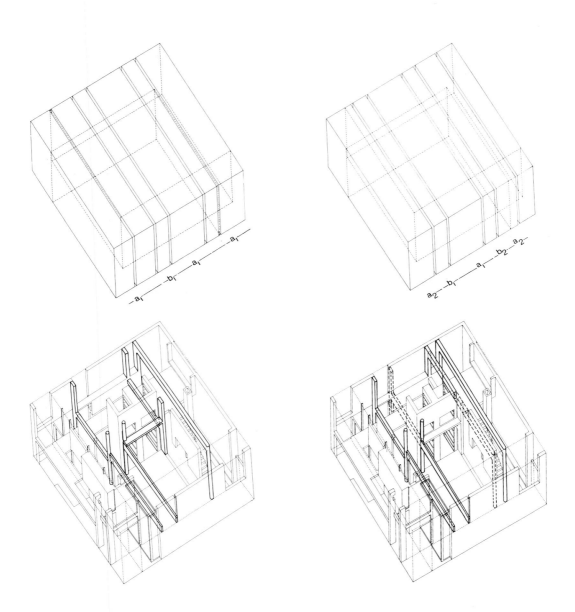

Axonometric diagrams of form and space as marked by columns and beams.

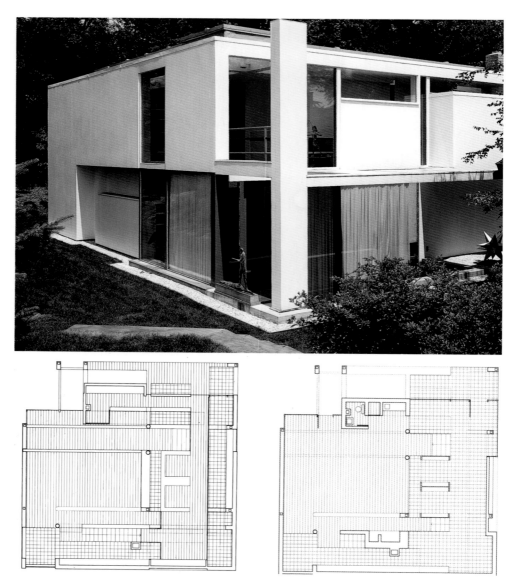

Upper-level plan (left); lower-level plan.

The structural function of columns and beams in House I is ambiguous.

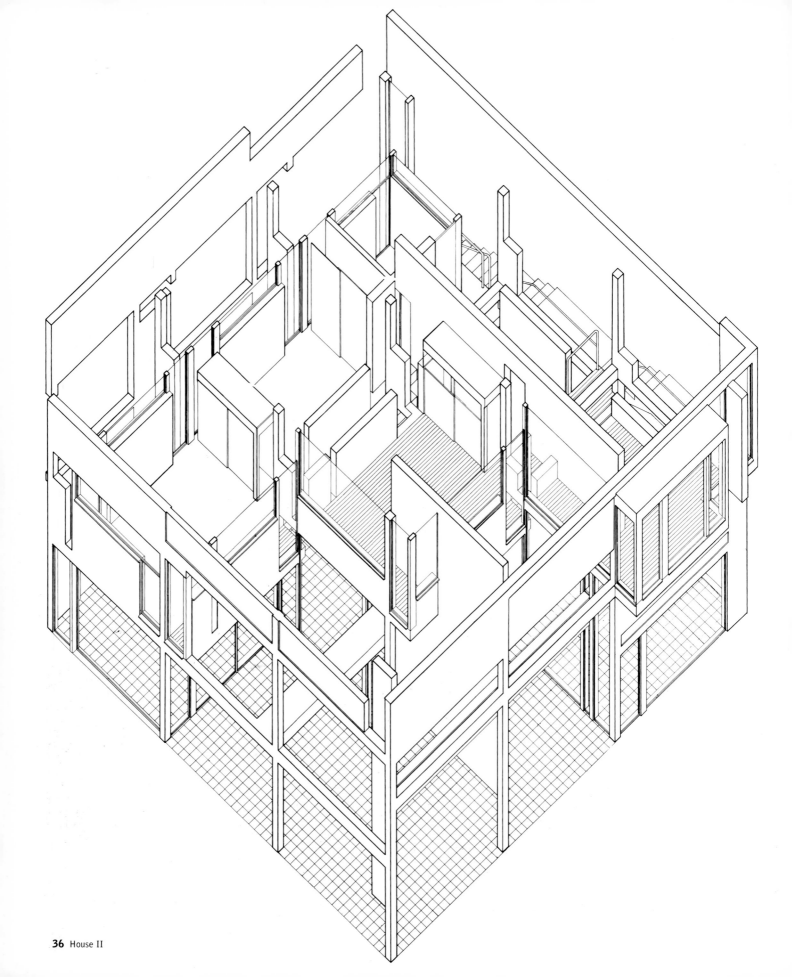

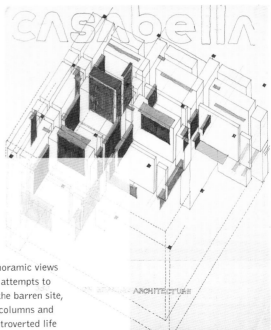

House II
1969–1970
Hardwick, Vermont

House II is situated on a 100-acre hilltop with broad panoramic views extending for twenty miles in three directions. The design attempts to simulate the presence of trees, which are nonexistent on the barren site, through the use of a sequence of columns and walls. The columns and walls frame the view and provide a transition from the extroverted life of summer to the introverted security of the winter fireplace.

Each of the two support systems – one of columns, the other of walls – is more than sufficient to meet the structural requirements of the house, which forces new readings. Either each system is supporting the house in part, or the two systems are completely supporting the house independently, or one system is only a sign of support. In this redundancy, an architectural sign is created: each system's function is to signify its own lack of function.

House II sheds its scale specificity by employing conventions of the architectural model in the actual object. The house looks like and is constructed like a model. Built of plywood, veneer, and paint, it lacks traditional details associated with conventional houses. Viewed without the external, scale-specific referent, House II becomes an ambiguous object that could be a building or a model.

Opposite: Axonometric perspective.
Right: West elevation.
Overleaf: House II northeast corner.

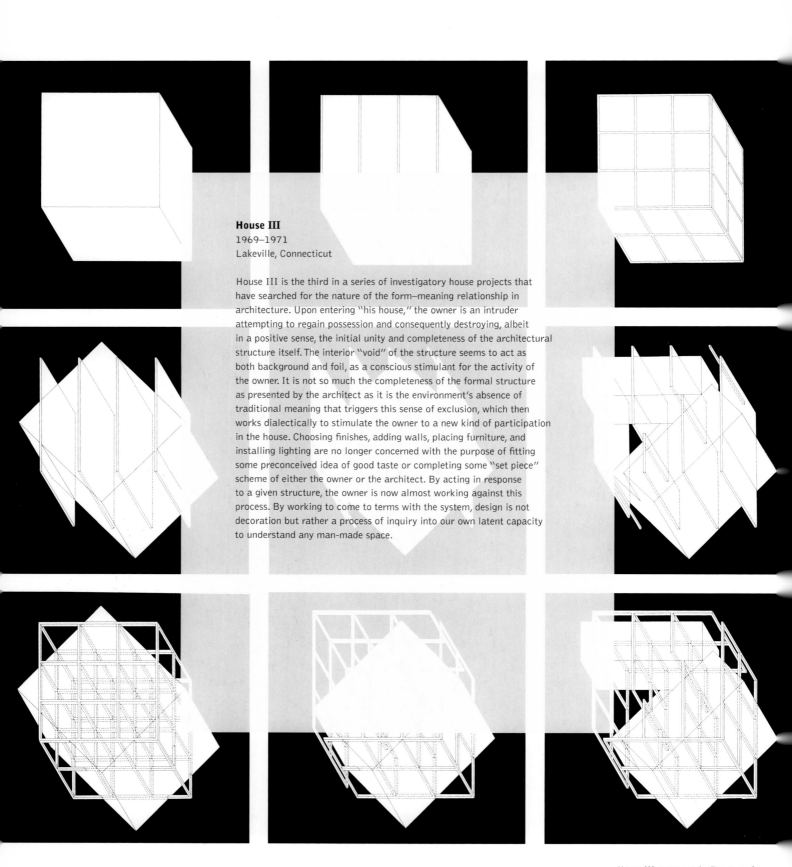

House III
1969–1971
Lakeville, Connecticut

House III is the third in a series of investigatory house projects that
have searched for the nature of the form–meaning relationship in
architecture. Upon entering "his house," the owner is an intruder
attempting to regain possession and consequently destroying, albeit
in a positive sense, the initial unity and completeness of the architectural
structure itself. The interior "void" of the structure seems to act as
both background and foil, as a conscious stimulant for the activity of
the owner. It is not so much the completeness of the formal structure
as presented by the architect as it is the environment's absence of
traditional meaning that triggers this sense of exclusion, which then
works dialectically to stimulate the owner to a new kind of participation
in the house. Choosing finishes, adding walls, placing furniture, and
installing lighting are no longer concerned with the purpose of fitting
some preconceived idea of good taste or completing some "set piece"
scheme of either the owner or the architect. By acting in response
to a given structure, the owner is now almost working against this
process. By working to come to terms with the system, design is not
decoration but rather a process of inquiry into our own latent capacity
to understand any man-made space.

House III axonometric diagrams of
form-meaning relationships.
Opposite: Study sketch.

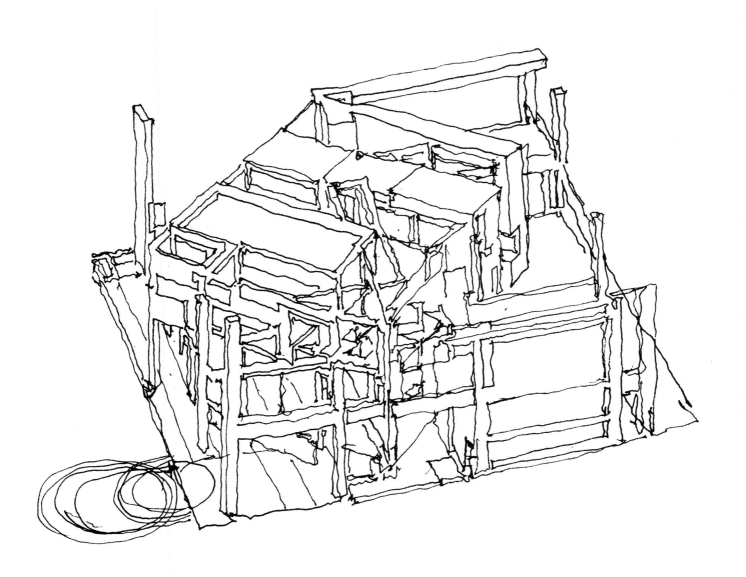

Overleaf: Pinwheeling beams and
planes do not reveal structural roles.

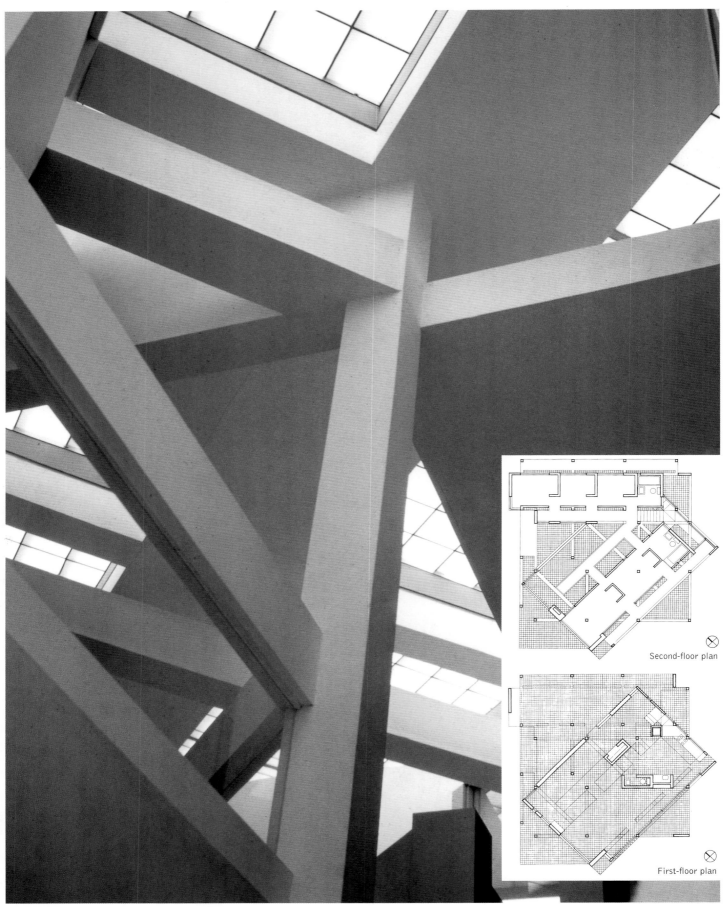

Second-floor plan

First-floor plan

FORMATIONAL

OBJECTIVES. OF WORK

EXAMINE THE NATURE OF SPATIAL OPPOSITIONS SUCH AS LINE V PLANE *JS*
TO SEE HOW VIRTUAL ... ... PLANE V VOLUME *VLVB*
PP ON SYSTEM ONCE ... SUM V ASUMM *MM*
USING OPPOSITIONS ... END V SIDE *E*
TRANSFORMATION ... CNTRPV NTRIP
EXT V ...
CENT V EDGE *aE*

House IV
1971
Falls Village, Connecticut

1. FROM COND...

INTENTION TO ...
BETWEEN EDGE AND ...
SUM ... AND ...

TO CHANGE ...
CUBE PRESS...

In House IV, a limited set of rules (shift, rotation, compression, extension) was applied to a limited set of elements (cubic volume, vertical planes, spatial nine-square grid). This transformational method establishes a code of spatial relationships within the syntactic domain of architectural language. The set of diagrams thus produced is recorded as both substance and indexical sign, which shift the focus away from existing conceptions of form in an intentional act of overcoming materiality, function, and meaning.

The transformational methods employed in House IV were specifically constructed to be largely self-propelling and therefore as free as possible from externally determined motives. A "logical formula," that is, a step-by-step procedural model, was established. Then basic elements such as line, plane, and volume were set into motion, resulting in an object that appeared to "design itself." Whether the result would be architecture or would have architectural features such as plan or façade was not a consideration of the process or a criterion for evaluation. In this sense, the problem was not to design an object but to search for and establish a transformational program free from traditional authorial constraints.

In House IV, in addition to the investigation of an autonomous process, the challenge to the hierarchical nature of configurational systems was extended to a certain dialectical relationship in architectural form, specifically the implicit hierarchy of the "favored partner" in dialectical pairs. Thus, if frontality/obliqueness is taken to be one such dialectic, with frontality the preferred point of view of modernism, in House IV the oblique view was equalized in importance with the frontal. Similarly, the simultaneously perceived was equalized with the sequentially perceived.

2.

3.

4.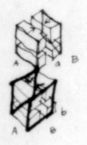

5.

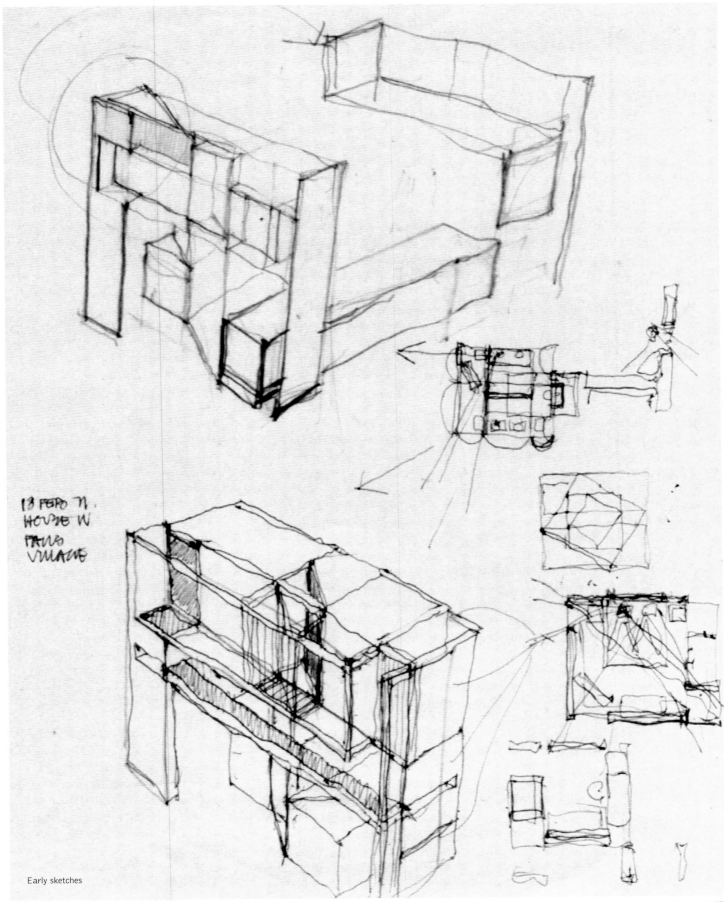

18 FEBO 71.
HOUSE IV
PAUS
VILLAGE

Early sketches

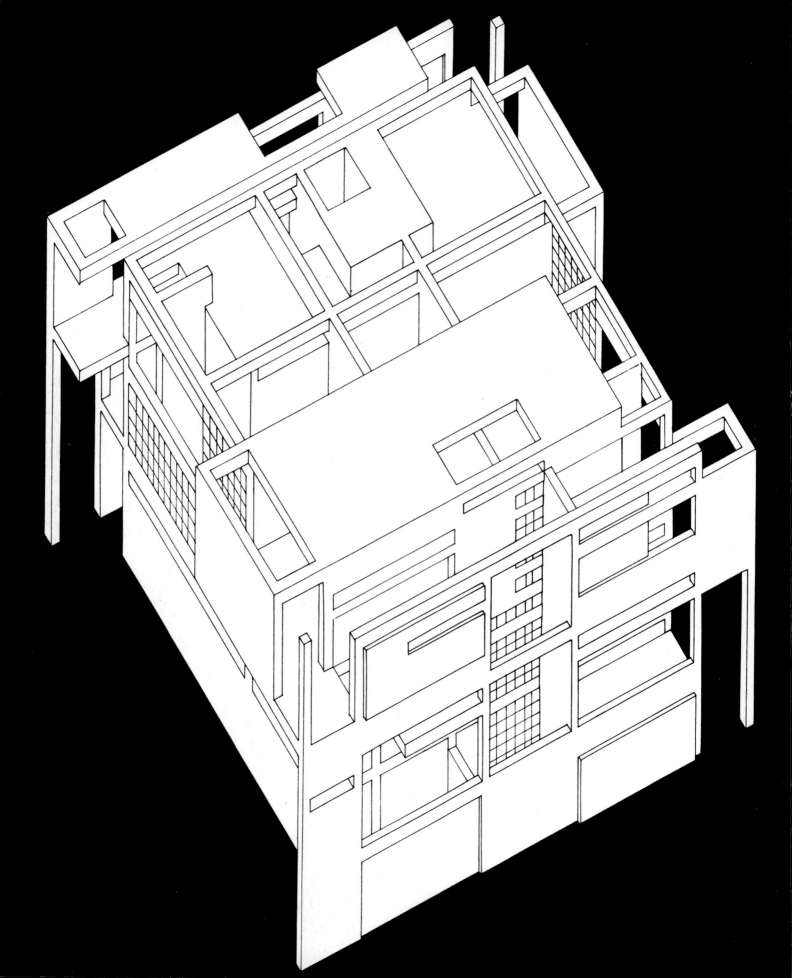

Above: Axonometric diagrams of volumes and planes in House IV.
Right: Study model. Opposite: Axonometric perspective.

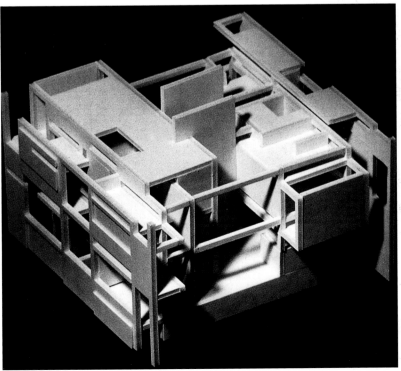

there seems to be a logical relationship between them, and further, that logic seems to be operative in a great deal of the art that is being produced at present. This logic involves the reduction of the conventional sign to a trace, which then produces the need for a supplemental discourse.

Within the convention of dance, signs are produced by movement. Through the space of the dance these signs are able to be coded both with relation to one another, and in correlation to a tradition of other possible signs. But once movement is understood as something the body does not produce and is, instead, a circumstance that is registered on it (or, invisibly, within it), there is a fundamental alteration in the nature of the sign. Movement ceases to function symbolically, and takes on the character of an index. By index I mean that type of sign which arises as the physical manifestation of a cause, of which traces, imprints, and clues are examples. The movement to which Hay turns—a kind of Brownian motion of the self—has about it this quality of trace. It speaks of a literal manifestation of presence in a way that is like a weather vane's registration of the wind. But unlike the weather vane, which acts culturally to code a natural phenomenon, this cellular motion of which Hay speaks is specifically uncoded. It is out of reach of the dance convention that might provide a code. And thus, although there is a message which can be read or inferred from this trace of the body's life—a message that translates into the statement "I am here"—this message is disengaged from the codes of dance. In the context of Hay's performance it is, then, a message without a code. And because it is uncoded—or rather uncodable—it must be supplemented by a spoken text, one that repeats the message of pure presence in an articulated language.

If I am using the term "message without a code" to describe the nature of Hay's physical performance, I do so in order to make a connection between the features of that event and the inherent features of the photograph. The phrase *"message sans code"* is drawn from an essay in which Roland Barthes points to the fundamentally uncoded nature of the photographic image. "What this [photographic] message specifies," he writes, "is, in effect, that the relation of signified and signifier is quasi-tautological. Undoubtedly the photograph implies a certain displacement of the scene (cropping, reduction, flattening), but this passage is not a *transformation* (as an encoding must be). Here there is a loss of equivalency (proper to true sign systems) and the imposition of a quasi-identity. Put another way, the sign of this message is no longer drawn from an institutional reserve; it is not coded. And one is dealing here with the paradox of a message without a code."[1]

It is the order of the natural world that imprints itself on the photographic emulsion and subsequently on the photographic print. This quality of transfer or trace gives to the photograph its documentary status, its undeniable veracity. But at the same time this veracity is beyond the reach of those possible internal

1.   Roland Barthes, "Rhetorique de l'image," [my translation]. *Communications*, no. 4 (1964), 42.

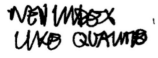

TRACE ELEMENTS

Stan Allen

From any crime to its author there is a trail. It may be – as in this case – obscure; but, since matter cannot move without disturbing other matter along its path, there always is – there must be – a trail of some sort. And finding and following such trails is what a detective is paid to do.

– Dashiell Hammett[1]

1. Dashiell Hammett, "House Dick" (1923) in *Nightmare Town* (New York: Vintage Crime, 1999), 46.

It has been pointed out that the conventional detective story has a paradoxical, and somewhat circular, narrative construction. From the crime that initiates the plot, the story moves forward in time, generally as a straight, linear narrative. But the trail that the detective follows leads back in time. The job of the detective is to reconstruct cause from effect, delving into the details of the crime and the lives of the suspects in a time before the story begins. As the narrative progresses, the details of the past accumulate. The circle closes when sufficient information has been gathered to reconstruct the decisive moments immediately before the crime. The reader is brought back to the starting point, now seen from a different perspective. This is part of the immense attraction that detective fiction enjoys: a story that is entirely conventional and straightforward in its narrative structure, and at the same time looping, circular, and topologically complex, all the while promising a satisfactory resolution. The rest is atmosphere.

49

Opposite: Eisenman reads Rosalind Krauss, "Notes on the Index: Seventies Art in America," October 3: 1977.

The simultaneous push/pull of narrative time might also explain the persistence of process-based design strategies in architecture. I want to tell a story (also retrospective) about the emergence – and persistence – of certain design practices that have their origin in an effort to rework architecture according to the codes of language and literature. These are in turn practices that owe something, if somewhat obliquely, to the operating principles of detective fiction: specifically, Peter Eisenman's early efforts to produce an architecture of greater rigor and conceptual density by codifying and rethinking the process of design itself. It is commonplace to speak today of design process, but it was Eisenman who first got us there, and we are still living with the consequences of that shift, often without thinking through its implications.

In the mid-1970s, when this story begins,[2] Eisenman was looking for ways to conceptualize the more complex geometries and elaborate transformational procedures that characterized his work at that time. One source was conceptual art. As Eisenman explored the parallels between his ideas and the practices of contemporary artists, Rosalind Krauss's well-known essay "Notes on the Index" was an important point of reference.[3] In this case, there are some clues, or at least parallels: Krauss delivered a version of her text as a lecture at the Institute for Architecture and Urban Studies in 1977, and the journal *October*, where the text first appeared, was originally published by the Institute, of which Eisenman was the director. I don't mean to suggest that Eisenman consciously modeled his design process on Krauss's text, but rather that the question of the index was in the air,

2. An early version of this text was originally written for a conference organized by K. Michael Hays and George Baird devoted to the architecture and theory of the 1970s that took place at Harvard University in 2001; the present version has been substantially reworked to address the theme of this book.

3. Rosalind Krauss, "Notes on the Index: Seventies Art in America," *October* 3 (Spring 1977): 68–81.

4. Charles Sanders Peirce, *Philosophical Writings of Peirce*, Justus Buchler, ed. (New York: Dover, 1955), 102. Further discussion of the index from: Thomas A. Sebok, "Indexicality," *The American Journal of Semiotics* 7, no. 4 (1990): 7ff.

50 TRACING EISENMAN

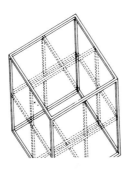

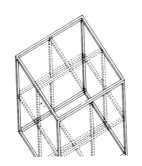

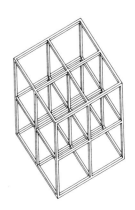

and would have been part of the intellectual atmosphere that surrounded Eisenman's thinking at that time.

The notion of the index is an old one, first articulated by the American pragmatist philosopher Charles Sanders Peirce in the late nineteenth century. The idea of the index played an important role in Peirce's semiotics, but it is worthwhile pointing out that this was not the version of semiotics current in architectural circles, which referred instead to Roland Barthes and Ferdinand de Saussure.

One easy way to exemplify the concept of the index, Peirce notes, is to think of imprints in the sand. For Peirce, the footprint that Robinson Crusoe found in the sand "was an Index to him that some creature was on his island." Indexical signs are bound to their referents through some form of contact, physical or otherwise: "An Index is a sign which refers to the Object that it denotes by virtue of being really affected by that Object."[4] Examples often given include animal tracks, fingerprints, handwriting, and medical symptoms. Or, as Dashiell Hammett puts it, "Since matter cannot move without disturbing other matter along its path, there always is – there must be – a trail of some sort." Yet, as the detective knows, the link between clue and crime is not always direct. Peirce takes note of this indirectness, placing the index under the category of "secondness." The index is doubly marked: by the definiteness of physical contact and by the uncertainty of interpretation. This uncertainty is a large part of the narrative motor of the conventional detective story. Because the clues point to the criminal only indirectly, it requires the interpretive powers

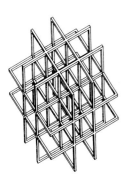

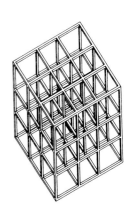

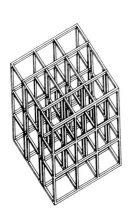

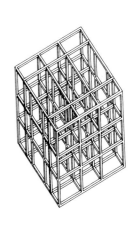

STAN ALLEN 51

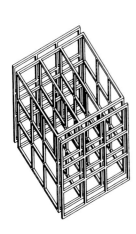

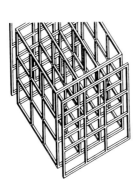

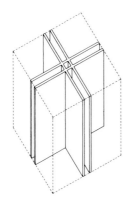
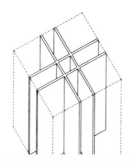
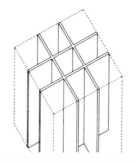
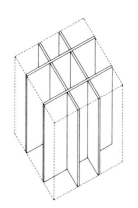

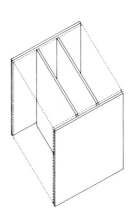
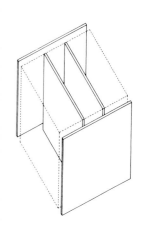

of the detective, revealed over the course of the story, to unravel the mystery. Detective work, like psychoanalysis, involves creating plausible narratives around disjunct clues. Indexical signs point back in time, eliciting a reconstruction of causes from effects. The index is an empty figure awaiting interpretation: "Such, for instance, is a piece of mold with a bullet-hole in it as a sign of a shot; for without the shot there would have been no hole; but there is a hole there, whether anybody has the sense to attribute it to a shot or not."[5]

Another distinguishing characteristic of indexical signs is their connection to the material world. Among signs, indexes are unique in that they are not ciphers in an abstract system, but physical artifacts. Some concrete mark is always left behind, and the materiality of the receptor surface is decisive: for example, the wet sand that holds the shape of the footprint; the light-sensitive coating of a photographic film; the polished surface of a glass that preserves an individual fingerprint.

Historian Carlo Ginzburg has suggested that the origins of a reading model based upon deciphering and interpreting clues might be traced back to early hunting practices where small signs ("prints in soft ground, snapped twigs, droppings, snagged hairs or feathers, smells, puddles, threads of saliva") led the hunter to his invisible quarry, or to a divinatory paradigm that worked through a close reading of minute, even trifling matters: "animals' innards, drops of oil on the water, heavenly bodies, involuntary movements of the body." Both worked through traces to approximate events that could not be directly experienced by the observer.[6]

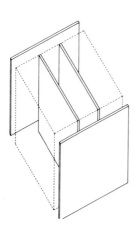
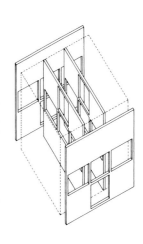

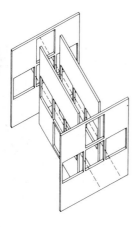
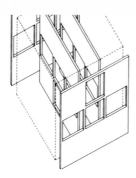
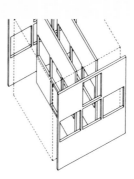
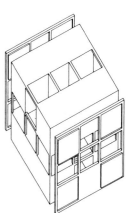

5. Peirce, *Philosophical Writings*, 104.

6. See "Clues: Roots of an Evidential Paradigm" in Carlo Ginzburg, *Clues, Myths and the Historical Method* (Baltimore: Johns Hopkins University Press, 1989), 96–125. Ginzburg compares the methods of Freud, Sherlock Holmes, and Giovanni Morelli, a nineteenth-century Italian physician and writer on art, inventor of a technique for authenticating works of art based on the study of small, often overlooked details: earlobes, fingernails, the shapes of toes.

In another important text of the Seventies, photography exemplifies the spatial and temporal displacement characteristic of the index. "A photograph," writes Susan Sontag, "is not only an image, … an interpretation of the real, it is also a trace, something directly stenciled off the real, like a footprint or a death mask."[7] Photography's truth value is directly linked to its indexical status. Photographs (like fingerprints, fossils, the tracks of gulls in the sand, the trajectories of electrons in a cloud chamber, or the image on the shroud of Turin) can be classified as indexical by virtue of the spatial connection of the object in question to the chemical surface of the photographic negative, as translated through the optics of the lens. The index, operating under the logic of metonymy, points a finger back over time to a moment of physical contact, now fixed and detached according to the logic of its own materiality (soft sand, fired clay, photographic film).

With new technologies of reproduction, it is worthwhile asking how far the indexical character can be maintained: Is an index still an index if the trace is processed through a coded representational system, even if all the information is preserved intact? Think of the difference between a digital scan and a photograph. Both register the traces of an object through reflected light, but in the case of the scan, the information is converted, bit by bit, into a digital code that permits its storage, retrieval, and manipulation. The dumb mechanical character of the index, and its corresponding immediacy (and its evidential authority), is bypassed. This is a question that I want to return to when we look at the

7. Susan Sontag, *On Photography* (New York: Delta, 1973), 154; as cited in Krauss, op. cit.

STAN ALLEN   53

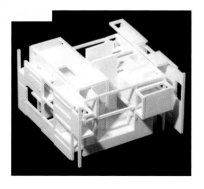

Opposite: House IV process diagrams.
Right: House IV presentation model.

operation of the index in architecture, where the physical immediacy of the index as described by Peirce can often be hard to obtain.

For Krauss, the capacity of indexical operations to short-circuit representational conventions based on resemblance is decisive. However, her notion of the index is filtered through an understanding based on photography and its impact on art practices. In the "Notes …" essay, Krauss employs the concept of the index to impart some consistency to the apparently heterogeneous art of the Seventies. In addition to photography, Krauss specifically mentions video, performance art, and earthworks. She takes note of the resulting displacement, and a consequent challenge to the conventional notion of the work of art. But she suggests that if examined from the point of view of the meaning-effects of indexical operations, there might be an underlying similarity in these apparently diverse practices. She proposes Roland Barthes' notion of a "message without a code" as a way of reading these works, and points to the consistent appearance of the "formal character of the indexical sign." In all these works, indexical operations take the place of art's traditional reliance on more mediated systems of representation. Unlike the minimalists of the preceding decade, these artists wanted to engage meaning in more specific terms than allowed by minimalism's generalized appeal to phenomenological presence. But they wanted to do so without reverting to the conventionalized codes of painting and sculpture. Indexical operations offered a model of signification that was at once highly specific, but did not rely on given symbolic

structures. Through the "snapshot-effect" of the index, the interpretation of the work is connected back to the process of its making. Minimalism's emphasis on making is reread in the context of evidential reconstruction: the index initiates a narrative of process. Like a photograph, each of these works freezes a moment in time, and calls for an interpretive effort on the part of the viewer to fill in the empty place of the indexical sign. The making of the work can be reconstructed from clues left behind.

However, it is important to note that Krauss is at pains to distinguish between these artists, who make use of the "formal character of the indexical sign," and earlier work, where a more direct, physical use of indexical procedures is present. All art is to some degree indexical. Classicism suppressed any trace of the hand of the artist; for many twentieth-century artists the distinguishing characteristic of a modern work was its ability to record its own making, and allow the viewer to participate vicariously in the act of creation. Cézanne's brushstrokes, Jackson Pollock's drips, or the slashed canvases of Lucio Fontana could all be understood as indexical signs in this sense. This is quite different from what Krauss had in mind. For Krauss, the distancing and codification of photographic operations is an important filter, and it is what distinguishes the work of the seventies from these high modernist predecessors. Although the essay is subtitled "Seventies Art in America," Krauss's primary points of reference are Jacques Lacan and Marcel Duchamp, and only four of the seventeen numbered sections even mention art of the seventies. Hers is a highly

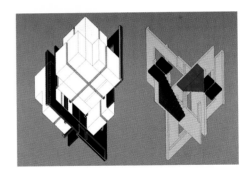

Opposite, above, and right:
House VI axonometric diagrams.

Left and below left: analytic
axonometric diagrams.
Below: House I .

mediated notion of the indexical sign, as exemplified by photography; that is to say, one that depends more on the formal characteristics of the index, and less on Peirce's criterion of physical contact. This difference is crucial when we move to a consideration of the operation of the index in architecture, especially as played out in Eisenman's practice. To make my own position clear, I think that Krauss's reading is at odds with Peirce's description of the indexical sign, and that something of the immediacy and the radical uncertainty that the index promises is lost in the process. Both Krauss and Eisenman, by insisting on the languagelike character of the indexical sign, seem to miss precisely what is most interesting about the index, which is that it totally bypasses codified language systems.

In his introduction to the book *Five Architects*, Colin Rowe famously described a divorce of the physique/flesh of modern architecture from its morale/word. By the middle of the seventies, it was commonly asserted that the solution to this perceived crisis of meaning was to see architecture itself as languagelike. Rather than see form and meaning as distinct entities always threatening to split apart, theorists looked at the many ways in which form and meaning were inexplicably intertwined. In separate *Oppositions* editorials published in 1976, Peter Eisenman and Mario Gandelsonas in different ways underlined this point. Gandelsonas pointed to the semiotic character of functionalist design strategies; Eisenman called for a "work on the language of architecture itself." I want to look more closely at the design operations that Eisenman proposes as part of this "work on language."

8. Diana Agrest and Mario
Gandelsonas, "On Practice," *A+U*
114 (March 1980): 35–36.

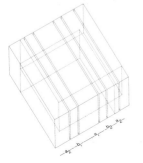  

Opposite: Colin Rowe, addition to
"Introduction" in **Five Architects**,
second edition, 1975.

For this edition, Colin Rowe wrote the following two special paragraphs, which should be added to the end of his Introduction.

These are reasonably important questions which it is ostrich-like not to consider. They propound problems which are not any less real becaus~~e~~ ... give them attention; a ... is immediately imp... rent from that which ... oncept of society and ... all indisputably bou... ; most of it makes a ... informa-tion explosi... ly second hand, what ... d pattern' (but, assun... akthrough is concern... the great merit of wh... not enor-mously sel... any very violent or s... ace them-selves in th... dio. Their posture ma... they are neither Ma... ntal soci-ological or ... to allevi-ate the pre... of poetry. There coul... ons; and, in a truly ... uld ever exist) what ... owledge-ment — as ... e people and *some* ... a general theory of p... it can be

Elsewhere, Diana Agrest and Mario Gandelsonas had asserted that it was both inevitable that architecture, as a social practice, would exhibit languagelike tendencies, and at the same time impossible that architecture could ever approach the transparency of discursive language.[8] If this is the case (and it is hard to argue otherwise), what would it mean to make architecture's languagelike character explicit? For Eisenman, who had by this time worked his way through Chomsky's linguistic theories, the notion of the index was one answer. Like the postminimalist artists discussed by Krauss, the index offered Eisenman a model of signification that was highly specific, but allowed him to bypass architecture's traditional semantic codes. And it dovetailed neatly with his already well-developed design procedures.

From the late 1960s until very recently, Eisenman's architecture has been "process" driven. That is to say, for Eisenman, architectural form is the outcome, or registration, of a series of design procedures. These procedures are under the control of the architect, carried out by graphic means, and have their own internal logic. That logic in turn is seen to be embedded in the architectural object as meaning and formal organization. This set of working procedures, I would argue, achieves a kind of conceptual clarity in the mid-seventies by reference to Krauss's notion of the index. And it is this same set of assumptions that later allows Eisenman to claim that his architecture is a kind of writing.

In *Five Architects*, Eisenman published not only the plans, sections, photographs, and descriptive axonometrics of his first two houses, but also an elaborate series of process

STAN ALLEN 57

faulted. Faults in detail may perhaps be recognized; but faults *in principle?* For, in terms of a general theory of pluralism, how can any faults in principle be imputed?

Which is to suggest that these five architects (who sometimes seem to regard buildings as an excuse for drawing rather than drawings as an excuse for building) are highly likely to be crudely manhandled

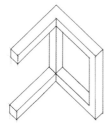

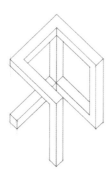

Sol LeWitt, two drawings
from the 131-piece **Schematic
Drawings for Incomplete Open
Cubes**, 1974.

diagrams. Each "project" as documented in the book is therefore an entire design process, and the built work has no more authority than any other graphic representation. Eisenman took a perverse pleasure in the fact that viewers often confused the built works with models, and he adapted the term "cardboard architecture" to underscore this collapse of object and representation. This notion of process and the concept-driven character of his work have often suggested an analogy to the work of conceptual artist Sol LeWitt. Eisenman's 1971 "Notes on Conceptual Architecture," for example, was consciously modeled on LeWitt's articles "Paragraphs on Conceptual Art" (1967) and "Sentences on Conceptual Art" (1969). However, despite a similar look and a predilection for axonometric representation, the intentions and results are distinct.

LeWitt's use of process is serial, exhaustive, and nonteleological. It has no beginning or end point. The diagrams are instead laid out for inspection and the viewers can move through the series in any direction whatsoever. The use of axonometric diagrams is no more than a simple means to make the idea clear. There is no distinction between work and diagram. The diagram is not simply a means to make the work, or something that disappears into the work, like a musical score or an architectural plan. For LeWitt, the diagram is the work and the work is the diagram. This is quite different from Eisenman's diagrams. Eisenman's diagrammatic series always begin with a simple form and describe a linear narrative of increasing complexity, with a fully realized building proposal at the end point. LeWitt's

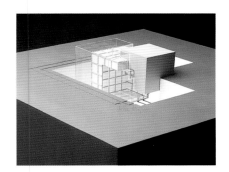

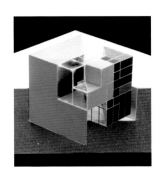

use of the diagram is itself a conscious critique of the notion of the fully realized "work of art." His series are instead always open, always provisional, and, unlike Eisenman's linear narratives, any point along the way is ultimately as important as the end point.

Eisenman's critique is distinct and directed at the terms of his own discipline. He uses the example of process-driven conceptual art as a means to make explicit the usually hidden aspects of the design process, giving them a transparency and internal logic that serves to critique the arbitrary nature of such procedures as normally practiced. However, he holds on to an idea of authorial intention, and sees the architect as the agent that endows the object with meaning – even if through a semiautomatic process. For Eisenman, design is the inscription of meaning into, or onto, the work by means of a series of more or less rigorous operations carried out by the designer. Eisenman as an architect imparts meaning to the building, which is in turn registered by its increasing complexity. This formal intricacy is intended to elicit a "decoding" operation as the viewer is invited to unpack the process of the making of the object, much as the indexical sign elicits a reconstruction of causes from effects, or a detective reconstructs a coherent narrative of the crime from scattered clues.

This could be clarified with an example of a project originally designed in the late seventies, but elaborated over the early part of the eighties, and that as such, marks Eisenman's new interest at that time in the writings of Jacques Derrida and the philosophy of deconstruction. In

STAN ALLEN   59

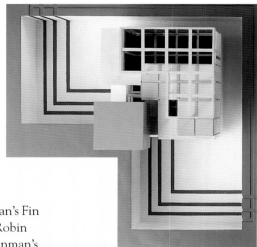

his 1985 review of the exhibition of Peter Eisenman's Fin d'Ou T Hou S at the Architectural Association, Robin Evans makes an explicit connection between Eisenman's claim that his architecture is a kind of writing, and an appeal to indexical procedures in the design process.[9] With the Fin d'Ou T Hou S [84] Eisenman invents a series of "morphological fictions" in order to construct a narrative of his procedures. In this case, he describes a process of pulling a smaller cube through a larger one as a way of explaining the final form of the building. Eisenman imagines that the traces of this process are registered – imprinted, or inscribed – in the material of the model as indexical signs. But for Evans, this requires a strange suspension of disbelief: "The nature of the material of which the thing is made of is inimical to it, so that the orthogonal crystalline cubic forms have to be thought of as having passed through a suitably soft, igneous phase." That is to say, the object has to be imagined as being momentarily composed of a soft material (like wet sand or soft clay) so that it might register the traces of these operations. This imprinting of signs, whereby the traces of the design process are embedded in the object, seems to be what allows Eisenman to speak of his architecture as being like writing. And consequently, by understanding design as inscription, a model of interpretation follows that presumes the viewer's ability to "read" the building by decoding the traces and reconstructing the narrative of design procedures.

For Evans, these fictions of process are implausible. For Eisenman, this is not at issue, and I am willing to accept this as an enabling fiction. The engagement with process

9. Robin Evans, "Not to be used for Wrapping Purposes," *AA Files* 10 (1985); reprinted in *Translations from Drawing to Building and Other Essays* (London: The Architectural Association, 1997).

Above: Fin d'Ou T Hou S elevation.
Above right: Model in plan view.

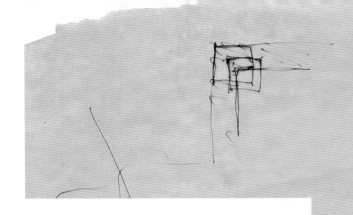

yields results not obtainable by conventional, more intuitive means. And Eisenman's method has the advantage of making explicit what is often hidden in an unexamined design process. Moreover, it has exposed something deeply embedded in the discipline itself. Making use of Giuseppe Terragni as a lever, Eisenman radicalized Rowe's analytical insights (which were retrospective, and explanatory), and reworked process as an explicit, internally consistent system of form generation. In doing so, he constructed a genealogy for his own work, tracing its origins back through Terragni and early modernism to Renaissance architecture. I am suggesting that we can take Eisenman at his word, and accept the idea that meaning can be inscribed into the building's formal structure through a series of geometrical transformations, while still remaining skeptical about the exact nature of the meanings produced.

An architecture that faithfully registers the architect's intentions through design process is almost by definition an architecture that has as its primary subject the internal workings of architecture as a discipline. If Eisenman has successfully exploited the capacity of the index to record the process of design, he is also locked into the evidential structure of the index, which can only point back to the operations of design and the private languages of architecture. Indexical signs, as described by Peirce, link physical artifacts and virtual meanings; hence their attraction for architects. Eisenman's indexes (like those Krauss described in the seventies) are more mediated, and inevitably work through codified geometries and

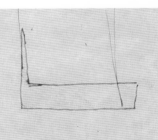

10. A story told around the Institute when I was a student in the late seventies (I have no idea if it is true) underlines this idea of the viewer/reader as "detective." The story goes that Eisenman gave a student drawings of House VI, noting that the house had been designed according to a strict series of geometrical transformations; could the student reconstruct that series from its end point? In other words, could he construct a plausible narrative from the clues left behind? Apparently the student came up with a perfectly logical series of geometrical operations that led flawlessly back to the starting point, but had absolutely nothing to do with the actual design process. There is nothing startling about this, (although apparently it surprised Eisenman at the time) but it does underscore the essentially arbitrary nature of the design process, and the impossibility of regulating meaning and interpretation.

11. Robin Evans, op. cit., 138.

representational systems. The meaning of the work is dominated by the structure of representation itself, which will always allow only partial access to the procedures of design.[10] His insistence on decoding, on the viewer as detective, limits the range of experience in the present.

Evans notes that Eisenman represents an exaggerated case of practices that are commonplace in thinking about architecture and design process. How often are the formal characteristics of a building explained by reference to the implication of fictional movement? Every time an architect refers to a rotated cube, a shifted grid, to inverted or compressed space, to warped axes, to hinges, joints, or to folded surfaces and aggregated volumes, he or she unconsciously implies movement. ("It is the verbs turned to adjectives that do it," notes Evans.[11]) In every case, some notion of the indexical sign, however mediated, is at work. This has been the one point of consistency as Eisenman has explored a wide range of formal and procedural vocabularies over the past thirty years. Regardless of the formal character of the operation, i.e., whether it is a shifted grid (1970s), scaling (1980s), or folded surfaces (1990s), the implication of narrative time and fictional movement persists. It is also one measure of Eisenman's enormous influence. Beyond specific references to his formal vocabulary (which are actually quite rare), any time we see work that justifies itself by reference to the history of its design process – interrogations of the body and representation from the late 1980s; architectural deconstruction, which understood form as the record of a violent collision; Libeskind's memory traces; the mapping

ouse II, study model in Plexiglas.

projects of the 1990s; or even today, the persistent student habit of explaining work by retracing the design process – we are in the territory first mapped out by Eisenman in the seventies with his investigations of the index. Since that time, an attention to process has been the explicit sign of a conceptually ambitious, theoretically driven work. And the underlying suggestion is that it is not just the artifact that matters, but how the artifact came to be – what the architect did in the course of the design process – that matters most.

But what was once a vital effort to rethink architecture's procedures has today ossified into a rigid formula. Indexical signs invariably point back in time, in this case to the event of design and the hand of the author. A closed circle results, in which the means of *interpreting* things are recycled as a model for *making* things. These operations work effectively to interrogate the means of representation, which are foregrounded in process, but they are powerless to engage any material not already implicated in the hermetic procedures of design. The result is a self-referential architecture, locked in the examination of its own history. The effect is to slow architecture down, rendering it incapable of responding to the rapidly changing demands of the city and its technologies. It is for this reason, rather than the implausibility of its enabling fictions, that many are rightly suspicious of the persistence of indexical procedures in design operations. Unable to engage the more radical possibilities of the index, they inevitably privilege the private language of design, and imply a retrospective model of interpretation.

If process is still important in architecture today, why not understand process as the unfolding life of the building and its site over time? The arrow of time in this case moves forward, not backward. Its origin is the moment when design is complete, the building is occupied, and the architect no longer in control. This is a process that design and construction can only initiate, or steer in a very general way. It is a process that unfolds in a complex interaction with the messy and unpredictable forces of life itself. Less narrative, less history; more atmosphere, more effect.

Process-driven work is still very much present and, ironically, often linked with digital design protocols, which had promised an architecture more adaptive and responsive to change. Given that computer modeling systems often work through deformations and transformations of geometric primitives, the use of the computer has, if anything, reinforced the sense of design as the outcome of formal manipulations. The most sophisticated examples of recent computer work employ design techniques that are characterized by mobility and change. The computer allows the designer to treat architecture as fluid matter that simulates movement and growth. But at a strategic point, these procedures arrest the formal dynamic and capture it as an indexical sign. The result is a snapshot of a dynamic process, but the objects themselves are incapable of responding to change in any way other than as visual metaphor. The dynamic interplay of change in the life of the building, city, or site remains untouched. Like trace elements left behind for the detective to analyze, these

House II, Hardwick, Vermont.

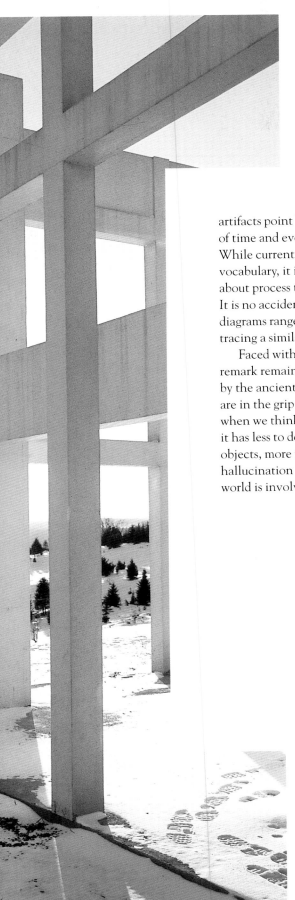

artifacts point back to their own origin, freezing a moment of time and evoking a chain of reconstructive interpretation. While current work presents an entirely different formal vocabulary, it is marked by the same underlying assumptions about process that Eisenman explored twenty-five years ago. It is no accident that these projects are often presented in diagrams ranged in series, beginning with simple forms and tracing a similar narrative of increasing formal complexity.

Faced with this persistence, Robin Evans's cautionary remark remains suggestive: "If we are still sometimes touched by the ancient idea that rocks are animate, we ourselves are in the grip of a similar sentiment amplified by language when we think of buildings as animated. In its modern form it has less to do with the willful breathing of life into inert objects, more to do with a willful unrealizing of them. The hallucination of a transcendental yet entirely corporeal world is involved."[12]

12. Robin Evans, op. cit., 138–39.

House VI
1972–1975
Cornwall, Connecticut

House VI is both an object and a kind of cinematic manifestation of the transformational process. Thus the object not only is the end result of its own generative history but also retains this history, serving as a complete record of it, process and product beginning to become interchangeable.

The space of perception in House VI is Euclidean, that is, it has a frontal orientation. However, there are unassimilable idiosyncrasies in the house – no compositional uniformity or proportional congruencies, a lack of dynamic balance, etc. – that resist a conventional perceptual relation. These "unassimilable idiosyncrasies" are signs of another geometrical order – topological – operating on a conceptual level.

In House VI, a particular juxtaposition of solids and voids produces a situation that is only resolved by the mind discovering a need to change their position. This mental attempt to reorder the elements is triggered by their precise size, shape, and juxtaposition. This produces a sense of tension or compression in a particular space that is not created through the actual position of walls but is in our conception of their potential location. The sense of warping, distortion, fluctuation, or articulation occurs because of the mind's propensity to order or conceptualize physical facts in certain ways, like the need to complete a sequence A–B or to read symmetries in a straight line.

House VI is not an object in the traditional sense – that is, the result of a process – but more accurately a record of a process. Like the set of diagrammed transformations on which its design is based, the house is a series of film stills compressed in time and space. Thus, the process itself becomes an object; not an object as an esthetic experience or a series of iconic meanings but an exploration into the range of potential manipulations latent in the nature of architecture, unavailable to us because they are obscured by cultural preconceptions.

Axonometric diagrams of House VI
(photo: rear elevation).

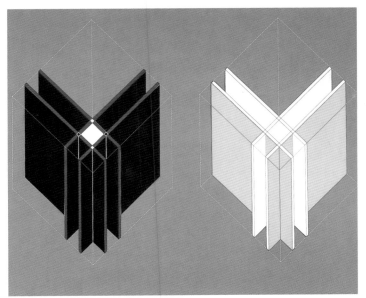
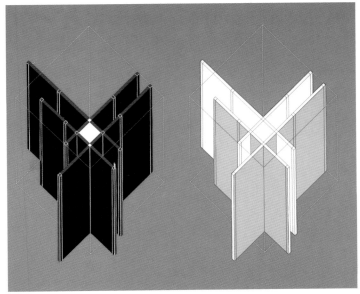

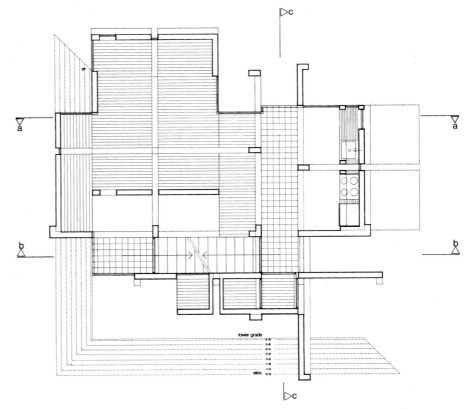

First-floor plan

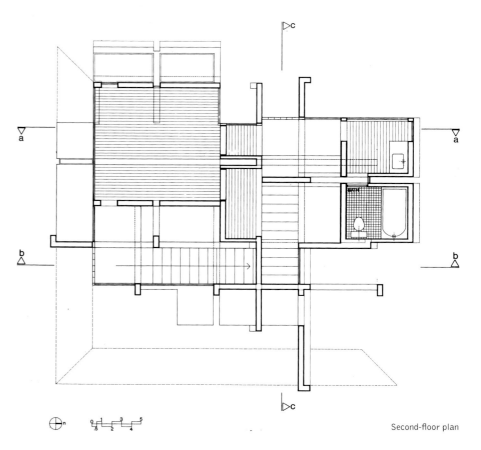

Second-floor plan

The ground is cut away from the front corner,
eliminating it as a datum for the house.
Opposite: Interior views.

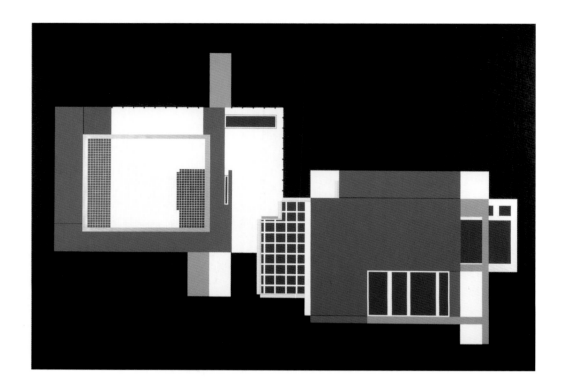

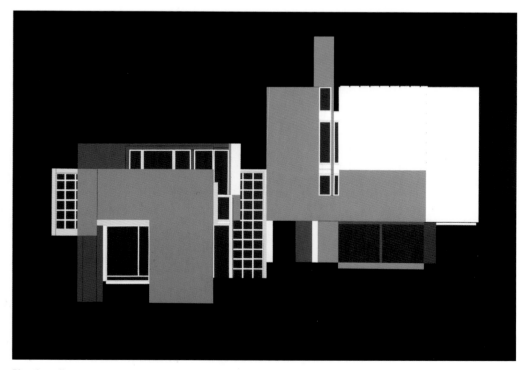

Elevation collages.

House X
1975
Bloomfield Hills, Michigan

Most houses are conceptually vertebrate. That is, in addition to their literal, necessary condition of structure they are metaphorically vertebrate. They have a center, usually a hearth or a stair; their roofs pitch from the center, and their construction exhibits a concern for an overall centrality. The center expresses both the functional core and conceptual unity of the house. In House X, the center is nothing.

The vertebrate house is also mimetic; it mirrors man's upright, axial condition. In an attempt to produce a conceptual distance between man and object, House X is nonvertebrate; to this extent, it is nonmimetic. There are no exposed linear elements – columns or beams. These are covered by solid vertical and horizontal surfaces, and further, two of the major horizontal living surfaces are void. This is a distortion of the Modern Movement's preferred section – two solid horizontal planes – as well as of the house's traditional mimesis of anthropocentric man, who stands on a solid horizontal surface and "dominates" the landscape.

The specific configurations of House X can be understood initially as the juxtaposition of four squares. This configuration is only an initial analogue, a heuristic device used to approach a more complex sign condition, which in itself is only a possible approximation of the reality it signifies. In fact, the final configuration is a cumulative attempt to dissolve its own seeming connection with any initial analogue. In other words, the final plan is only a series of traces that refer, in a sense, forward to a more complex and incomplete structure rather than backward to a unitary, simple, and stable structure. It thus becomes a kind of pre-distillation of a more complex "future" condition.

Presentation model (above) and axonometric model.

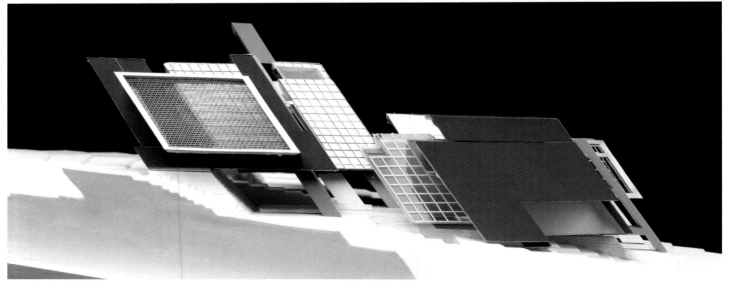

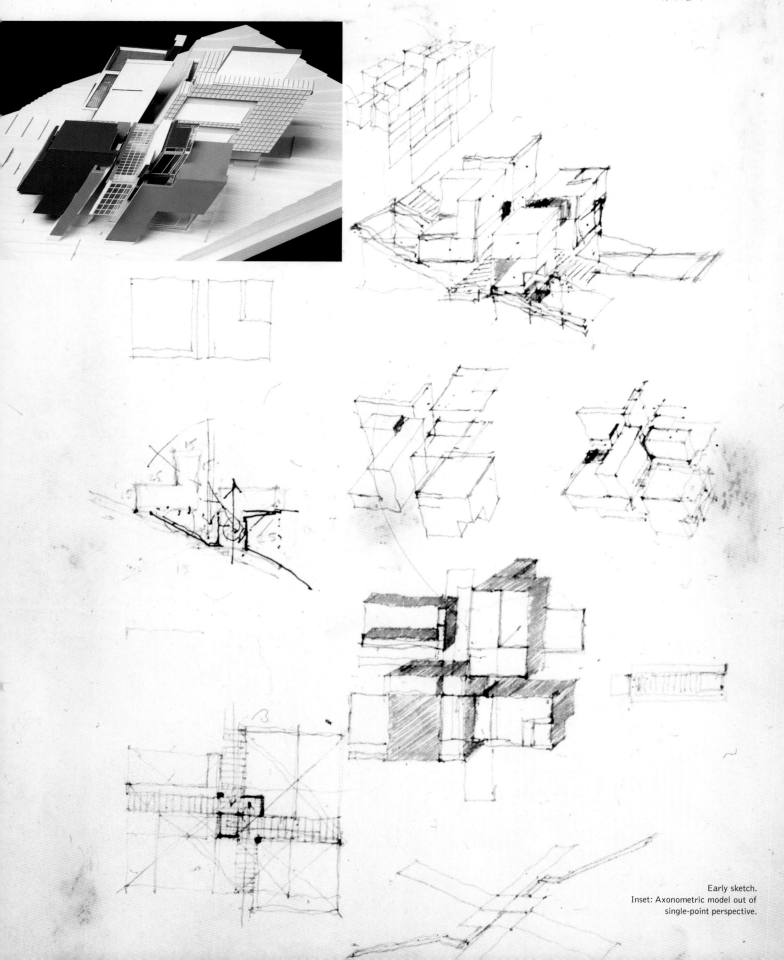

Early sketch.
Inset: Axonometric model out of
single-point perspective.

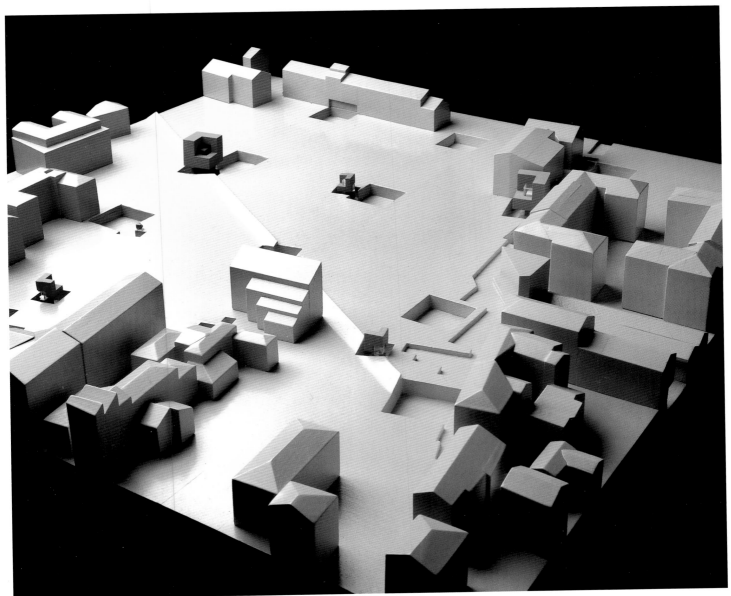

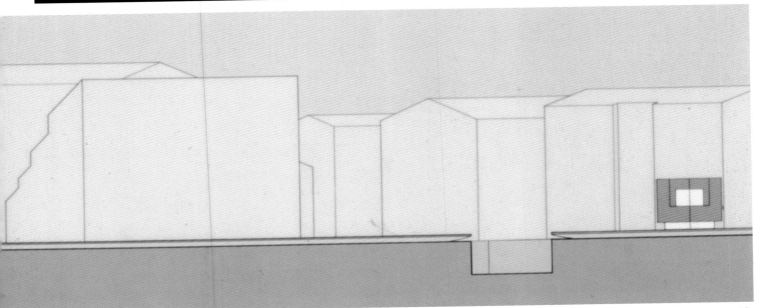

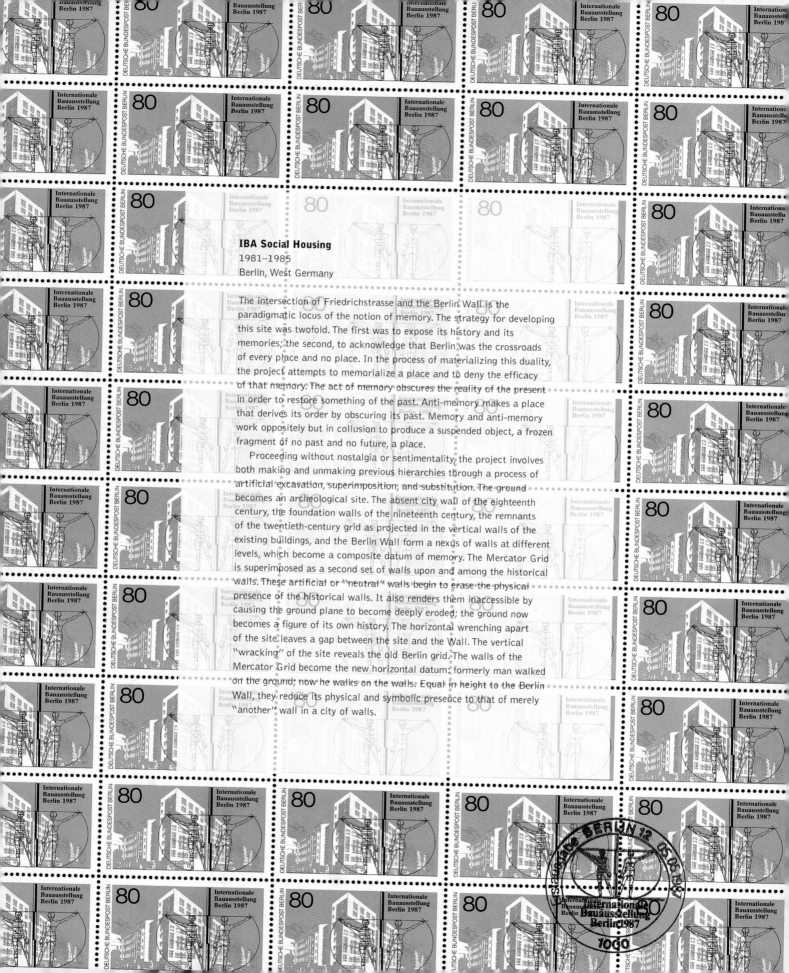

IBA Social Housing

1981–1985

Berlin, West Germany

The intersection of Friedrichstrasse and the Berlin Wall is the paradigmatic locus of the notion of memory. The strategy for developing this site was twofold. The first was to expose its history and its memories; the second, to acknowledge that Berlin was the crossroads of every place and no place. In the process of materializing this duality, the project attempts to memorialize a place and to deny the efficacy of that memory. The act of memory obscures the reality of the present in order to restore something of the past. Anti-memory makes a place that derives its order by obscuring its past. Memory and anti-memory work oppositely but in collusion to produce a suspended object, a frozen fragment of no past and no future, a place.

Proceeding without nostalgia or sentimentality, the project involves both making and unmaking previous hierarchies through a process of artificial excavation, superimposition, and substitution. The ground becomes an archeological site. The absent city wall of the eighteenth century, the foundation walls of the nineteenth century, the remnants of the twentieth-century grid as projected in the vertical walls of the existing buildings, and the Berlin Wall form a nexus of walls at different levels, which become a composite datum of memory. The Mercator Grid is superimposed as a second set of walls upon and among the historical walls. These artificial or "neutral" walls begin to erase the physical presence of the historical walls. It also renders them inaccessible by causing the ground plane to become deeply eroded; the ground now becomes a figure of its own history. The horizontal wrenching apart of the site leaves a gap between the site and the Wall. The vertical "wracking" of the site reveals the old Berlin grid. The walls of the Mercator Grid become the new horizontal datum: formerly man walked on the ground; now he walks on the walls. Equal in height to the Berlin Wall, they reduce its physical and symbolic presence to that of merely "another" wall in a city of walls.

Left: Conceptual diagrams of IBA site.
The building façade carries the grid of the ground plane.

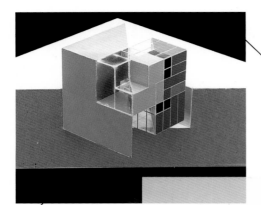

Fin d'Ou T Hou S
1983

The first premise of the Fin d'Ou T Hou S is that the world can no longer be understood in relation to any "absolute" frame of reference defined by man. If one accepts this presupposition, then the concept of extrinsic or relative value becomes meaningless, and the traditional rationalism merely arbitrary. Fin d'Ou T Hou S suggests that the architectural object must become internalized so that its value lies in its own processes. Those programmatic requirements that had previously been seen as the causes must now become the effects of architecture. This "folly," unlike most of modern architecture, is neither rational architecture in the traditional sense nor the traditional arbitrary folly. It proposes an intrinsic value system as an alternative to a context of arbitrariness; it is true to its own logic. Faced with an object that admits no discursive element external to its own processes, our customary role as subject is futile, and we are bereft of our habitual modes of understanding and appraising architecture. Fin d'Ou T Hou S requires a new reader, one willing to suspend previous modes of deciphering in favor of an attitude of receptive investigation.

While Fin d'Ou T Hou S claims to be self-definitive, it does not claim to be self-explanatory. This process records its own history at every point in its development, but no one step, including the last, is any more than an artificial representation of a single frame from a seamless continuity, which would be self-explanatory if it could be recreated. Traditionally, the need for a score or text devalued the architectural project. Fin d'Ou T Hou S is presented as a score of its process; text is provided in the form of a presentation and critique of decomposition as architectural process, and an explanation of the analyses and processes discovered in the initial configuration. The "house" itself is proposed as an approximation of decomposition, not an example of it.

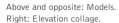

Above and opposite: Models.
Right: Elevation collage.

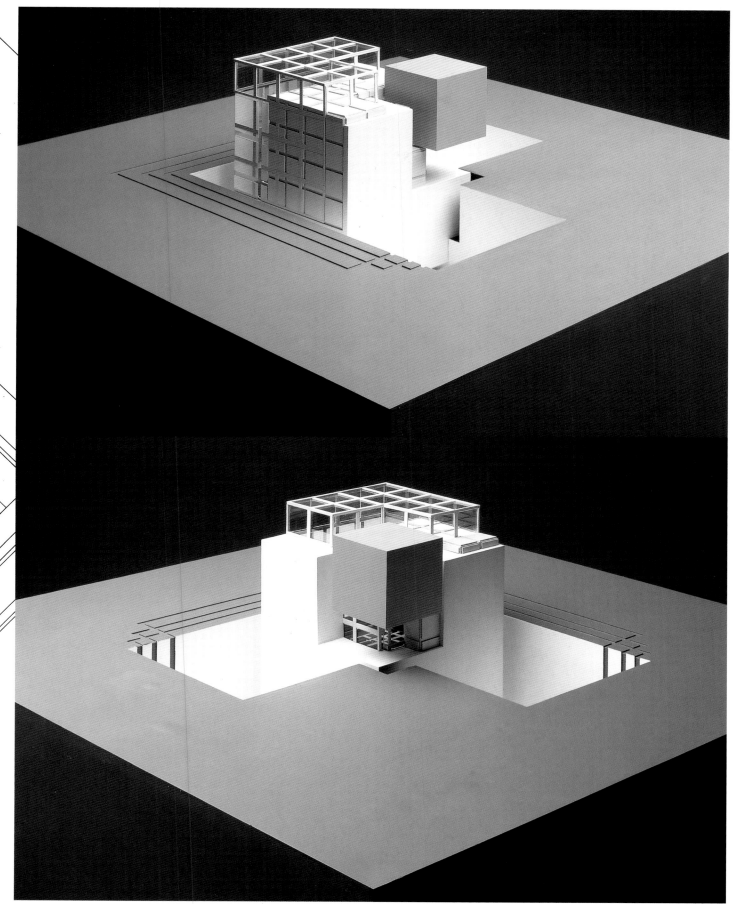

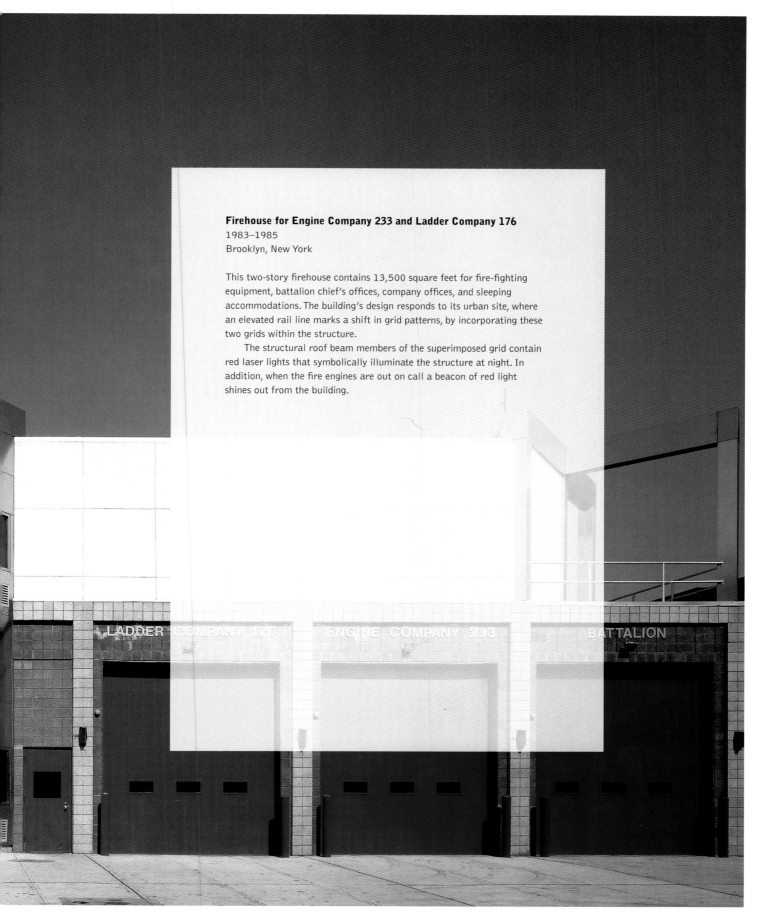

Firehouse for Engine Company 233 and Ladder Company 176
1983–1985
Brooklyn, New York

This two-story firehouse contains 13,500 square feet for fire-fighting equipment, battalion chief's offices, company offices, and sleeping accommodations. The building's design responds to its urban site, where an elevated rail line marks a shift in grid patterns, by incorporating these two grids within the structure.

The structural roof beam members of the superimposed grid contain red laser lights that symbolically illuminate the structure at night. In addition, when the fire engines are out on call a beacon of red light shines out from the building.

Ground-floor plan and second-floor
barracks plan, rotated 45 degrees.

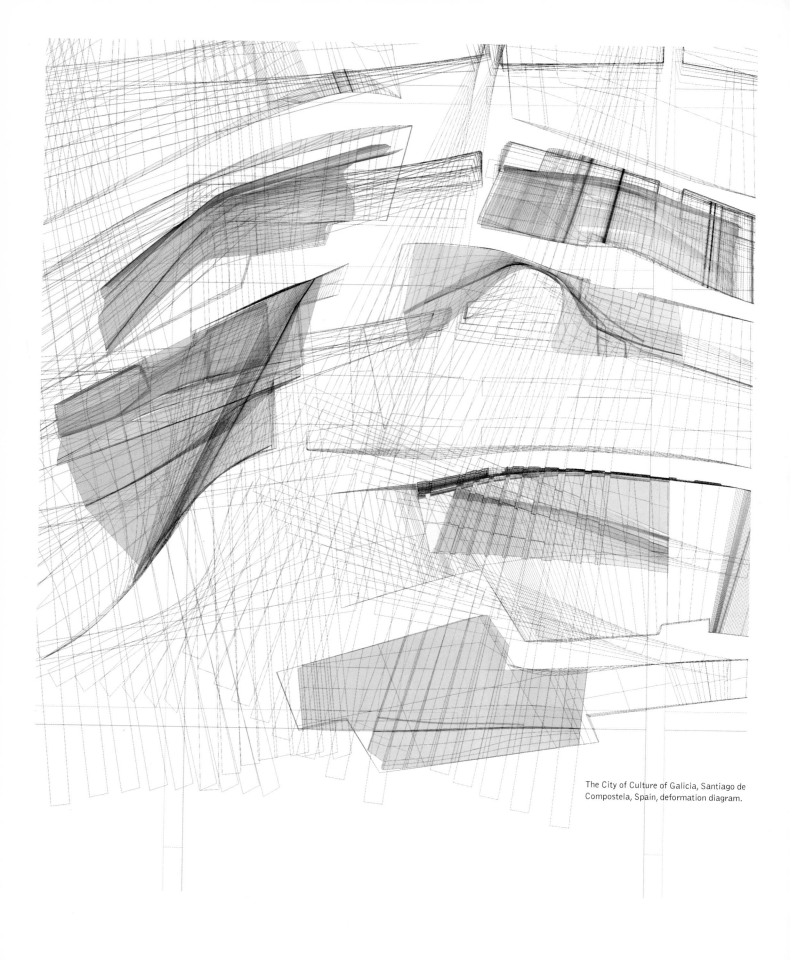

The City of Culture of Galicia, Santiago de
Compostela, Spain, deformation diagram.

EUPHORIC RATIO

Sarah Whiting

The detective novel can coerce the self-shrouding world into revealing itself in this manner only because it is created by a consciousness that is not circumscribed by that world. Sustained by this consciousness, the detective novel really thinks through to the end the society dominated by autonomous Ratio – a society that exists only as a concept – and develops the initial moments it proposes in such a way that the idea is fully realized in actions and figures.[1]

– Siegfried Kracauer

1. Siegfried Kracauer, "The Hotel Lobby," in *The Mass Ornament: Weimar Essays*, Thomas Y. Levin, trans. and ed. (Cambridge: Harvard University Press, 1995), 174.

For Siegfried Kracauer, capitalism's most fetid by-product was *Ratio*: pure rationality drained of all meaning. Despite the fact that mathematical ratios construct precise relationships, they nevertheless possess a now-you-see-me, now-you-don't quality – their real impact radiates from the underlying relationships that oscillate back and forth across the simple device of their double dots (:). Kracauer believed that the detective novel permitted a peek around the edges of rationalism's pseudo-mythical façade, behind which lay a space filled with the ricocheting irrationalities of modern life. Although detective stories construct precise, complex scenarios, Kracauer pointed out that even the genre's best-selling page-turners – those with the most twisting and turning of organizational frameworks – never added up to more than unmemorable, albeit amusing distractions.[2] For

2. See Thomas Y. Levin, "Introduction," in Siegfried Kracauer, *The Mass Ornament*, for a more complete discussion of Kracauer's study of the detective genre as well as his interest in/ horror of *Ratio*.

Kracauer, the incongruous union of exactitude, complexity, and ephemerality was precisely what made the detective story the perfect encapsulation of *Ratio*.

Kracauer's *Ratio* was balanced upon a 1920s fulcrum of sorts, a view of the world that was delicately perched amidst enlightened positivism, late humanism, and burgeoning modernity. With the advantage of hindsight, it is possible to understand this *Ratio* as a kind of see-saw of sensibilities, poised to tip in the ensuing decades but impossible to know in which direction (which is precisely why Kracauer's text is so evocative). In this essay, I will examine the subsequent "tilt" of this *Ratio* as it pertained to modern architecture, and in particular to what can be termed *The Crisis of the Modern Subject*. I will take up this topic through a brief discussion of Rudolf Wittkower and Colin Rowe with the aim of concentrating on a discussion of *Ratio* and the subject in the work of Peter Eisenman.

To ask "what is *Ratio*'s relation to architecture?" is at once obvious and absurd, especially to the fifty-years'-worth of architecture students who fed upon the formalist diet of Colin Rowe's "Mathematics of the Ideal Villa."[3] *Ratios* are the inescapable ether underlying architecture, like rhythm to music or hue to painting. They constitute architecture's most base, most innate, most identifiable viscera, informing our grasp of architecture in the most exact of ways (proportions) and yet never failing to effervesce into that vast enigma known as architectural *meaning*. Their precise rationality is inextricably intertwined with the inchoate sensibilities that they generate. Vitruvius himself used the term *ratiocination*

3. Colin Rowe, "The Mathematics of the Ideal Villa" (1947), in *The Mathematics of the Ideal Villa and Other Essays* (Cambridge: MIT Press, 1976).

Colin Rowe, analytic diagram of Palladio's Villa Malcontenta, first published in **Architectural Review**, 1947.

(the process of reasoning) specifically to mean "architectural theory," thereby infusing theory with inference. The first subset of Vitruvius' *venustas* (the second category of the firmness, beauty, and delight triad) was *ordinatio*, the detailed proportioning of each part of the building as well as the proportional relations of the parts to the building as a whole. As Vitruvius insisted, "Without symmetry and proportion no temple can have a rational design, unless, that is, there is a precise relationship between its parts, as in the case of a well-built human body."[4] Here, *Ratio*'s dependence upon the certainties of measure unfailingly succumbs to the vagaries of vastness, to architecture's incessant attempts to affect synthesis in the broadest possible (in this case "humanist") sense. Arguably, it is precisely at this moment – the confluence of exactitude and generality – that *Ratio* yields its greatest potential. Whether in pursuit of commodity, firmness, or delight, it is *Ratio* that incites architecture's subject, without whom *ratiocination* would be for naught.

Perhaps unwittingly, Kracauer brought to the fore a crisis that underlay architecture throughout the twentieth century. The advent of modernism carried with it the dissolution of the singular, collectivist subject that the Vitruvian *Ratio* sought to create. Kracauer's writings are filled with the entropic fallout (the "isolated anonymous atoms"[5]) of modern life. Across the last seven or eight decades, few issues have marked architecture as profoundly as has *The Crisis of the Modern Subject*. In simplified terms, twentieth-century architects have had two responses to this condition: 1) *This Crisis is Really Interesting* and 2) *We Have to Fix This*

4. Vitruvius, *De architectura III. i.i* (Loeb, vol. I: 158) as translated in Hanno-Walter Kruft, *A History of Architectural Theory from Vitruvius to the Present*, trans. Ronald Taylor, Elsie Callander, and Antony Wood (New York: Princeton Architectural Press, 1984), 27. The original, 1914 English translation of Vitruvius' *Ten Books on Architecture* by Morris Hicky Morgan admittedly places less emphasis on the term *rational* (New York: Dover Publications, 1960), 72.

5. Kracauer, *The Mass Ornament*, 182.

6. Peter Eisenman, "Misreading," in *Houses of Cards* (New York: Oxford University Press, 1987), 177.

7. On the distinction between singularity and originality, please see Rosalind Krauss, "The Originality of the Avant-Garde" in Krauss, *The Originality of the Avant-Garde and Other Modernist Myths* (Cambridge, MA: MIT Press, 1985; 1993): 151–70. For Eisenman's own reference to Krauss and singularity, see Peter Eisenman, "Diagram: An Original Scene of Writing," in *Diagram Diaries* (New York: Universe, 1999), 51."

Crisis. Peter Eisenman has been a long-time player in the Really-Interesting-Crisis camp. Colin Rowe was Eisenman's most visible counterpart among the Fix-Its. Paradoxically, both responses are thoroughly indebted to *Ratio* as a central discursive tenet. Eisenman's *Ratio* produces an architecture that "would necessarily create anxiety and distance,"[6] resulting in a subject ultimately at odds with him- or herself. Put another way, while Vitruvius's collective ambitions yield to the "face-to-face with nothing" vacuity of Kracauer's lobby, Eisenman's subject is separated not only from other individuals – *à la* Kracauer – but, even more radically, from his or her own subjectivity. It is this necessary anxiousness that constitutes the very root of Eisenman's commitment to the definition of "singularity" in architecture.[7] In a career that has oscillated among forms, histories, and disciplines, Eisenman's redefined subjects – his composite objective/subjective *Ratios* – have reveled in architecture's capacity to renew itself from within the *Ratio*-busting maelstrom of the present. Rowe's *Ratio*, on the other hand, resuscitated liberal humanism in the guise of a rewritten modernism: "our jurist is obliged to consult the old and existing; and it is only by reference to these that a genuine innovation can be proclaimed."[8] In stark contrast to Eisenman's radically individuated subject, Rowe's subject was a reinvigorated collective whose common ground lay in the transcendent nature of supra-linguistic formal systems.

Rowe's coupling of meaning and order underscored his own affiliation with his mentor Rudolf Wittkower, whose *Architectural Principles in the Age of Humanism* of 1949

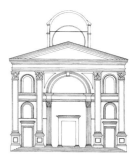

Above and opposite:
Michele Funari, drawings of Alberti's Sant'Andrea at Mantua, in **Formal Design in Renaissance Architecture from Brunelleschi to Palladio** (Rizzoli, 1995).

8. Rowe, as cited in R.E. Somol, *In Form Falls Fiction: Misreading the Avantgarde in Contemporary Architecture* (Ph.D. Diss., University of Chicago, 1997),30. Somol's chapter "The Law of the Colon" (30–62) offers one of the best existing studies of Rowe's interpretation of and influence on the American context.

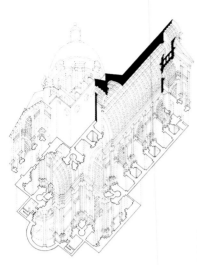

9. See Rudolf Wittkower, *Architectural Principles in the Age of Humanism* (1949; rpt. New York: W.W. Norton, 1971). See also Alina Payne, "Rudolf Wittkower and Architectural Principles in the Age of Modernism," *JSAH* 53 (September 1994): 322–42.

jettisoned intuitive or empathetic theories of reception in favor of understanding Renaissance esthetics as a rational belief in *numerical* order. Wittkower tied architecture not to psychology but to science, mathematics, and music.[9] For Wittkower as for his student Rowe, "The conviction that architecture is a science and that each part of a building, inside as well as outside, has to be integrated into one and the same system of mathematical ratios, may be called the basic axiom of Renaissance architects."[10] The *meaning* of those ratios, according to Wittkower, resided in their ability to codify a harmonious, divinely ordered universe where man's place would always be as precise as any column's. In describing Alberti's Santa Maria delle Carceri, he writes: "Its majestic simplicity, the undisturbed impact of its geometry, the purity of its whiteness are designed to evoke in the congregation a consciousness of the presence of God – of a God who has ordered the universe according to immutable mathematical laws, who has created a uniform and beautifully proportioned world, the consonance and harmony of which is mirrored in His temple below."[11] Wittkower unapologetically idealizes not only the harmony of the Renaissance ratios, but also the harmony between man's place in the world and architecture's definition of that world. Given that he is writing in the 1940s, one can imagine that Wittkower was deliberately, even longingly looking back to a period where such a harmony might be attainable.[12] Colin Rowe's continuation of this harmonic vision owed much to his mentor. His "Mathematics of the Ideal Villa" article, also written in the 1940s, extended a

10. Wittkower, *Architectural Principles*, 101.

11. Ibid., 21.

12. As Alina Payne notes, although Wittkower's *Architectural Principles* was published in 1949, the book originated in three articles dating from the early 1940s. Payne, op. cit. fn. 14: 325.

ings, but which he regarded as general. Indeed, Rome for him was still supremely

, their large scale

similar argument about the relationship between science, architecture, and modernism. Like Wittkower, Rowe correlated order with lived harmony; he opened his text with references to Virgilian dreams of happiness and virtue emanating from both Palladio's and Le Corbusier's rationalized oeuvres, although he does acknowledge that harmony is more artificially sustained in Le Corbusier's post-world-war world. Le Corbusier (as interpreted by Rowe) offers a perfect illustration of *Ratio* being used, as Kracauer said, to promote a *calculated*, constructed worldview that exists only as pure concept: "*Ratio* flees from reason and takes refuge in the abstract."[13] The difference between Palladio and Le Corbusier is significant: the former uses *Ratio* as a mirror for the perfect world that *is*, while the latter uses *Ratio* to offer a window on to a world that he thinks *ought to be*. However, these views collapse into one another inasmuch as both *Ratio*-types promulgate a world where architecture's meaning emanates from its formal order.

Eisenman leaves no doubt about his loyalties to the form/meaning alliance. His is an entire career committed to formal research, to what could fondly be termed *Ratio ad nauseam* inasmuch as we are always left unsettled by his work. Eisenman's *Ratio* meters the alienated, hidden, inconsistencies of contemporary life – hardly the stuff of harmonious continuity, let alone perfection. If Rowe pulled an idealized history forward, Eisenman pushes a vertiginous present back into history. If modernism brought us a spectacular (if occasionally harrowing) panorama of our collective future, Eisenman gives us an unnerving view into

13. Kracauer, *The Mass Ornament*, 84.

ics and he would
m. For his plans
and *commodité*
ground of a
recently, pos-
re, one may
ents which if
eminiscent of his
he Byzantine
there is also
ts of mechanics.
emple of love
s are fitted with

something of
he Virgilian
which is repre-
elf very readily to
between the
e gap between
receives its most
mpelling as the
as at the Malcon-
with sophisti-
tual feat which
cies in the pro-

ed classicist with
ranslates this
the continued

96   TRACING EISENMAN

validity that he finds it to possess. The reference to the Pantheon in the superim-posed pediments of the Malcontenta, to the thermae in its cruciform salon, the ambiguity, profound in both idea and form, in the equivocal conjunction of tem-ple front and domestic block; these are charged with meaning, both for what they

NOT A FORMALIST AT ALL
BUT CHARGED WITH
MEANING

the agitated matter of our individuated *now*. Perhaps nothing is more significant in this transition than the relocation of *The Crisis of the Modern Subject*. One might think of this relocation in terms of labor, or, to circumvent the Marxist-capitalist baggage that such a term evokes, in terms of *effort*. Eisenman deploys a canonically modern device by requiring that the contemporary subject be active, that he or she exert effort in situating him- or herself in space. And yet his subject radically diverges from the classic (read: Rowe-ian) Crisis response in that this effort results in individuation rather than an imposed collectivity. And herein lie the seeds of dissenting opinions vis-à-vis Peter Eisenman: Is Eisenman's homeopathic approach to architecture a valid antidote to the failings of modernism's allopathy? Is "an architecture of good intentions" even possible in a world whose subjectivities find themselves drowning in the profoundly disquieting anxieties of contemporary life? Or, perhaps most importantly, should we be at all invested in the notion that architecture carries with it any possibility of reinvigorating the health of The Subject?

* * *

Taped discussion about an Eisenman submission runs like this: "If you want nonrelevant housing, this is nonrelevant housing," says Voice One. "I object intensely," responds Voice Two. "Look at the violence that architect has used on the client. He's got a 6'9" x 6'9" bedroom, and all of that construction …" A third Voice breaks in, concluding that "the architect's concerns have nothing to do with people who encounter the building; it's an abstraction." Is there a vote on this? It's "No" of course.[14]

SARAH WHITING   97

14. John Morris Dixon recalling the P/A Design Awards jury deliberation over Peter Eisenman's entry (one of his houses), Editorial, *Progressive Architecture*, March 1972.

House IV plan.

Eisenman rereads Colin Rowe, "The Mathematics of the Ideal Villa," in **The Mathematics of the Ideal Villa and Other Essays** (MIT Press, 1992 edition).

Peter Eisenman is famously and frequently accused of being a "mere formalist." Truth be told, Eisenman's work is not what most critics would define as "user-friendly." But to ask whether this architecture has anything to do with people is ridiculous at best and inane at worst. The form of this question belies not simply a misreading of Eisenman but (far more worrisome) a wholesale ignorance of what has transpired in architecture culture over the last one hundred years. This is not to say that Eisenman is somehow above reproach; we are all well enough versed in the critical project to recognize that a purely critical project rings hollow without offering some form of projective counterpart.[15] And few would question that a 6'-9" square bedroom leaves something to be desired. But does the absence of the rhetoric of "goodness" (swirling around us today in a heavily coded, halo-bathed, apparently obligatory discourse) necessarily signify a lack of interest in the occupation of these spaces?

In his own description of House III [40], Eisenman refers to the owner as an "intruder," a subject to be "stimulated" and re-cast by architecture rather than merely living among the mirrors of "imposed taste."[16] Eisenman's compulsory role for the owner of the house is directly related to the understanding that architecture necessarily *creates* its audience, and that in so doing, alters the previous existence of this audience's members. "If we speak of, say, Renaissance art," Rosalind Krauss explains regarding a parallel scenario, "we are not just referring to objects that look different from the ones that preceded (or followed) them by virtue of a transformed set of organizing rules. We are speaking

15. See *Assemblage* 41, especially Whiting, Eisenman, and Somol on the question of the critical.

16. Peter D. Eisenman, "House III: To Adolf Loos and Bertolt Brecht," *Progressive Architecture* (May 1972): 92.

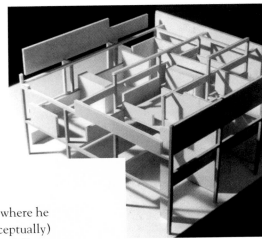

House II model.

17. Rosalind Krauss, "Death of a Hermeneutic Phantom: Materialization of the Sign in the Work of Peter Eisenman," in Eisenman, op. cit.: p. 180.

as well of a different conception of a viewer and where he stands (spiritually, intellectually, politically, perceptually) vis-à-vis the object."[17] What then, is Eisenman's "different conception" of the viewer, and how does that conception correspond to the changing formal manipulations of his architecture over his career?

Eisenman's house projects aimed at liberating architecture from the burden of program. By the 1960s – a decade during which Eisenman studied, wrote about, and began building architecture – modernism's creed "form follows function" was so deeply embedded within architecture culture that it had been reduced to a mere caricature. Eisenman's response to this was to develop a "Cardboard Architecture," stripped of functions and, consequently, neutralized in terms of social, political, and technological assignations:

Cardboard is used to shift the focus from our existing conception of form in an aesthetic and functional context to a consideration of form as a marking or notational system. The use of cardboard attempts to distinguish an aspect of these forms which are designed to act as a signal or a message and at the same time the representation of them as a message.[18]

18. Peter D. Eisenman, "House I, 1967," in *Five Architects: Eisenman, Graves, Gwathmey, Hedjuk, Meier*, ed. Arthur Drexler (New York: Oxford University Press,1972), 15.

Eisenman's goal was (and continues to be) to distill the structure of architecture's form in an effort to find meaning *established by* as opposed to *associated with* architecture. Rowe had similarly focused upon architecture's autonomy – architecture *qua* architecture – but had done so by resuscitating the *Ratio* of pre-modernity. Meaning for Rowe came from the proportional relationships that, he

SARAH WHITING 99

argued, transcended history. Deploying the comparative method of the nineteenth-century German art historian Heinrich Wölfflin, Rowe demonstrated the mathematical correspondences of planar and elevational proportioning systems. Because these proportional correspondences reappeared in different projects from different historical moments, Rowe argued in his early writings that the meanings of the buildings analyzed were tied to their formal characteristics, not to the politics, economics, or social conditions of their times, nor to the functional requirements of their programs.

Taking his cue from Rowe, who was a friend and mentor when he wrote his doctoral thesis at Cambridge, Eisenman similarly eschewed architecture's dependence upon socio-political contexts. But, already in his dissertation, Eisenman began turning away from Rowe's particular formalism in favor of an architectural analysis that foregrounded *process* over *object*. Rowe's humanist excavations carried with them the scent of immutability, of Truth. Whether located within a modern or premodern ethos, for Eisenman the certainties of a particular *Ratio* could not be reconciled with the essential instabilities of life today. "While Wittkower's and Rowe's diagrams essentially relied on an analysis of the formal as a stable and *a priori* condition, my diagrams contained the seeds of something else: they proposed the possible opening up of the formal interiority of architecture to concerns of the conceptual, the critical and perhaps to a diagramming of a preexistent instability in this interiority."[19] Noam Chomsky's linguistic theories of deep structure and

19. Peter Eisenman, "Interiority: Grids," in *Diagram Diaries* (New York: Universe, 1999), 48. For more on Eisenman's foregrounding of process, see Stan Allen's "Trace Elements" in this book.

20. Peter Eisenman, "From Object to Relationship II: Giuseppe Terragni's Casa Giuliani Frigerio," *Perspecta* 13/14 (1971): 41.21. ref

Rosalind Krauss's poststructuralist art historical criticism enabled Eisenman to bring these "seeds" to maturation by offering a theoretical milieu within which he could redefine the formalist role given to *Ratio* and, in so doing, render it less stable, less neutral: "While formal analysis is a valuable art-historical method, in itself it can become merely descriptive – an exercise in intellectual gymnastics," Eisenman explained, justifying his opportunistic instrumentalization of architectural history.[20] Instead of seeking a *Ratio* based on proportional typologies, Eisenman turned formal analysis into a "probing device to uncover traces"[21] of the unstable, the atypical, and the unforeseen. The effect was profound: *Ratio* at this point became a tool of critique/production, thereby leaving behind its role as a measure of conformance.

Eisenman's 1971 article, "From Object to Relationship II: Giuseppe Terragni's Casa Giuliani Frigerio," reveals this recasting of *Ratio*'s purview. Springboarding from Chomsky, who argued that deep structure determines a semantic reading, Eisenman identified three semiotic categories for architecture: *pragmatic* (functionalism), *semiotic* (iconography, or the relationship between symbols and their referents), and *syntactic* (structuralism, or the relationship of symbol to symbol). Eisenman used Terragni's 1920s and 30s modernism to demonstrate how an architecture that foregrounds the syntactic – its "deep structure" – offers both a conceptual and perceptual reading, thereby expanding architecture's meaning, generating new meanings by releasing architecture from humanism's grip.[22]

SARAH WHITING   101

21. Ibid.

22. See Eisenman, "Postfunctionalism" in *Oppositions* 6 (Fall 1976) for his explanation of how architecture can shed both functionalism and iconography so that its meaning would come from architecture itself, rather than man.

House IV study model.

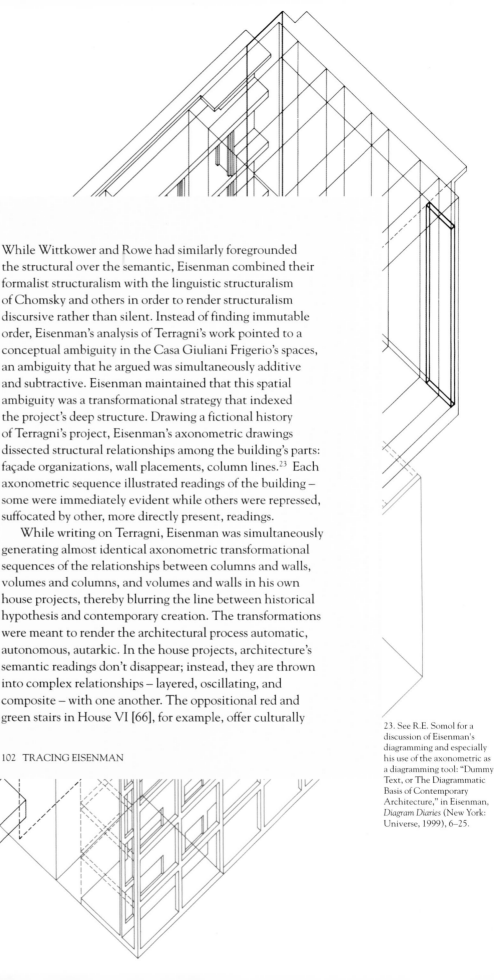

While Wittkower and Rowe had similarly foregrounded the structural over the semantic, Eisenman combined their formalist structuralism with the linguistic structuralism of Chomsky and others in order to render structuralism discursive rather than silent. Instead of finding immutable order, Eisenman's analysis of Terragni's work pointed to a conceptual ambiguity in the Casa Giuliani Frigerio's spaces, an ambiguity that he argued was simultaneously additive and subtractive. Eisenman maintained that this spatial ambiguity was a transformational strategy that indexed the project's deep structure. Drawing a fictional history of Terragni's project, Eisenman's axonometric drawings dissected structural relationships among the building's parts: façade organizations, wall placements, column lines.[23] Each axonometric sequence illustrated readings of the building – some were immediately evident while others were repressed, suffocated by other, more directly present, readings.

While writing on Terragni, Eisenman was simultaneously generating almost identical axonometric transformational sequences of the relationships between columns and walls, volumes and columns, and volumes and walls in his own house projects, thereby blurring the line between historical hypothesis and contemporary creation. The transformations were meant to render the architectural process automatic, autonomous, autarkic. In the house projects, architecture's semantic readings don't disappear; instead, they are thrown into complex relationships – layered, oscillating, and composite – with one another. The oppositional red and green stairs in House VI [66], for example, offer culturally

23. See R.E. Somol for a discussion of Eisenman's diagramming and especially his use of the axonometric as a diagramming tool: "Dummy Text, or The Diagrammatic Basis of Contemporary Architecture," in Eisenman, *Diagram Diaries* (New York: Universe, 1999), 6–25.

Peter Eisenman, analytic axonometric drawing of Giuseppe Terragni, Casa Giuliani Frigerio.

established, immediate semantic readings of stop and go: the red, upside-down stair, which cannot be ascended, says "stop," while the functional green stair, leading up to the second floor, indicates "go." But a conceptual reading of the two colors interferes with this iconic one: red and green combine to make gray. Eisenman's choice of these two particular colors was a deliberate effort to tangle color's symbolic value with its purely indexical use by literally graying it out. Over the course of his career Eisenman has continued to rely upon shades of oppositional, rather than complementary, colors, establishing his own self-referential, notational palette, which has differentiated itself from the high modernist primary color palette of red, yellow, blue, as much as it has from the late modern naturalist palette of pale yolk yellows, robin's egg blues, and avocado greens.[24]

24. Author's conversation with Eisenman, May 30, 2003.

Already in these early projects, Eisenman began to conceive of *Ratio* in an altogether new manner. Regulated acts of compositional disposition – governing the placement of walls, columns, and openings according to time-honored proportioning rules – had predicted architecture's correctness for hundreds of years. Now, in a no less regulated manner, *Ratio* was being used to establish architecture's "instability," its appetite for multifarious meaning. The weighty consecration that *Ratio* had both assumed and assured for so long was here being confronted by willfully transient super-meanings, minor-meanings, and counter-meanings at every turn. The early house projects rendered a simple object – a cube – complex by transforming it to reveal its "deep structure" – that is, the relations among its inherent

SARAH WHITING   103

House VI, stair details.

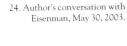

House VI, interior detail.

elements, its columns and surfaces. Looking at these projects
is like seeing double several times over: displacements,
shifts, rotations, and multiplications turn a single object
into many. Describing House VI (although the comment
could refer to any of the projects), Eisenman explained that
"this work is an attempt to transcend our traditional view
of designing, seeing, understanding our environment. It is
an attempt to alienate the individual from the known way
in which he perceives and understands his environment to
an environment which presents [itself] through a logical
structure of space … spatial relationships [that] are both
perceptual and conceptual."[25]

25. Peter Eisenman, *Houses
of Cards* (New York: Oxford
University Press, 1987), 150.

Alienating the viewer from norms, expectations,
and habits served as a wake-up call, a shocking view into
new spatial possibilities. In moving away from Rowe and
Wittkower, Eisenman moved closer to the early twentieth-
century work of the Russian formalists, including Viktor
Shklovsky, Osip Brik, and other members of the *Opoyaz*
group. The Russian formalists' strategy of *ostranenie*
("estrangement" or "defamiliarization") and, subsequently,
in Germany, Bertolt Brecht's parallel theory of *Verfremdung*
("estrangement" or "alienation") had the aim of startling
the reader, the viewer, or the audience member into a new
consciousness by "free[ing] socially conditioned phenomena
from that stamp of familiarity which protects them against
our grasp today"[26] – that is, by taking the familiar and
making it unfamiliar. To do this in literature or theater is to
shift course in midsentence or to interrupt an explanation,
a conversation, a proposition. But how to do the same in

26. Bertolt Brecht, "A Short
Organum for the Theatre"
(1949), in *Brecht on Theatre: The
Development of an Aesthetic*, ed.
and trans. John Willett (New
York: Hill & Wang, 1994), 37.
For an extended discussion of
Brecht's theory of *Verfremdung*
and its relation to Russian theories
of *ostranenie*, see Juliet Koss's
excellent essay "Playing Politics
with Estranged and Empathetic
Audiences: Bertolt Brecht and
Georg Fuchs," *South Atlantic
Quarterly* 96:4 (Fall 1997),
809–20.

architecture, which is fixed and which purports to stabilize our sense of being?

In the first houses, Eisenman achieved this estrangement through his choreography of excessive transformations. Layer upon layer of shifts, redundancies, rotations, and dislocations place the object as well as its systemic underpinnings just beyond our grasp. The surfeit of process (and the form that process begets) in these houses assures us that this is not merely the evacuated abstraction of a reductivist sensibility. These projects thrive on their proliferate excess. *Ratio* provokes this flux with an eye on stimulating its dynamic rather than taming its unruliness. The very transformations that are sequential – as evidenced by the series of diagrams accompanying each house design – ultimately collapse back onto themselves, becoming contradictory or even cannibalistic. In House II, for example, the deliberate redundancy of two structural systems (load-bearing walls and columns) results in a notational excess that catapults the subject into a suspended state, floating within the crossed-wires of the object's spatial codes. Eisenman's originality lies precisely here, in the recasting of *Ratio*'s subject-object relationship.

* * *

Across architectural history, *Ratio* has served as a kind of radiant heat for the reception of objects. To a greater or lesser degree, *Ratio* percolated outward from architects' calibrations of objects, thereby controlling how those objects affect us as subjects. Even under modernism, typically assumed to have been a radical departure from its antecedents, *Ratio*'s object-

ON READING ARCHITECTURE

to-subject outward radiance was maintained: what mattered most was an object's capacity to transform a model, modern subject into an idealized figure with idealized political and social capacities. Since at least the sixties, this object-subject model has become more complicated, more tangled in the complexity of the "subject studies" (in architecture and in extra-architectural disciplines) that emerged over recent decades. From situationism to identity politics, from cross-programming to cultural hybridity, today's subject continuously bobs about in the effluvium of pluralist difference. Not only can objects no longer be expected to determine our reactions to them, for many architects objects themselves have become emblems of heterogeneity. This is a clear departure from pre–World War II modernism. In much recent architectural practice, the subject appears to have assumed the role of the object (the radiator). Mapping and indexing abound in contemporary projects that strive to look multiple, diverse, and absorbent. These projects are avowedly opposed to totalization, leading their architects to seek techniques such as collage and fracturing in their endless pursuit of appearing minor.

Few would counter the assertion that Peter Eisenman is not, never has been, and never will be interested in appearing minor. And while it might well be interesting to discuss Eisenman's ambitious personality, it is more fruitful in this context to focus upon his architectural ambitions. While Eisenman subscribes to certain tenets of both modernism and postmodernism, the radiance in his projects emanates neither from the object nor the subject. Instead,

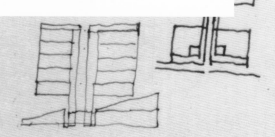

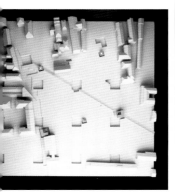

Presentation model for
Cannaregio, Venice, Italy.

Eisenman has collapsed the object and subject into one
another, denying them the tidy polar relationship that has
conventionally guided their use throughout architectural
history. Where his ambition differs from modernism is
that Eisenman's subject *and* object emerge from formal
manipulations; neither one is conclusive or singular. In other
words, while the modernist project was meant to form a
particular subject, Eisenman is more intent on transforming
subjectivity, inciting possibilities without predicting them.

Eisenman started with the modernist project of
estrangement, but then quickly expanded his scope to a
project of engagement. His "Cities of Artificial Excavation"
projects – Cannaregio [76], Berlin [80], Long Beach [129],
La Villette [140], and the Wexner Center [112] – evenly
arrayed historical and fictional information about a project's
site, history, and context, permitting subjects to rearrange
that information as they wanted. The subject was engaged
in writing the project's narrative, assembling it from the
material provided. This strategy was modern in its desire
to use architecture to affect a subject, and postmodern in
its flattening out of source material, rendering all "origins"
equal and hence simultaneously valuable and suspect.
The maintainence of this duality is crucial in grasping the
difference between Eisenman's excavation projects and
Colin Rowe/Fred Koetter's *Collage City*. For Rowe/Koetter,
the pastiche of collected references represents the demotion
of the object in deference to a particular enlightened liberal
subject – the book's juxtapositions serve as examples of
conformance being adapted to pluralist desires so that

SARAH WHITING   107

Sketches for IBA Social Housing at
Checkpoint Charlie, Berlin, West Germany.

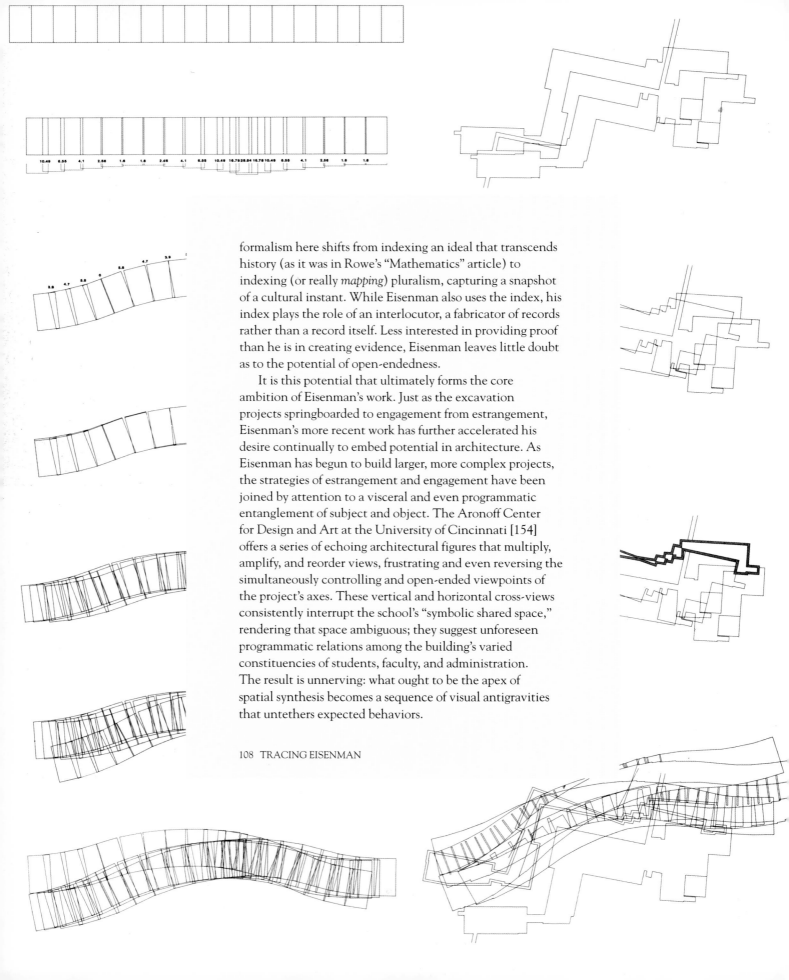

formalism here shifts from indexing an ideal that transcends history (as it was in Rowe's "Mathematics" article) to indexing (or really *mapping*) pluralism, capturing a snapshot of a cultural instant. While Eisenman also uses the index, his index plays the role of an interlocutor, a fabricator of records rather than a record itself. Less interested in providing proof than he is in creating evidence, Eisenman leaves little doubt as to the potential of open-endedness.

It is this potential that ultimately forms the core ambition of Eisenman's work. Just as the excavation projects springboarded to engagement from estrangement, Eisenman's more recent work has further accelerated his desire continually to embed potential in architecture. As Eisenman has begun to build larger, more complex projects, the strategies of estrangement and engagement have been joined by attention to a visceral and even programmatic entanglement of subject and object. The Aronoff Center for Design and Art at the University of Cincinnati [154] offers a series of echoing architectural figures that multiply, amplify, and reorder views, frustrating and even reversing the simultaneously controlling and open-ended viewpoints of the project's axes. These vertical and horizontal cross-views consistently interrupt the school's "symbolic shared space," rendering that space ambiguous; they suggest unforeseen programmatic relations among the building's varied constituencies of students, faculty, and administration. The result is unnerving: what ought to be the apex of spatial synthesis becomes a sequence of visual antigravities that untethers expected behaviors.

Promise here is forever offset by a calculated frustration. These are spaces predicated on unfulfilled glimpses of spatial order, on glances of a *Ratio* whose conclusion is replaced with an innately architectural potential. The curve of the main stair and the numerous vertical and horizontal cross axes and planes create an infinite number of vanishing points; there is no "correct" *point* from which to view. Even in the main auditorium, the central view to the stage is distracted: mysterious and alluring balcony spaces pull the eye upward and out; slits of fluorescent lighting follow the chevron pattern in the ceiling, suggesting not only the original building, but also the possibility of a light space directly above the auditorium; and, finally, the angled planes – neither parallel nor converging – that form the walls of the auditorium draw the eye in innumerable directions.

What Eisenman started with the Aronoff Center, he has almost infinitely multiplied in the more than one-million-square-foot project under construction for The City of Culture of Galicia in Spain [308]. Composed of six parts – a Music Theater, Galician Library, Museum of Galician History, New Technology Center, and a Central Services Building, as well as an arboretum – the project constitutes a 173-acre reformulation of a hilltop above the historic pilgrimage city of Santiago de Compostela. If the Aronoff Center created anxieties by eliminating *Ratio*'s traditional stabilities (proportions, axes, and perspectives), it did so mainly within the building's interior, focusing on activating the space between the old building and the new addition. Even if the addition bore a curious relation to its

Opposite: Aronoff Center for
Design and Art, process diagrams.
Below: Section model.
Above: Main auditorium.

SARAH WHITING 109

27. Dante, *La Vita Nuova*, chapter 7.

surroundings, it barely disturbed the figure-field relationship that architecture has traditionally had to the ground upon which it sits. At Santiago, Eisenman's destabilized *Ratio* now engages landscape and urbanism as well as architecture: the hilltop has been both carved and extracted, making it impossible to tell where landscape ends and building starts. Spaces between and within buildings are rendered similarly ambiguous, making it possible to redefine programs typically associated with either interiors or exteriors.

The City of Culture will become a new pilgrimage site for Galicia, transforming subjects not through religion but through a *Ratio* that plays architecture, landscape, and urbanism off one another. Santiago was one of medieval Christendom's most important pilgrimage destinations: in *La Vita Nuova*, Dante classified those who travel for the sake of serving the Supreme Being as follows: "Those who travel across the seas [to the Holy Land] may be called 'palm-bringers' and those who visit Rome can be called 'Rome-goers,' but the title of 'pilgrims' belongs to those only who are going to or coming from the House of Galicia, the holy grave of the apostle James."[27] The possibilities of transformation are the point of any pilgrimage site, but change doesn't come easily: at Santiago, just like at the Aronoff and all of Eisenman's other projects, those subjected to this architecture will never experience the luxury of being passive. Instead, they will be snared in an atmosphere of calculated estrangement whose vertiginous, agitating, and even frustrating qualities are laced with the ever-hopeful opiate of transformation. No mere project of detached

The City of Culture of Galicia, Santiago de Compostela, Spain, deformation diagram (right) and Periodicals Library (above).

abstraction, the *Ratio*-maelstrom that comes with the collapse of the subject and the object into one another belies an almost euphoric optimism about architecture's infinite possibilities.

My deepest thanks to Cynthia Davidson for her extraordinary patience, Peter Eisenman for the productive incentive imposed by his lack thereof, and Ron Witte for *everything*.

SARAH WHITING   111

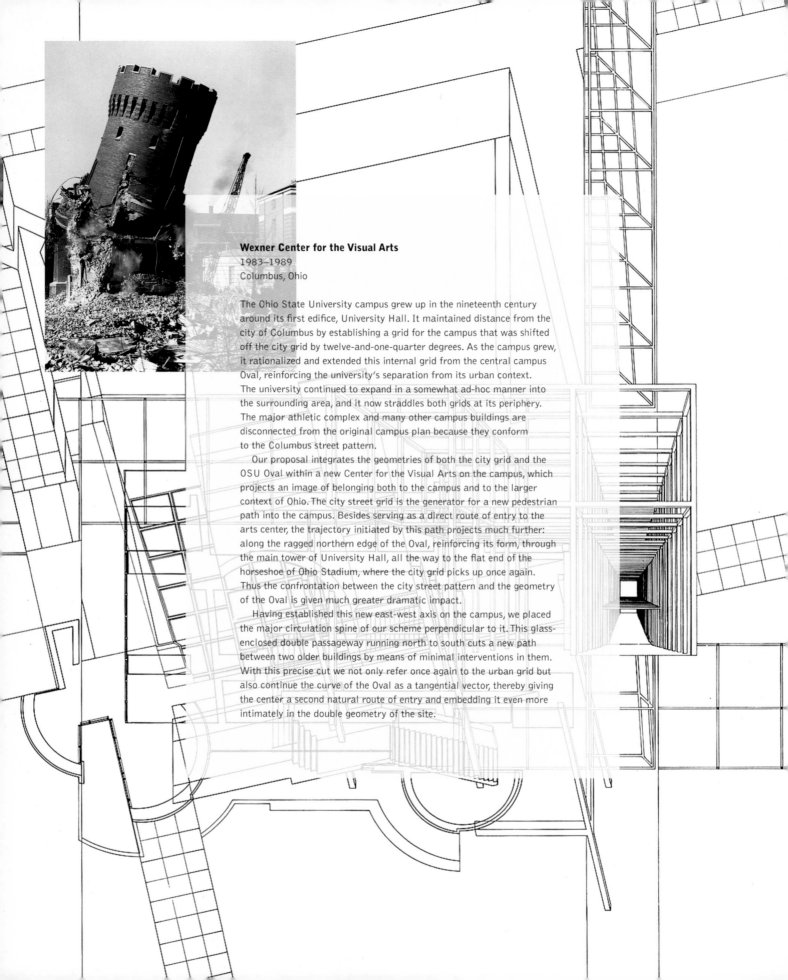

Wexner Center for the Visual Arts
1983–1989
Columbus, Ohio

The Ohio State University campus grew up in the nineteenth century around its first edifice, University Hall. It maintained distance from the city of Columbus by establishing a grid for the campus that was shifted off the city grid by twelve-and-one-quarter degrees. As the campus grew, it rationalized and extended this internal grid from the central campus Oval, reinforcing the university's separation from its urban context. The university continued to expand in a somewhat ad-hoc manner into the surrounding area, and it now straddles both grids at its periphery. The major athletic complex and many other campus buildings are disconnected from the original campus plan because they conform to the Columbus street pattern.

Our proposal integrates the geometries of both the city grid and the OSU Oval within a new Center for the Visual Arts on the campus, which projects an image of belonging both to the campus and to the larger context of Ohio. The city street grid is the generator for a new pedestrian path into the campus. Besides serving as a direct route of entry to the arts center, the trajectory initiated by this path projects much further: along the ragged northern edge of the Oval, reinforcing its form, through the main tower of University Hall, all the way to the flat end of the horseshoe of Ohio Stadium, where the city grid picks up once again. Thus the confrontation between the city street pattern and the geometry of the Oval is given much greater dramatic impact.

Having established this new east-west axis on the campus, we placed the major circulation spine of our scheme perpendicular to it. This glass-enclosed double passageway running north to south cuts a new path between two older buildings by means of minimal interventions in them. With this precise cut we not only refer once again to the urban grid but also continue the curve of the Oval as a tangential vector, thereby giving the center a second natural route of entry and embedding it even more intimately in the double geometry of the site.

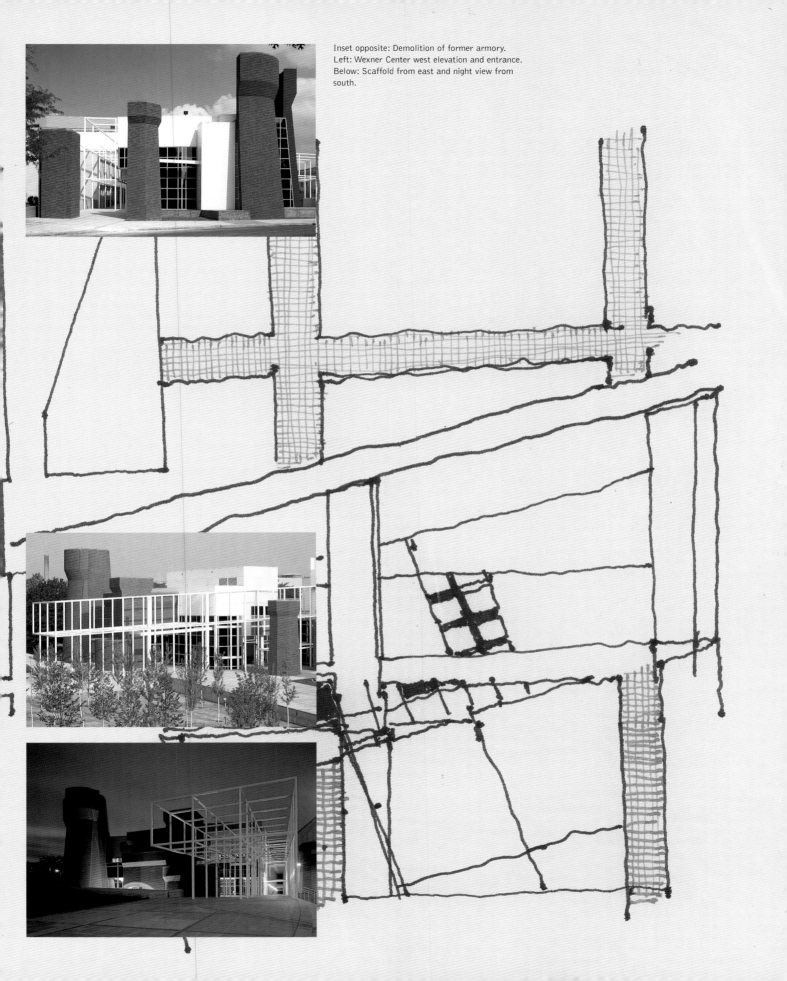

Inset opposite: Demolition of former armory.
Left: Wexner Center west elevation and entrance.
Below: Scaffold from east and night view from
south.

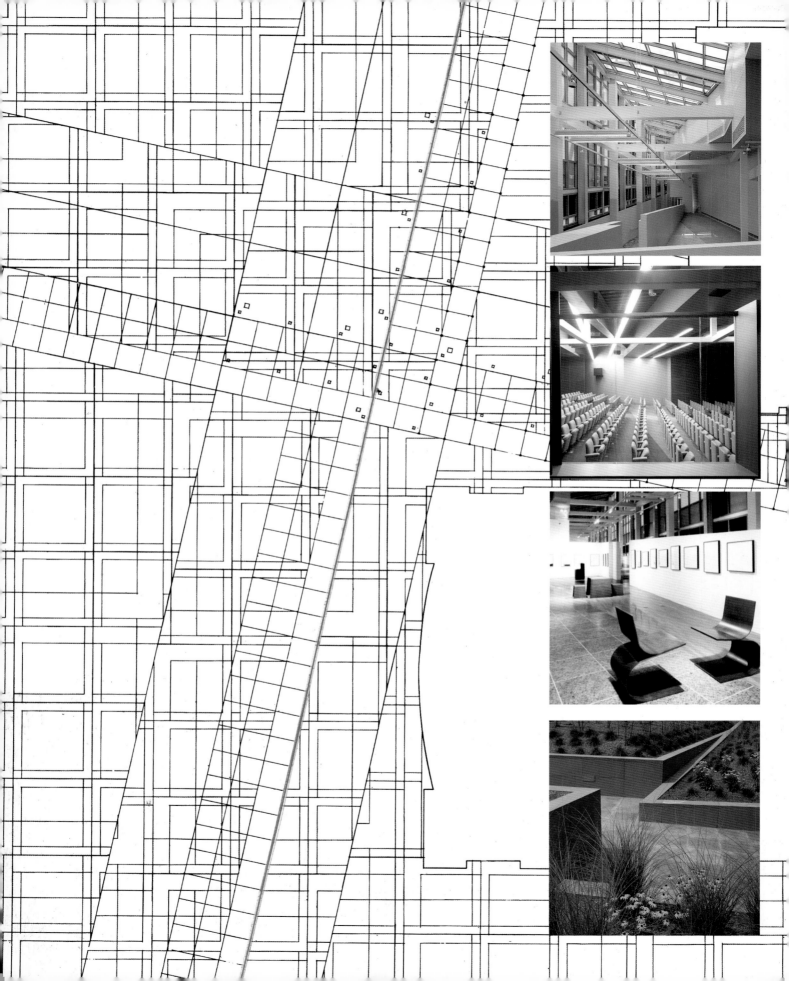

Opposite: Diagram of Wexner grid, shifted 12.25 degrees off campus grid, with interior and exterior views.

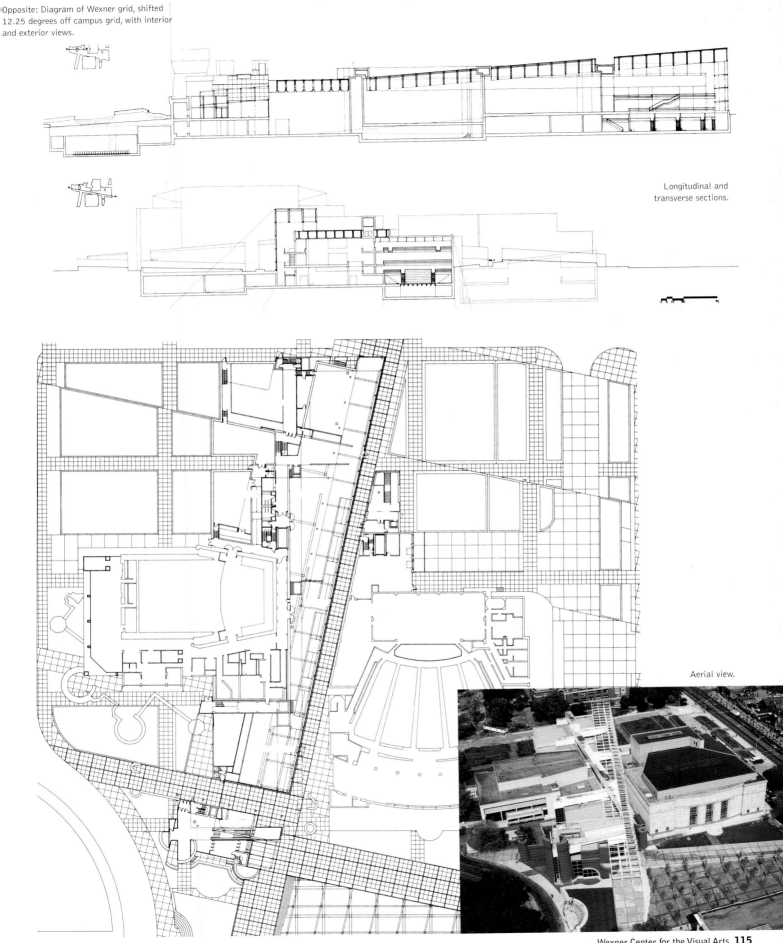

Longitudinal and transverse sections.

Aerial view.

Exterior scaffold runs parallel to interior ramp connecting galleries.

Moving Arrows, Eros, and Other Errors
1985
Verona, Italy

In 1530, Luigi Da Porto wrote "Giulietta e Romeo" to account for
two closely situated but separate castles in the Italian hill town of
Montecchio. In 1554, Matteo Bandello created another version of the
story, removing the lovers to Verona, where Shakespeare also located
his play of about 1596. Romeo and Juliet are fictional characters who
"lived" in real places. Our project attempts to uncover the story of a
site and retell it with architectural metaphors in drawings and models.

Through the multiple versions of the story, a setting is created
at more than one scale, thus undermining the anthropocentric
obsession with human scale that has dominated architecture since
the Renaissance. Scaling entails the use of three mutually dependent,
destabilizing concepts: discontinuity, which confronts the metaphysics
of presence; recursiveness, which confronts origin; and self-similarity,
which confronts representation and the esthetic object. First, the "site"
is confronted as a privileged presence — a context that is knowable and
whole. Images in three scales are superimposed so that no one scale is
preeminent. The images are revealed in excavations, both symbolizing
and making real the idea of uncovering a story. Illusion and reality
collide, and past, present, and future remain in perpetual flux. By
treating the site not simply as a presence but as both a palimpsest
and a quarry, containing traces of both memory and immanence,
the site can be thought of as nonstatic.

Theories of the site as present origin presume that the moving arrow
and the still arrow are the same, yet putting one's hand in front of both,
one quickly discovers the difference. Even though a picture of one arrow
would be virtually indistinguishable from the other, the moving arrow
contains where it has been and where it is going; it has a memory and
an immanence that are not present to the observer of its image — they
are essential absences. Hence the project title.

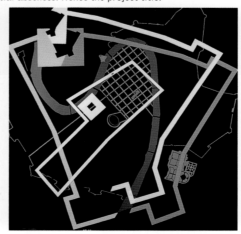
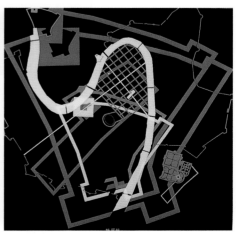

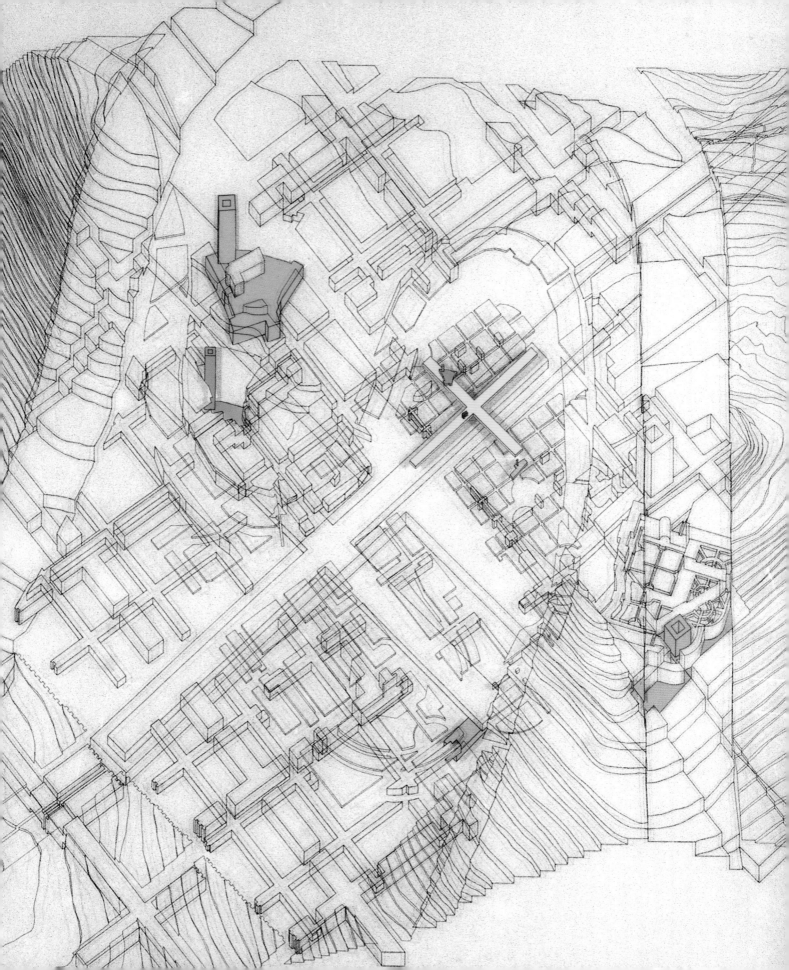

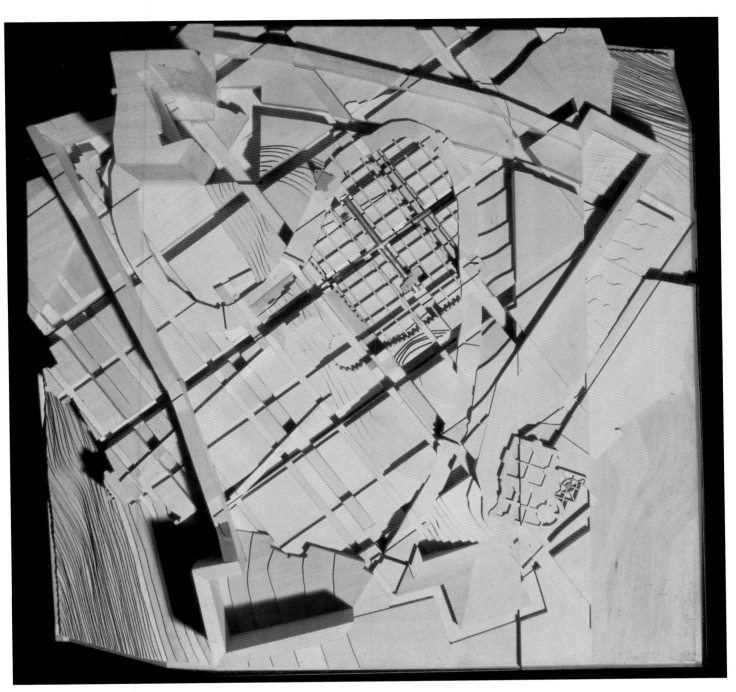

Site models.

Jewelry, Tableware, Hardware
1986
Textiles
1990

The jewelry designed for Cleto Munari proposes a different relationship to the human wearer. Mimetic of neither human form nor human proportion, each piece denies any connection to or embellishment of the human form. They are not decorative or representational but, rather, are part of a scaled continuum of objects from the ring to a building. More like ritual objects that carry mystical and unconscious meanings, the pieces are to be worn on symbolic occasions. It is clear that they mean, but what they mean can never be known.

The limited-edition plates for Swid Powell and door handles manufactured by FSB GmbH for the Wexner Center for the Visual Arts [112] are variations on the grid patterns of the Wexner Center.

The patterns for a collection of fabrics with Knoll, called Snakes and Ladders, are derived from diagrams from several architectural projects. The arc of the oar-stroke that defined the landscape for the Banyoles Olympic Hotel [170], the snaking wire-frame diagram of the addition to the Aronoff Center for Design and Art [154], and the Boolean Cube diagram for the Carnegie Mellon Research Institute [144] are each, in their woven repetitions, the basis for uniquely patterned and colored upholstery fabrics.

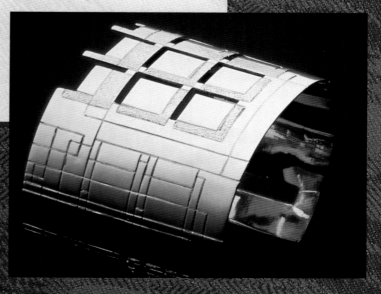

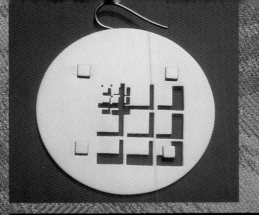
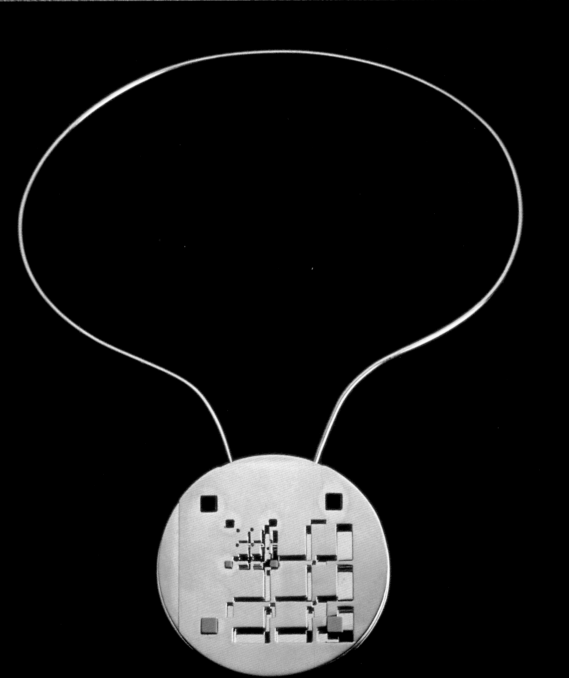

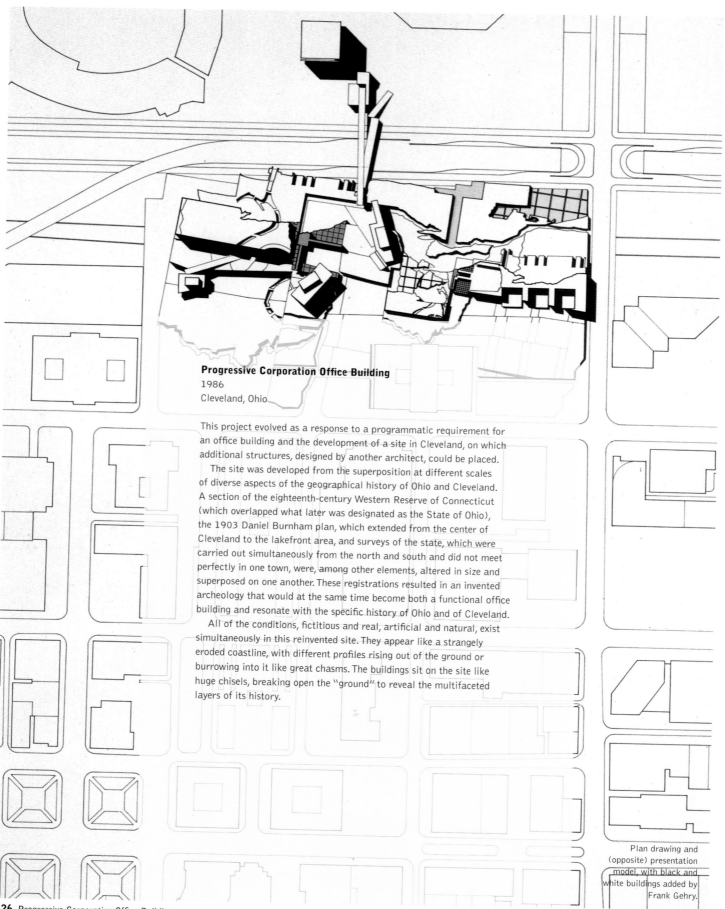

Progressive Corporation Office Building
1986
Cleveland, Ohio

This project evolved as a response to a programmatic requirement for an office building and the development of a site in Cleveland, on which additional structures, designed by another architect, could be placed.

The site was developed from the superposition at different scales of diverse aspects of the geographical history of Ohio and Cleveland. A section of the eighteenth-century Western Reserve of Connecticut (which overlapped what later was designated as the State of Ohio), the 1903 Daniel Burnham plan, which extended from the center of Cleveland to the lakefront area, and surveys of the state, which were carried out simultaneously from the north and south and did not meet perfectly in one town, were, among other elements, altered in size and superposed on one another. These registrations resulted in an invented archeology that would at the same time become both a functional office building and resonate with the specific history of Ohio and of Cleveland.

All of the conditions, fictitious and real, artificial and natural, exist simultaneously in this reinvented site. They appear like a strangely eroded coastline, with different profiles rising out of the ground or burrowing into it like great chasms. The buildings sit on the site like huge chisels, breaking open the "ground" to reveal the multifaceted layers of its history.

Plan drawing and (opposite) presentation model, with black and white buildings added by Frank Gehry.

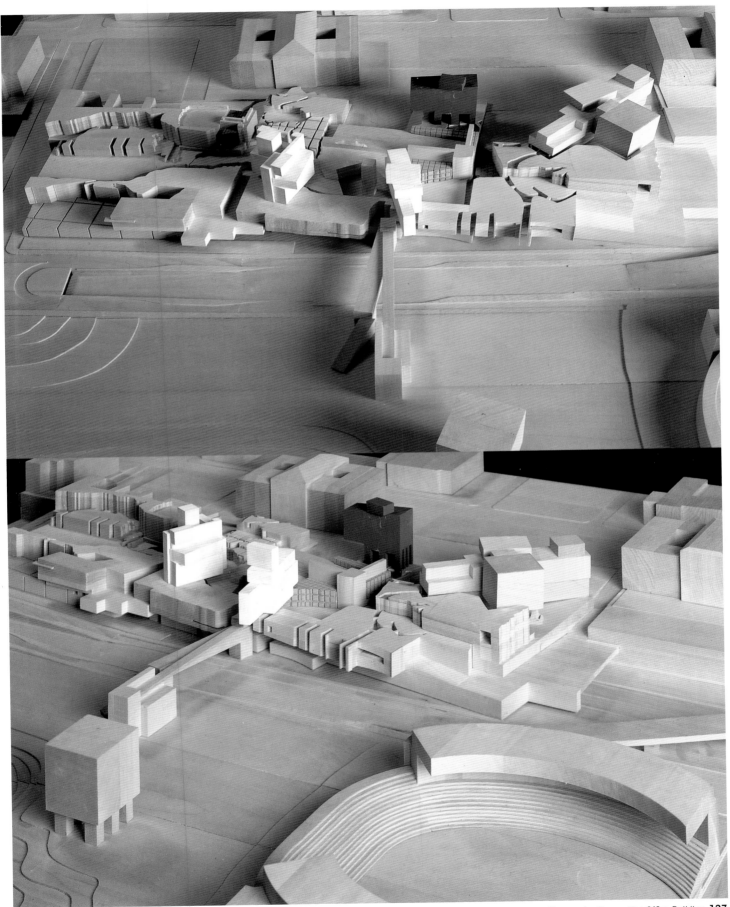

University Art Museum

1986

Long Beach, California

On a twenty-three-acre site adjacent to the main campus entrance of California State University at Long Beach, we developed the program and architectural design for a museum of contemporary experimentation. Located in an arboretum, the design allowed the museum to be discovered and perceived as if it were an archeological artifact.

The project is the outcome of a history "given to" the building. This "history" was compiled from a series of significant dates, beginning with the settlement of California in 1849, the creation of the campus in 1949, and the projected "rediscovery" of the museum in the year 2049. The idea was to imagine the site 100 years after the founding of the university, and 200 years after the gold rush. The building takes its form from the overlapping registration of several maps: of the ranch that once occupied the site, of the campus, and of the changing configurations of fault lines, a river, a channel, and the coastline. The "superposition" of these maps reveals analogical relationships that were obscured when some notations, such as social delineations, were accorded more importance. For example, the relationship of the channel at the edge of the museum site is similar to the relationship of the river to the entire campus site. Thus the building can be seen as an artifact, relating past and present conditions in a way that alludes to past, present, and possible future conditions. In addition, an elevated walkway, symbolic of the famous Southern California seacoast pier developments of the 1920s, provides a link between the north and south areas of the arboretum, traversing above and through the museum precinct.

Opposite: Plan view of presentation model and detail (right).

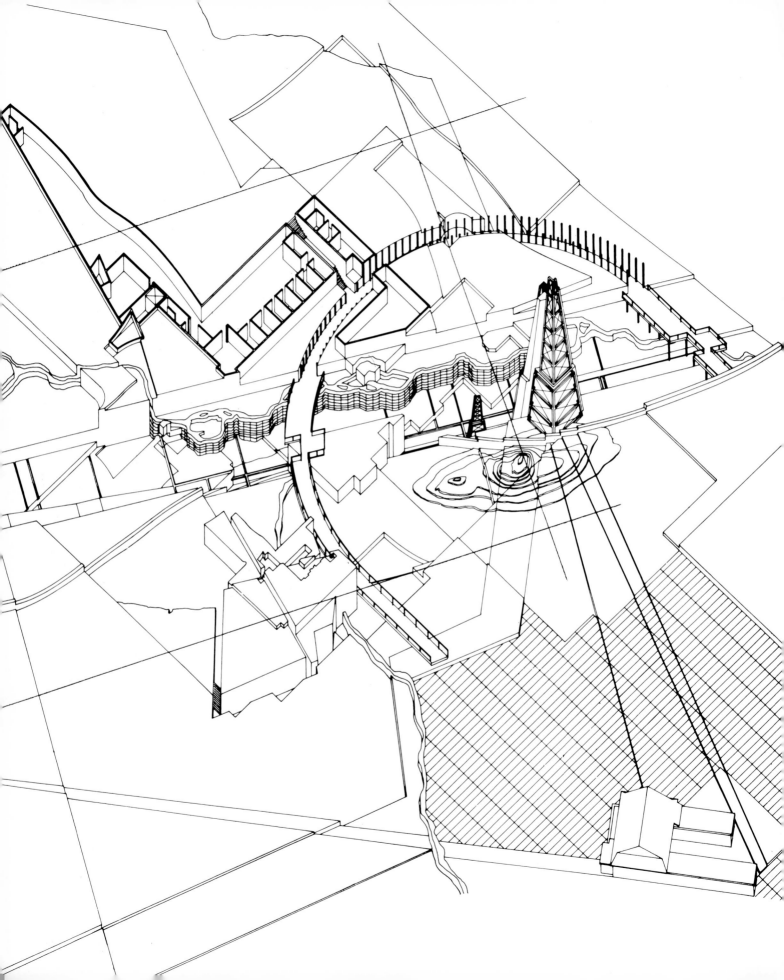

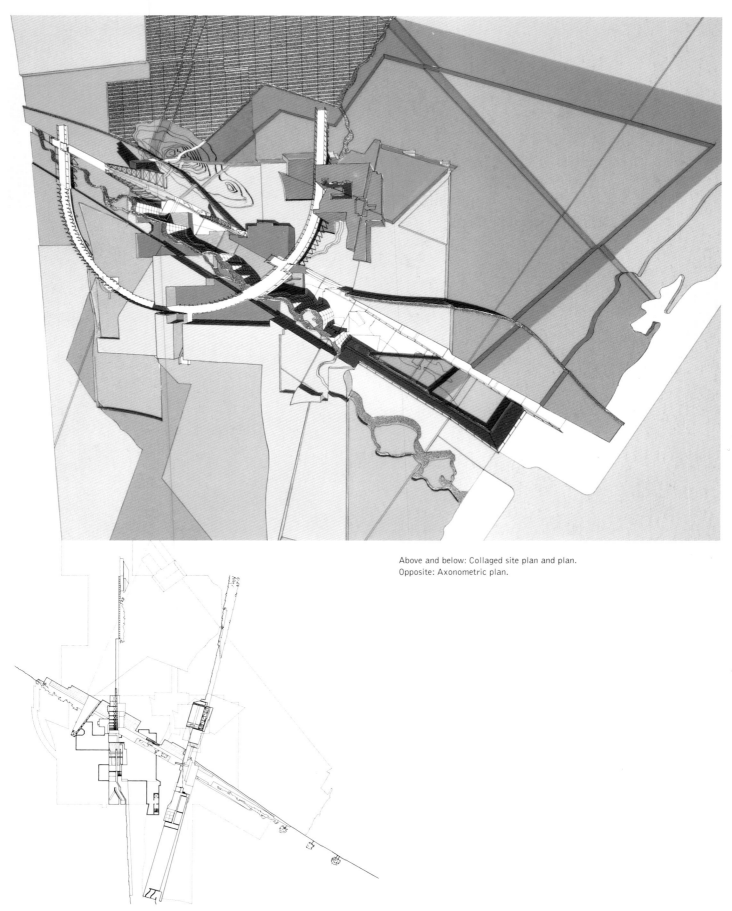

Above and below: Collaged site plan and plan.
Opposite: Axonometric plan.

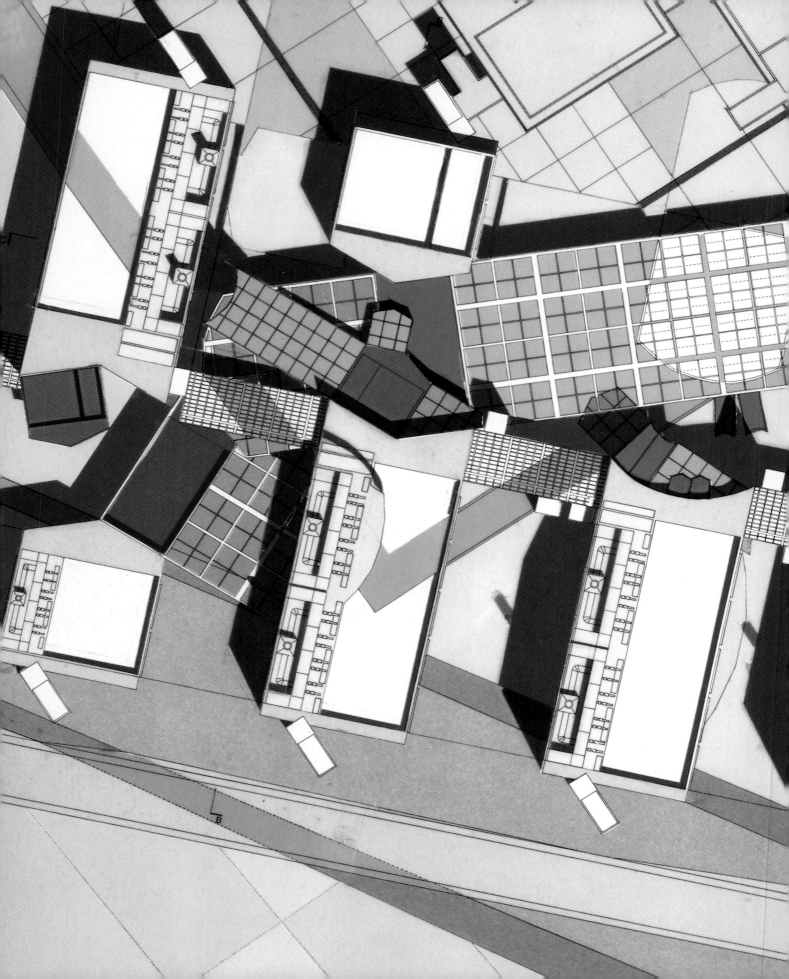

Biocenter
1987
Frankfurt am Main, Germany

An ambiguity between structure and ornament is produced in the design of the Biocenter for J.W. Goethe University by creating an analogy between architectural and biological processes. Biologists explain the construction of proteins by using four geometric figures, each with a specific color that symbolizes the DNA code. The shapes of the inner faces of these figures are capable of locking together in pairs. The blueprint for every protein is encoded in long sequences of these paired figures to form a double-strand chain. Using an analogy between biological construction and architectural construction, this chain can be transposed into architectural form in such a way that it produces an architecture symbolic of the discipline it houses.

In the Biocenter, the biologists' figures are overlaid on the site in a row along the base of a zigzagging band, following the precise sequence of the DNA chain for the protein collagen, which produces the necessary tensile strength of structure (as in bone). Rather than simply representing the physical configuration of the DNA, however, the project articulates the three most basic processes by which it produces proteins: replication, transcription, and translation. Each of these processes was used to transform the base figures progressively. By architecturally subjecting the biologists' figures to the very processes they describe, the interdisciplinary boundaries between architecture and biology are blurred. The final project is therefore neither simply architectural nor simply biological. Rather, it is an addition to a science complex that in itself can be naturally expanded, like the DNA double-helix model, as future use demands.

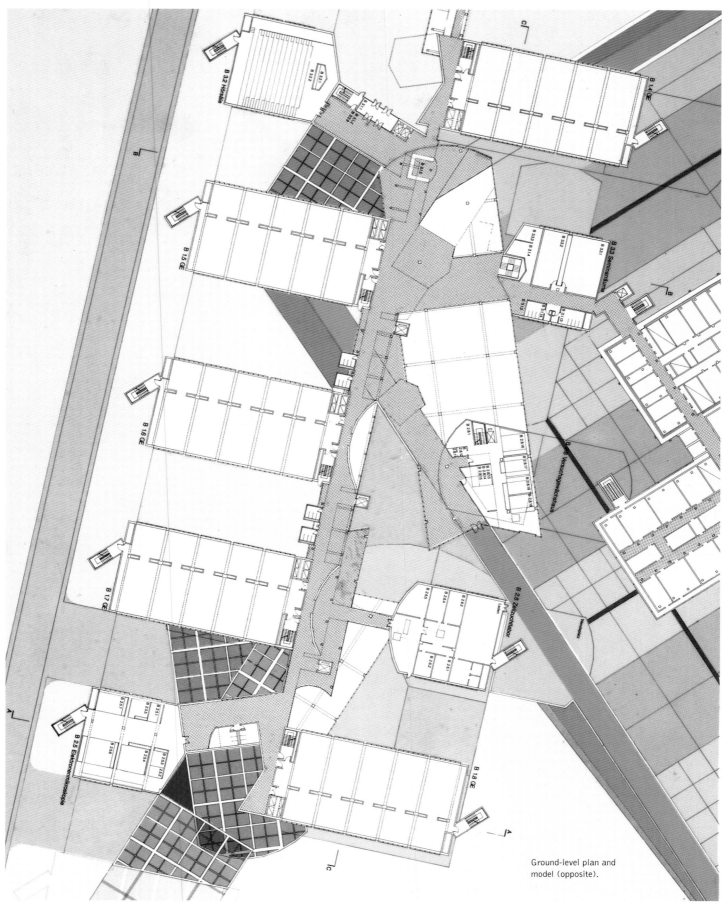

B 3.2 Hörsäle

B 3.21

B 3.22

B 1.4 QE

B 1.5 QE

B 3.33 Seminarräume

B 333

B 332

B 331

B 1.6 QE

B 2.6 Versuchsgewächshaus

B 2.6 Zahlzuchtlabor

B 1.7 QE

B 2.5 Elektronenmikroskopie

B 1.8 QE

Ground-level plan and model (opposite).

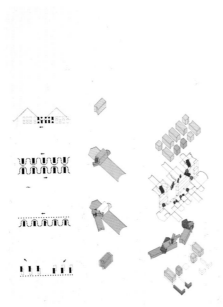

Perspective and concept diagrams (above).

Fuller Toms Loft
1987
New York, New York

The site for this project was a 4,000-square-foot loft in Lower Manhattan, and the program was to transform it into a living space and a small painting studio. The space is essentially an irregular rectangle in the proportions of 100 to 40. The shortest side faces onto Broadway, which, because it is a diagonal in the regular grid of New York, causes the adjacent sides of the loft to be joined at obtuse angles. The idea for this project is similar to the idea for our project for the Wexner Center for the Visual Arts in Columbus, Ohio [112] — a relationship between two grids; but the important differences were twofold: first was a question of scale; second was the question of an internal insertion.

The idea was to insert a foreign body into the existing context in such a way as to produce a disorienting relationship between old and new. The non-right-angle geometry of the site and the intersection of two grids were used to produce a condition in which no single geometry was dominant in either the vertical or horizontal dimensions. This produced the effect of displacing and destabilizing the conventional devices of orientation in urban space.

Often when one is in a given room, because of its complex relationship with other rooms, it is difficult to orient oneself to the context of the city, to the simple coordinates of north and south. While there appears to be a dominant vertebrate system of order in the loft, it is fractured when another system is introduced. In a sense, there is here an order within an order and a scale within a scale.

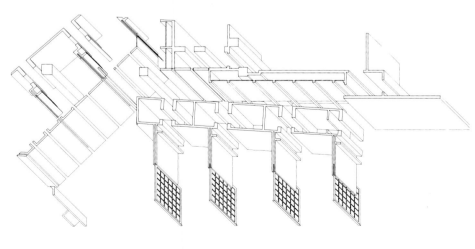

Interior views and axonometric (above).

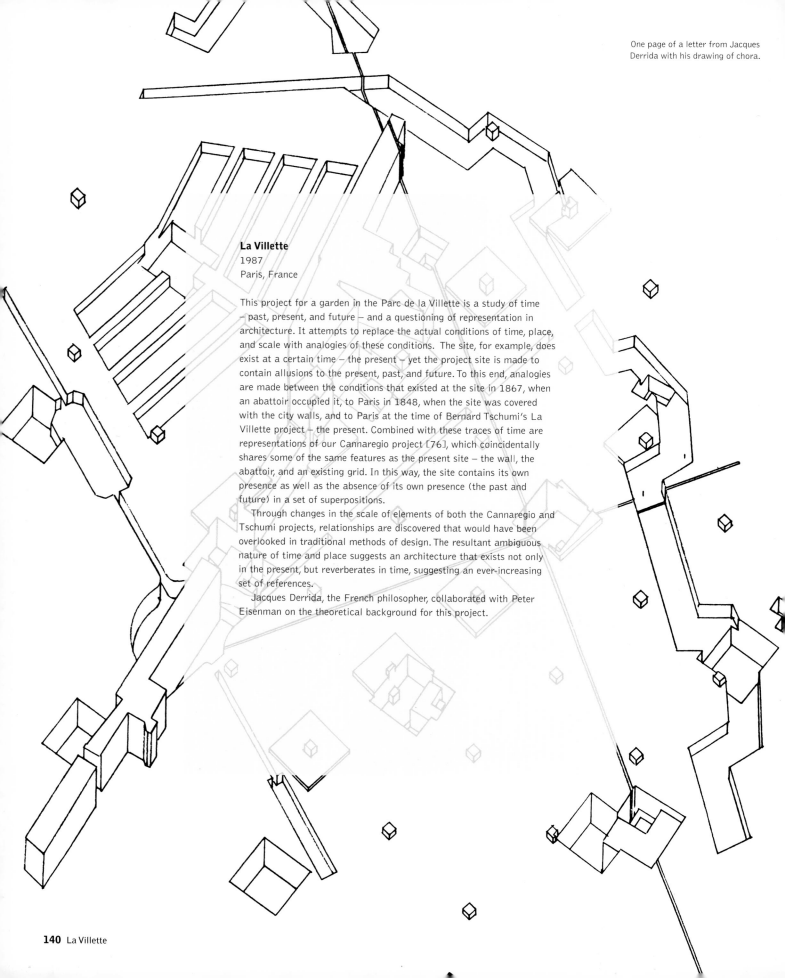

La Villette
1987
Paris, France

This project for a garden in the Parc de la Villette is a study of time – past, present, and future – and a questioning of representation in architecture. It attempts to replace the actual conditions of time, place, and scale with analogies of these conditions. The site, for example, does exist at a certain time – the present – yet the project site is made to contain allusions to the present, past, and future. To this end, analogies are made between the conditions that existed at the site in 1867, when an abattoir occupied it, to Paris in 1848, when the site was covered with the city walls, and to Paris at the time of Bernard Tschumi's La Villette project – the present. Combined with these traces of time are representations of our Cannaregio project [76], which coincidentally shares some of the same features as the present site – the wall, the abattoir, and an existing grid. In this way, the site contains its own presence as well as the absence of its own presence (the past and future) in a set of superpositions.

Through changes in the scale of elements of both the Cannaregio and Tschumi projects, relationships are discovered that would have been overlooked in traditional methods of design. The resultant ambiguous nature of time and place suggests an architecture that exists not only in the present, but reverberates in time, suggesting an ever-increasing set of references.

Jacques Derrida, the French philosopher, collaborated with Peter Eisenman on the theoretical background for this project.

DEPARTMENT OF COMPARATIVE LITERATURE
1113 BINGHAM HALL

très solide ressemblerait à la fois à une trame, à
un crible ou une grille (GRID) et
à un instrument de musique à corde (CHORD).

(piano, harpe, lyre?)

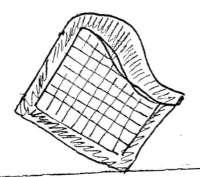

En tant que grille, grid, etc. il aurait un
certain effet intéressant et
certain 2x/102t avec le aura permis de lui et de crible
sélectif qui aura permis de lui et de crible
les 3 sites et les 3 couches (PDE, BT, CV) etc.
En tant qu'instrument à corde il ferait
figurer le choral le choral work.

Orchestration Je crois que rien ne devrait être
inscrit sur cette sculpture, à moins que peut-être,
sauf le titre et une disposition n'y figurent quelque
part (Choral works, by ... –1986...) – A discuter,
entre autres choses.

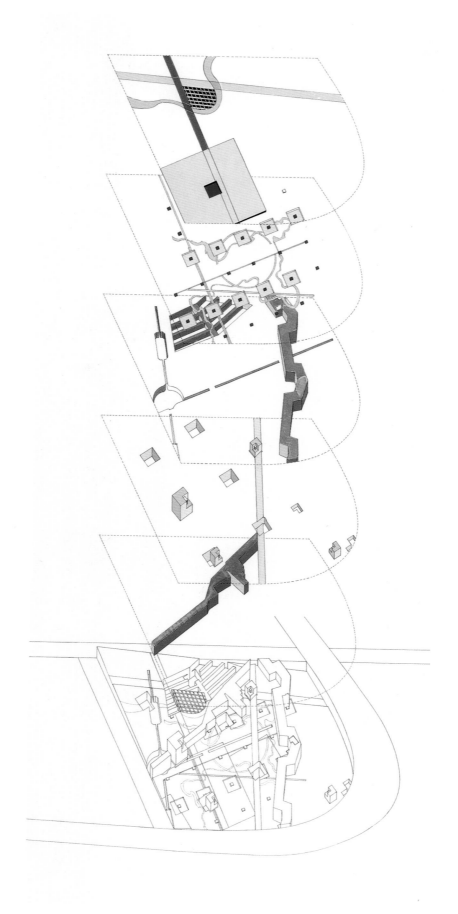

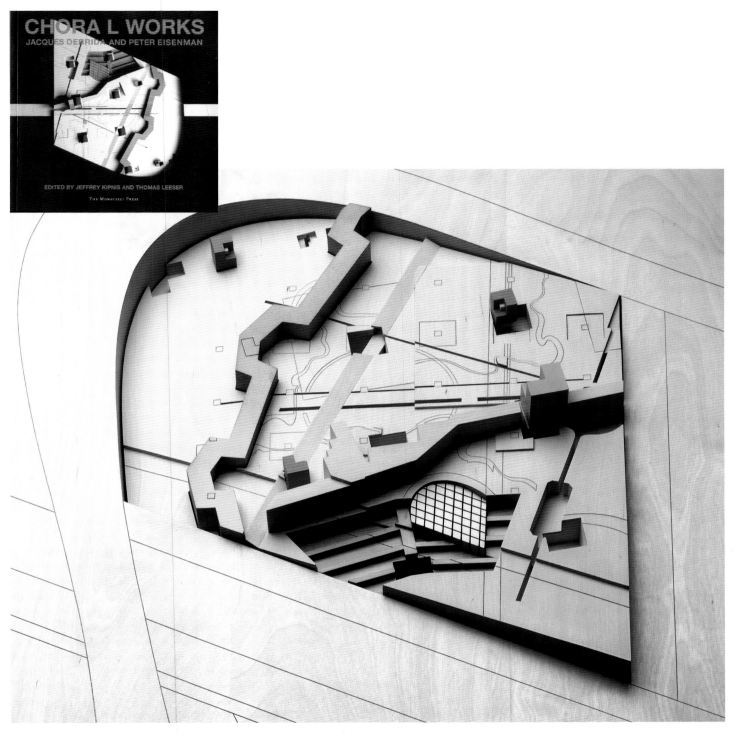

CHORA L WORKS
JACQUES DERRIDA AND PETER EISENMAN

EDITED BY JEFFREY KIPNIS AND THOMAS LEESER

THE MONACELLI PRESS

Opposite: Exploded axonometric drawing.
Above and right: Presentation model and
section study.

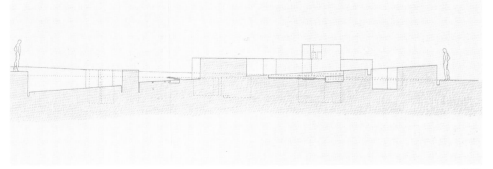

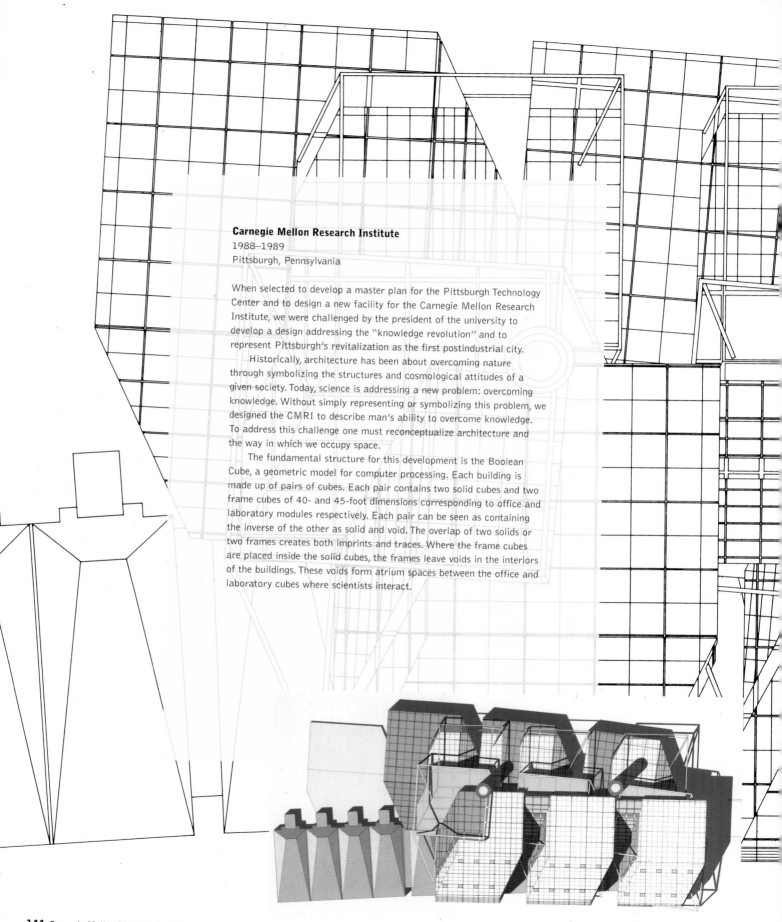

Carnegie Mellon Research Institute
1988–1989
Pittsburgh, Pennsylvania

When selected to develop a master plan for the Pittsburgh Technology Center and to design a new facility for the Carnegie Mellon Research Institute, we were challenged by the president of the university to develop a design addressing the "knowledge revolution" and to represent Pittsburgh's revitalization as the first postindustrial city.

Historically, architecture has been about overcoming nature through symbolizing the structures and cosmological attitudes of a given society. Today, science is addressing a new problem: overcoming knowledge. Without simply representing or symbolizing this problem, we designed the CMRI to describe man's ability to overcome knowledge. To address this challenge one must reconceptualize architecture and the way in which we occupy space.

The fundamental structure for this development is the Boolean Cube, a geometric model for computer processing. Each building is made up of pairs of cubes. Each pair contains two solid cubes and two frame cubes of 40- and 45-foot dimensions corresponding to office and laboratory modules respectively. Each pair can be seen as containing the inverse of the other as solid and void. The overlap of two solids or two frames creates both imprints and traces. Where the frame cubes are placed inside the solid cubes, the frames leave voids in the interiors of the buildings. These voids form atrium spaces between the office and laboratory cubes where scientists interact.

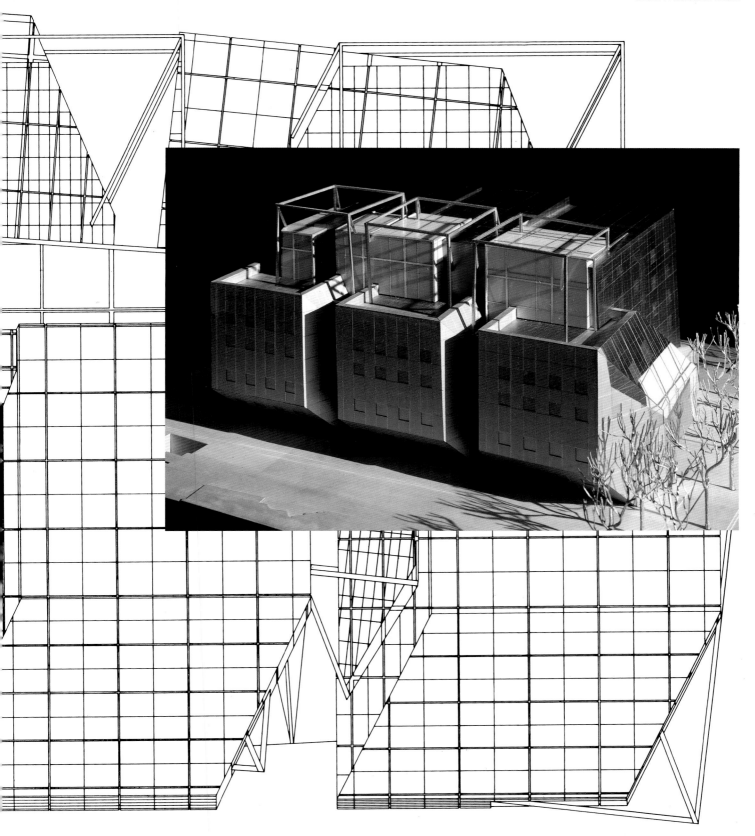

Solid

Frame

Phased Spacing

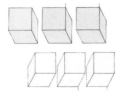

Progressive Spacing

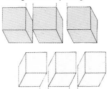

Asymptotic Curve and Tilt

Intersection

Positive Imprint

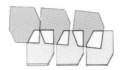

Phased Spacing

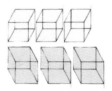

Progressive Spacing

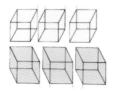

Asymptotic Curve and Tilt

Elevation

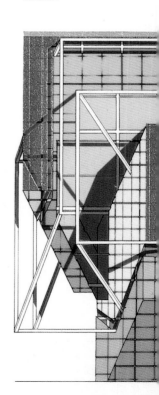

Intersection

Negative Imprint

Negative Trace

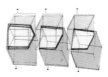

5—N Intersection

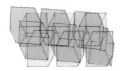

5—A Imprints

5—N Traces

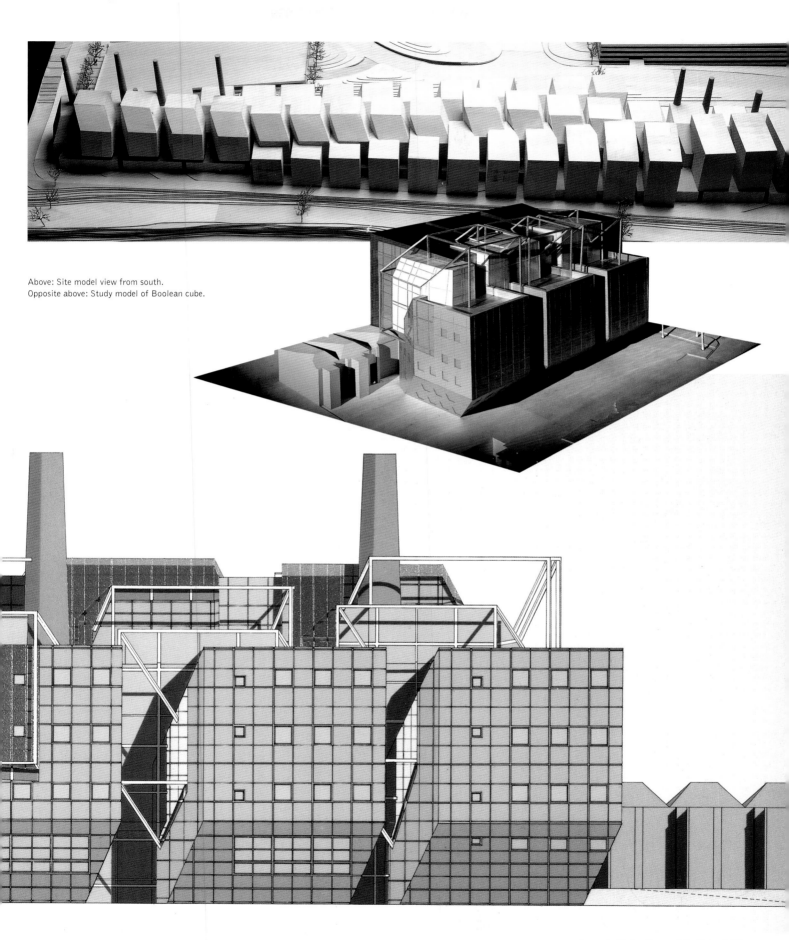

Above: Site model view from south.
Opposite above: Study model of Boolean cube.

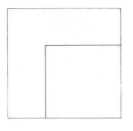 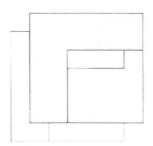 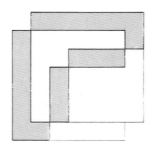 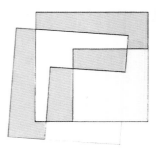

Guardiola House

1988

Cadiz, Spain

The idea of place, or topos, has always been central to man's relationship to his environment. This design for a house examines the meaning of place and how it has been affected by a changing understanding of the world. Since Roman times, man has defined place as the mark of his struggle to overcome nature. Today the traditional forms of place-making are in question because technology has overwhelmed nature, making the rational grids and radial patterns of the past obsolete. In addition, modern thought has found unreasonableness within reason, the illogical within logic. Thus architecture must ask whether marking man's conquest of nature is still significant, as well as acknowledge that place (topos) has always contained "no place" (atopia). This breakdown of the traditional forms of place also affects the traditional categories of figure/ground and frame/object.

Since classical times there has been another definition of place, which suggests the simultaneity of two traditionally contradictory states. In Plato's **Timaeus**, the receptacle (**chora**) is defined as something between place and object, between container and contained. For Plato, the receptacle is like the sand on the beach: it is not an object or a place, but the record of the movement of water, which leaves traces of high-tide lines and scores of imprints – erosions – with each wave.

This house is the manifestation of a receptacle in which the traces of logic and irrationality are intrinsic components of the object/place. It exists between the natural and the rational, between logic and chaos. It breaks the notion of figure/frame because it is figure and frame simultaneously. Its tangential L-shapes penetrate three planes, always interweaving. These fluctuating readings resonate in the material of the house, which, unlike a traditional structure of outside and inside, neither contains nor is contained, and the imprinted forms that record movements of the pattern are no longer frame or object.

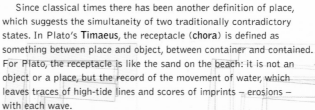

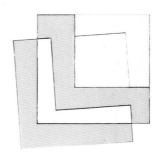

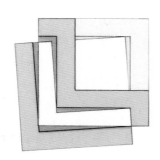 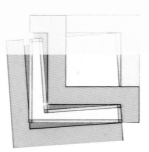  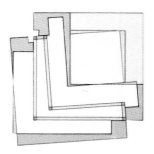

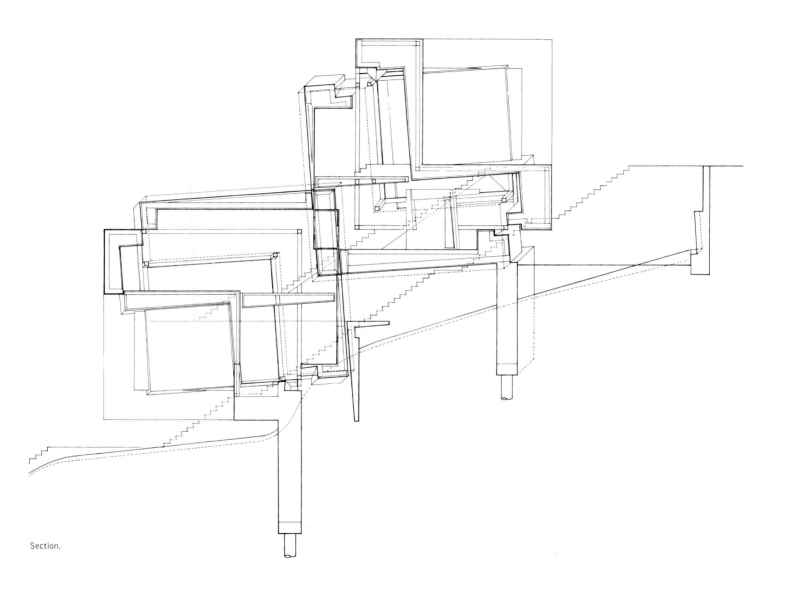

Section.

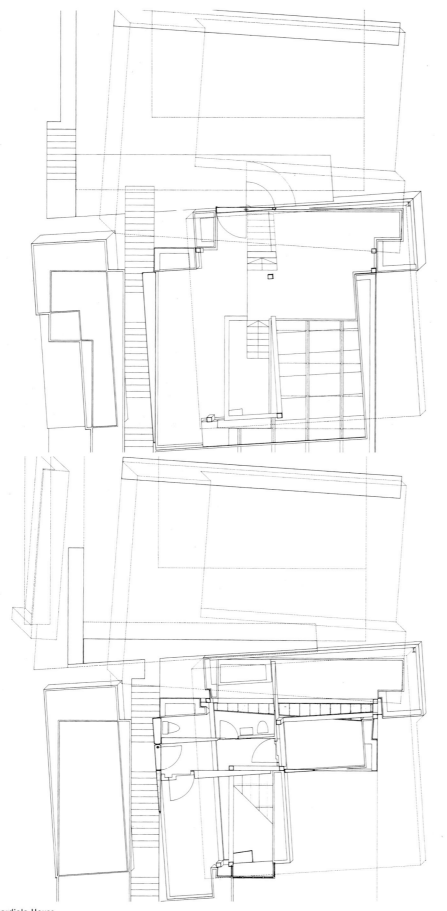

Plans and structural model.

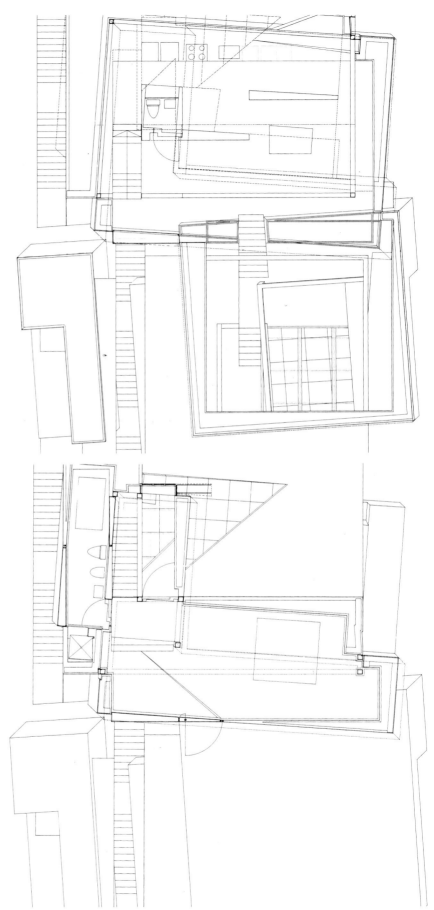

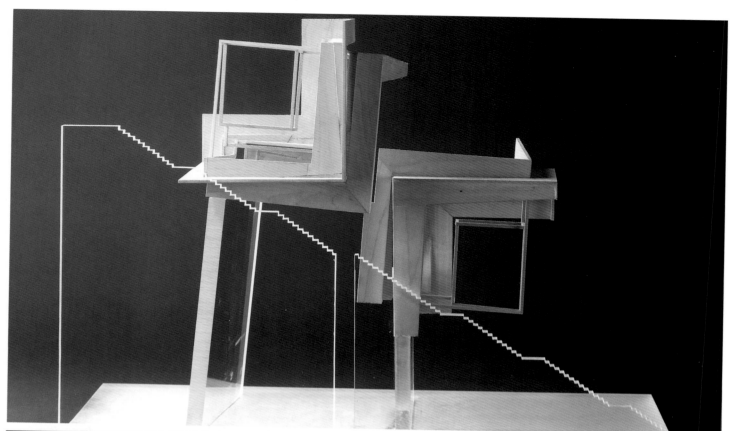

Study model from southeast.
Opposite: Structural model.

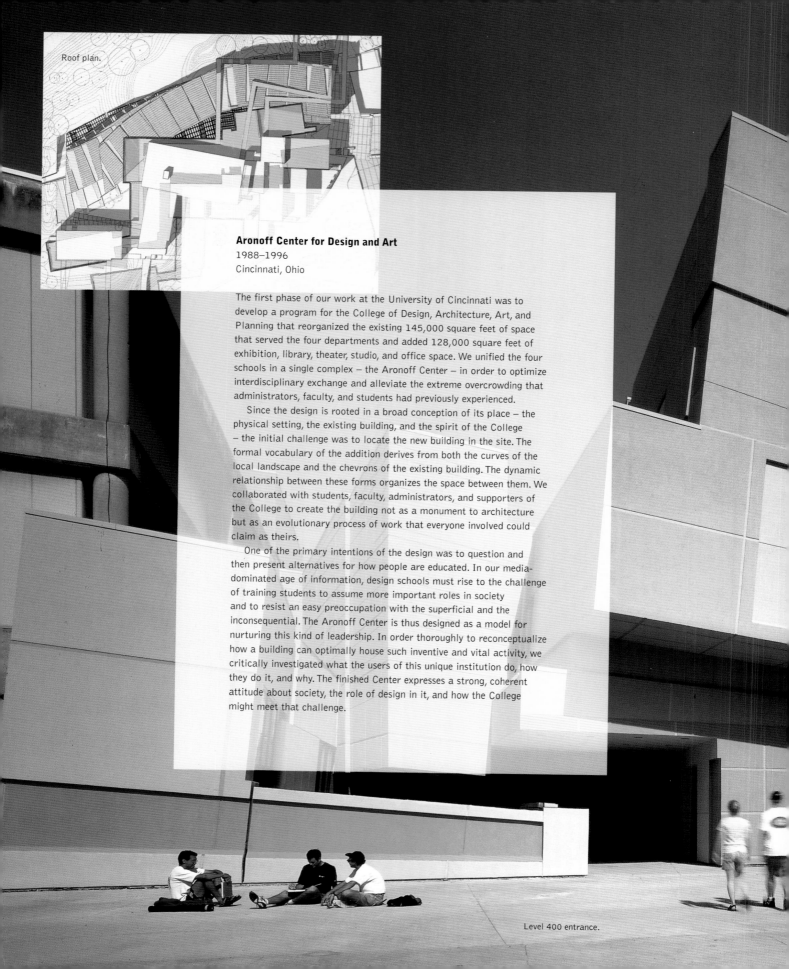

Roof plan.

Aronoff Center for Design and Art
1988–1996
Cincinnati, Ohio

The first phase of our work at the University of Cincinnati was to
develop a program for the College of Design, Architecture, Art, and
Planning that reorganized the existing 145,000 square feet of space
that served the four departments and added 128,000 square feet of
exhibition, library, theater, studio, and office space. We unified the four
schools in a single complex – the Aronoff Center – in order to optimize
interdisciplinary exchange and alleviate the extreme overcrowding that
administrators, faculty, and students had previously experienced.

Since the design is rooted in a broad conception of its place – the
physical setting, the existing building, and the spirit of the College
– the initial challenge was to locate the new building in the site. The
formal vocabulary of the addition derives from both the curves of the
local landscape and the chevrons of the existing building. The dynamic
relationship between these forms organizes the space between them. We
collaborated with students, faculty, administrators, and supporters of
the College to create the building not as a monument to architecture
but as an evolutionary process of work that everyone involved could
claim as theirs.

One of the primary intentions of the design was to question and
then present alternatives for how people are educated. In our media-
dominated age of information, design schools must rise to the challenge
of training students to assume more important roles in society
and to resist an easy preoccupation with the superficial and the
inconsequential. The Aronoff Center is thus designed as a model for
nurturing this kind of leadership. In order thoroughly to reconceptualize
how a building can optimally house such inventive and vital activity, we
critically investigated what the users of this unique institution do, how
they do it, and why. The finished Center expresses a strong, coherent
attitude about society, the role of design in it, and how the College
might meet that challenge.

Level 400 entrance.

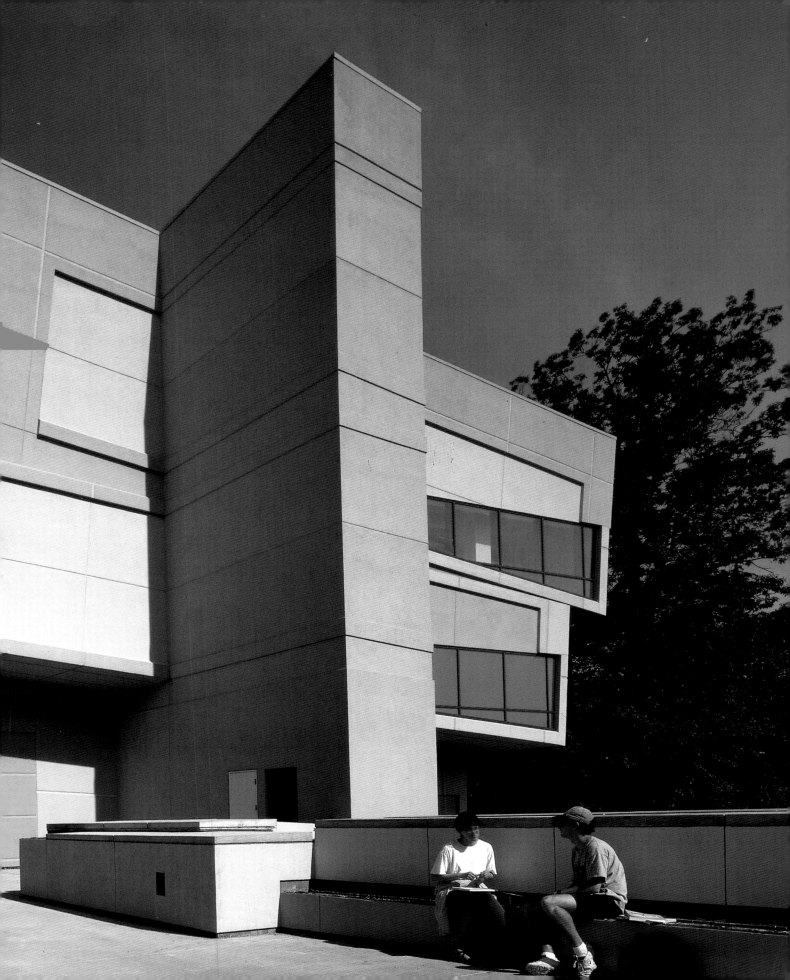

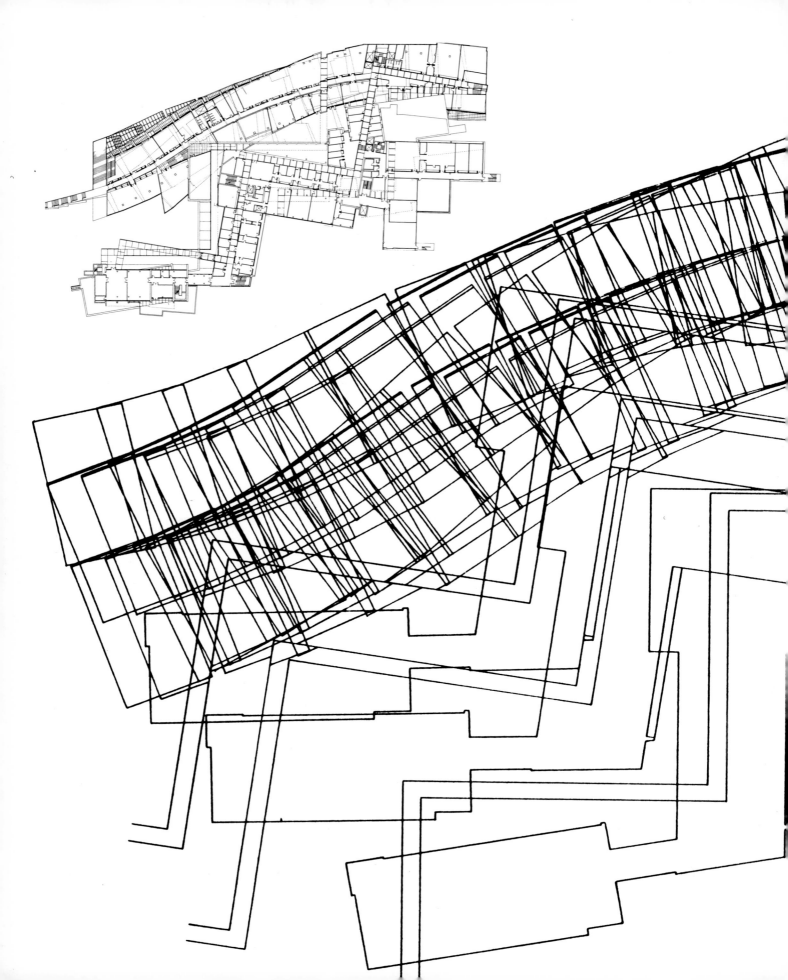

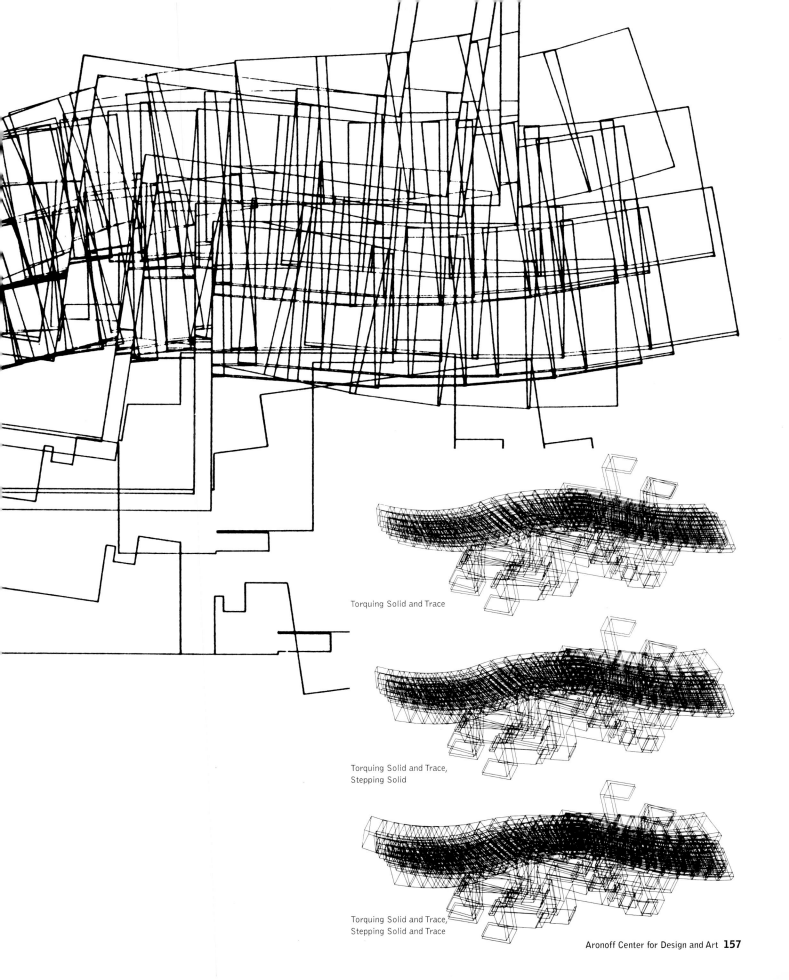

Torquing Solid and Trace

Torquing Solid and Trace,
Stepping Solid

Torquing Solid and Trace,
Stepping Solid and Trace

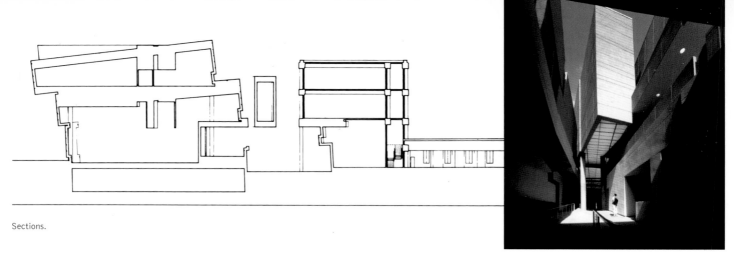

Sections.

Level 300 entry from parking deck.

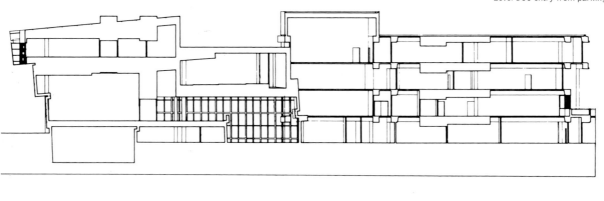

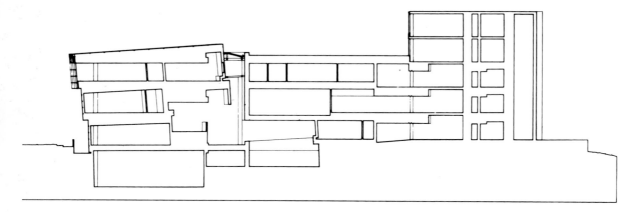

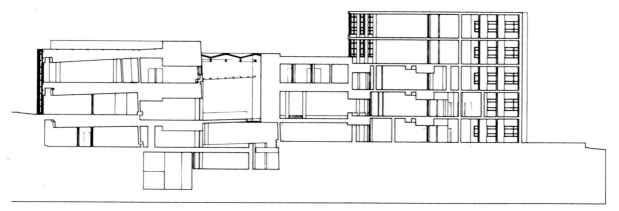

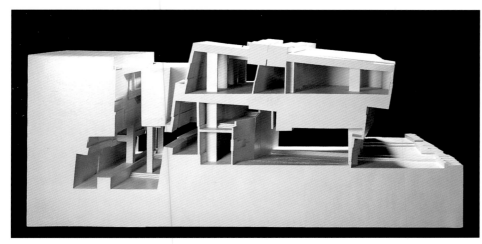

Left: Sectional model.
Below: View from the art gallery.

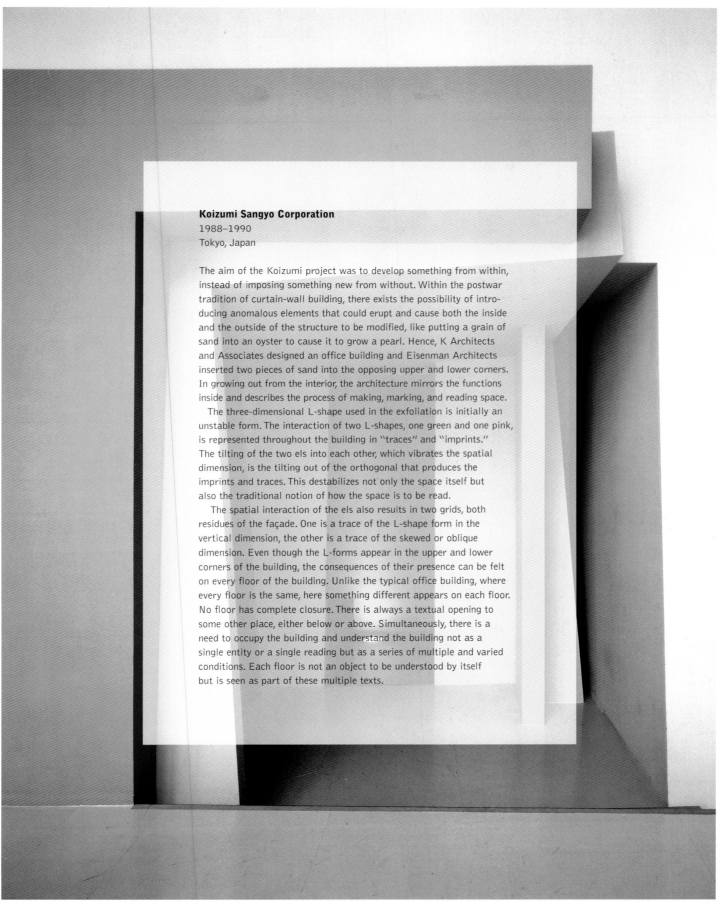

Koizumi Sangyo Corporation
1988–1990
Tokyo, Japan

The aim of the Koizumi project was to develop something from within, instead of imposing something new from without. Within the postwar tradition of curtain-wall building, there exists the possibility of introducing anomalous elements that could erupt and cause both the inside and the outside of the structure to be modified, like putting a grain of sand into an oyster to cause it to grow a pearl. Hence, K Architects and Associates designed an office building and Eisenman Architects inserted two pieces of sand into the opposing upper and lower corners. In growing out from the interior, the architecture mirrors the functions inside and describes the process of making, marking, and reading space.

The three-dimensional L-shape used in the exfoliation is initially an unstable form. The interaction of two L-shapes, one green and one pink, is represented throughout the building in "traces" and "imprints." The tilting of the two els into each other, which vibrates the spatial dimension, is the tilting out of the orthogonal that produces the imprints and traces. This destabilizes not only the space itself but also the traditional notion of how the space is to be read.

The spatial interaction of the els also results in two grids, both residues of the façade. One is a trace of the L-shape form in the vertical dimension, the other is a trace of the skewed or oblique dimension. Even though the L-forms appear in the upper and lower corners of the building, the consequences of their presence can be felt on every floor of the building. Unlike the typical office building, where every floor is the same, here something different appears on each floor. No floor has complete closure. There is always a textual opening to some other place, either below or above. Simultaneously, there is a need to occupy the building and understand the building not as a single entity or a single reading but as a series of multiple and varied conditions. Each floor is not an object to be understood by itself but is seen as part of these multiple texts.

Above: Interior view.
Left: Section of Eisenman L-shapes in K Architects' proposal.

Concept diagrams.

Street level insertion.

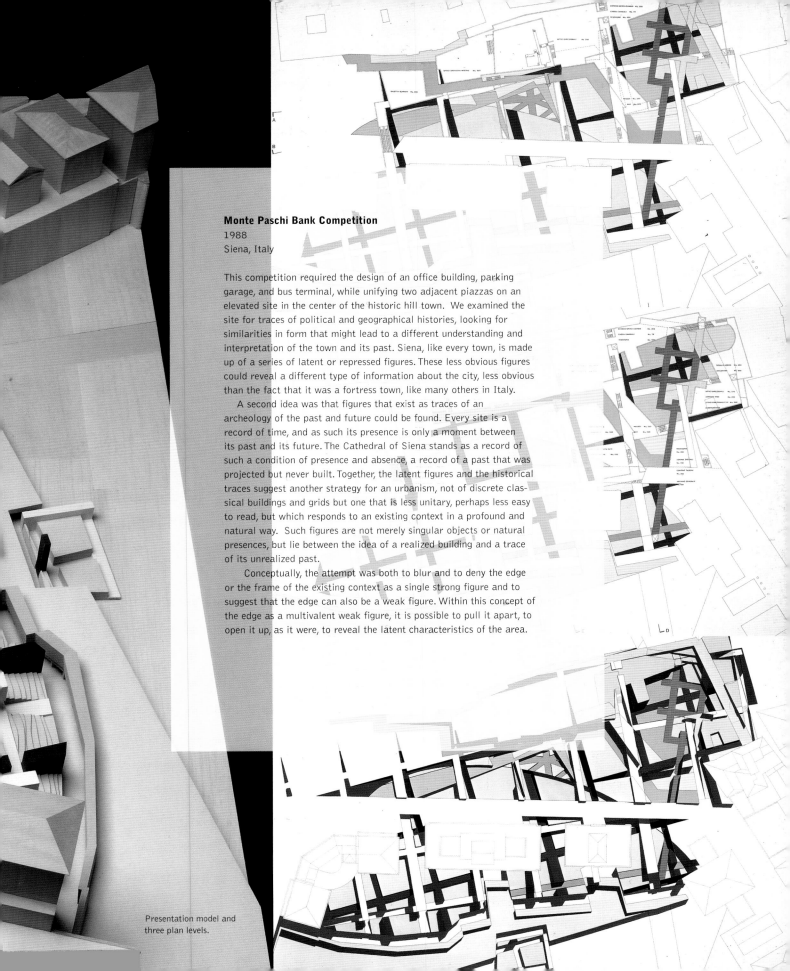

Monte Paschi Bank Competition
1988
Siena, Italy

This competition required the design of an office building, parking garage, and bus terminal, while unifying two adjacent piazzas on an elevated site in the center of the historic hill town. We examined the site for traces of political and geographical histories, looking for similarities in form that might lead to a different understanding and interpretation of the town and its past. Siena, like every town, is made up of a series of latent or repressed figures. These less obvious figures could reveal a different type of information about the city, less obvious than the fact that it was a fortress town, like many others in Italy.

A second idea was that figures that exist as traces of an archeology of the past and future could be found. Every site is a record of time, and as such its presence is only a moment between its past and its future. The Cathedral of Siena stands as a record of such a condition of presence and absence, a record of a past that was projected but never built. Together, the latent figures and the historical traces suggest another strategy for an urbanism, not of discrete classical buildings and grids but one that is less unitary, perhaps less easy to read, but which responds to an existing context in a profound and natural way. Such figures are not merely singular objects or natural presences, but lie between the idea of a realized building and a trace of its unrealized past.

Conceptually, the attempt was both to blur and to deny the edge or the frame of the existing context as a single strong figure and to suggest that the edge can also be a weak figure. Within this concept of the edge as a multivalent weak figure, it is possible to pull it apart, to open it up, as it were, to reveal the latent characteristics of the area.

Presentation model and three plan levels.

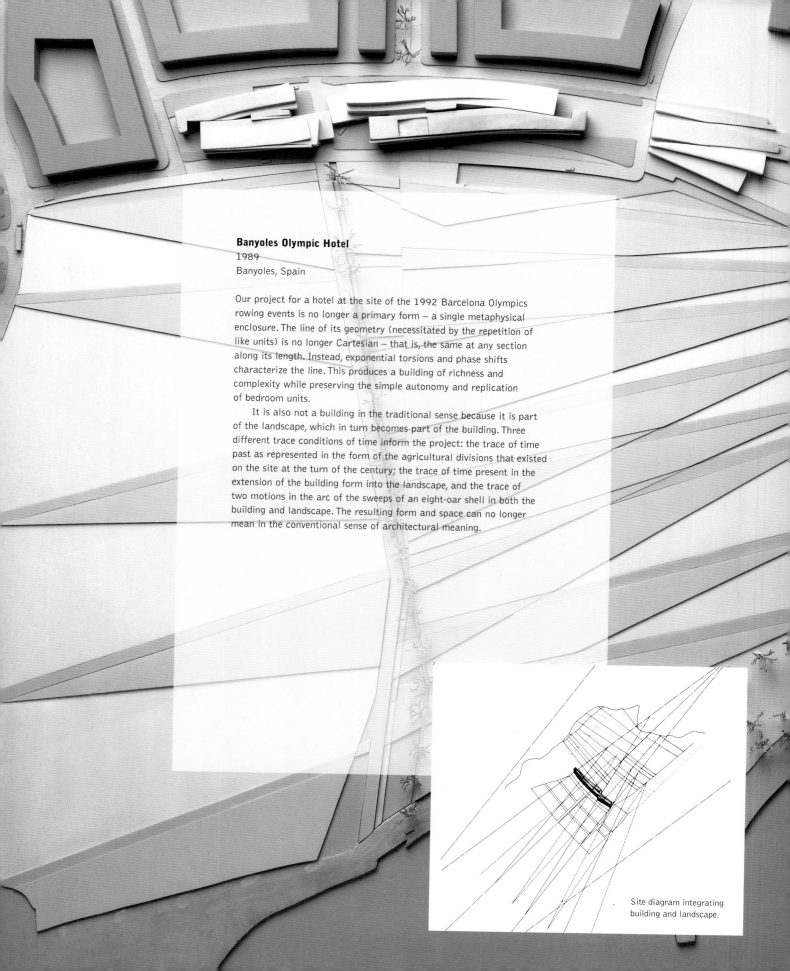

Banyoles Olympic Hotel
1989
Banyoles, Spain

Our project for a hotel at the site of the 1992 Barcelona Olympics rowing events is no longer a primary form – a single metaphysical enclosure. The line of its geometry (necessitated by the repetition of like units) is no longer Cartesian – that is, the same at any section along its length. Instead, exponential torsions and phase shifts characterize the line. This produces a building of richness and complexity while preserving the simple autonomy and replication of bedroom units.

It is also not a building in the traditional sense because it is part of the landscape, which in turn becomes part of the building. Three different trace conditions of time inform the project: the trace of time past as represented in the form of the agricultural divisions that existed on the site at the turn of the century; the trace of time present in the extension of the building form into the landscape, and the trace of two motions in the arc of the sweeps of an eight-oar shell in both the building and landscape. The resulting form and space can no longer mean in the conventional sense of architectural meaning.

Site diagram integrating building and landscape.

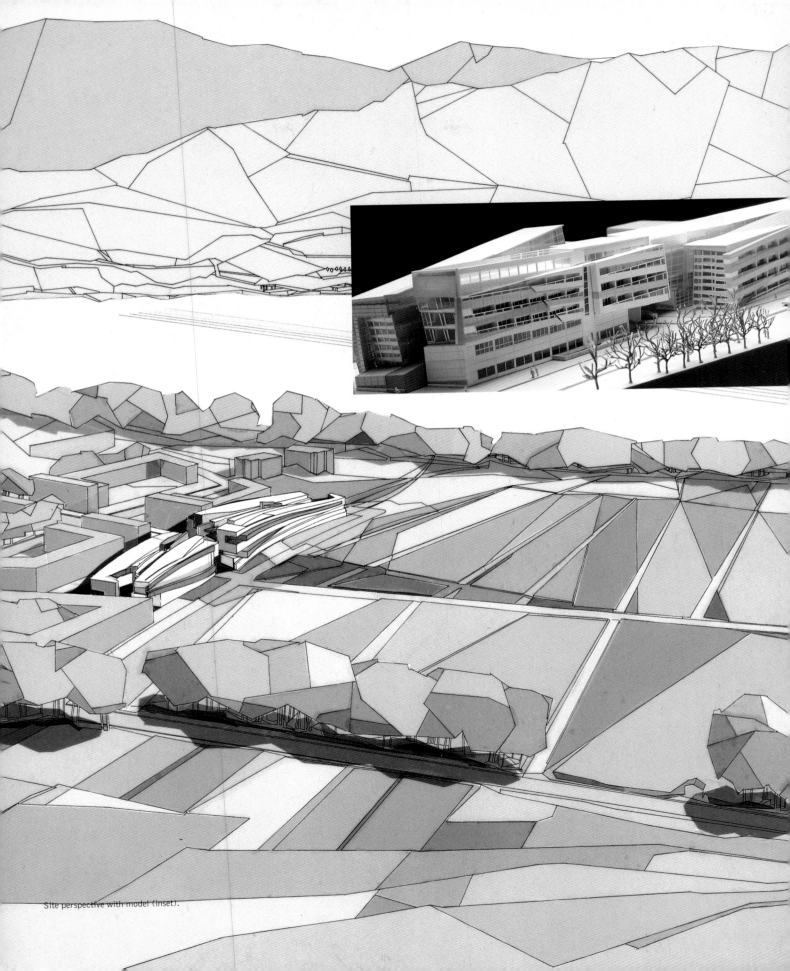

Site perspective with model (inset).

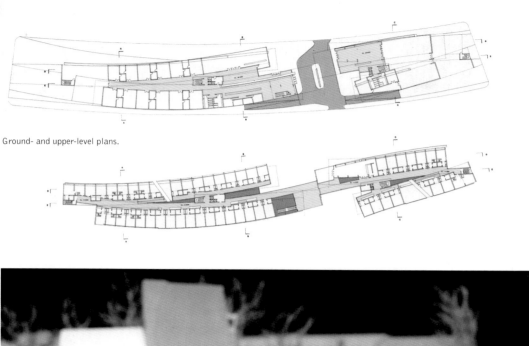

Ground- and upper-level plans.

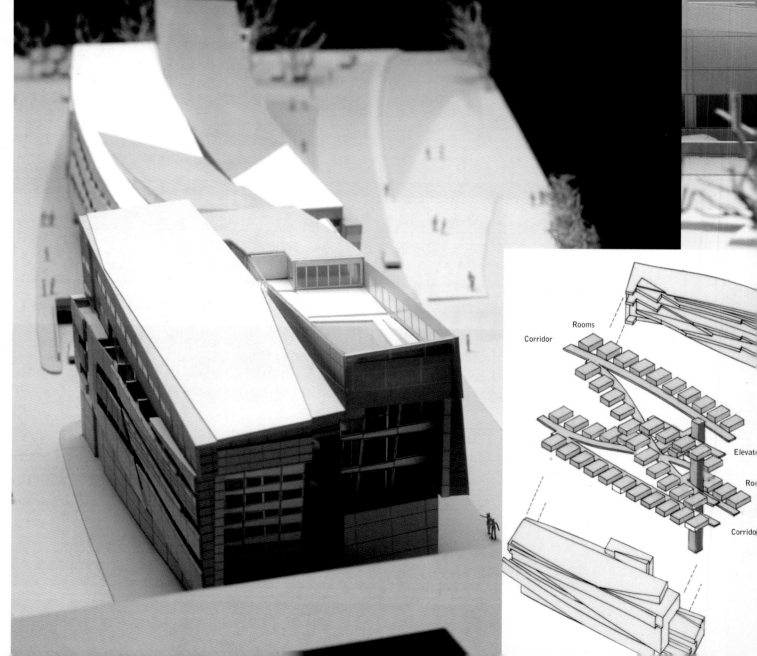

Corridor

Rooms

Corridor

Elevat

Ro

Corrido

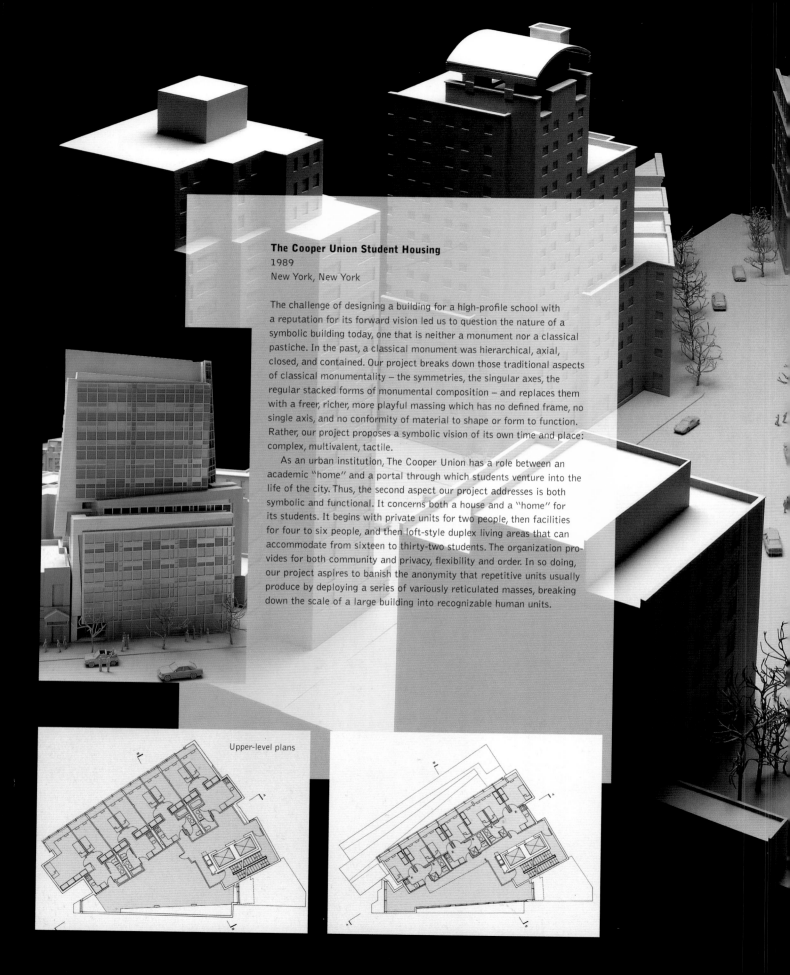

The Cooper Union Student Housing
1989
New York, New York

The challenge of designing a building for a high-profile school with
a reputation for its forward vision led us to question the nature of a
symbolic building today, one that is neither a monument nor a classical
pastiche. In the past, a classical monument was hierarchical, axial,
closed, and contained. Our project breaks down those traditional aspects
of classical monumentality – the symmetries, the singular axes, the
regular stacked forms of monumental composition – and replaces them
with a freer, richer, more playful massing which has no defined frame, no
single axis, and no conformity of material to shape or form to function.
Rather, our project proposes a symbolic vision of its own time and place:
complex, multivalent, tactile.

As an urban institution, The Cooper Union has a role between an
academic "home" and a portal through which students venture into the
life of the city. Thus, the second aspect our project addresses is both
symbolic and functional. It concerns both a house and a "home" for
its students. It begins with private units for two people, then facilities
for four to six people, and then loft-style duplex living areas that can
accommodate from sixteen to thirty-two students. The organization provides for both community and privacy, flexibility and order. In so doing,
our project aspires to banish the anonymity that repetitive units usually
produce by deploying a series of variously reticulated masses, breaking
down the scale of a large building into recognizable human units.

Upper-level plans

figure no. 1

Clamato™ Juice
16 fl. oz. (1 pt.)

"the talented mr. tracer", tracing eisenman, 2005

Fig. 1

Fig. 2

THE TALENTED MR. TRACER

Greg Lynn

What is being traced and who am I following? Picture this: standing in a football stadium parking lot is a gray-haired, professorial gentleman pouring Clamato juice (fig. 1) and vodka into a stainless steel thermos set amidst a sea of uncooked sausages and freshly baked Italian rolls arrayed across the tailgate of a rented Chevrolet. Looking through wire-frame spectacles in the shape of Le Corbusier's round plastic frames, only in nickel-plated steel (fig. 2), and wearing a hand-tailored, striped Egyptian cotton shirt in one of two primary colors, not yellow, with collar detached, top button open and all other buttons straining in a pattern of rippling scallops immortalized by Leon Krier in a drawing published on the last page of the book *House X*, wool slacks in one of five shades of gray (no belt), blue blazer with brass buttons, and a slack bow tie in one of three primary colors (fig. 7) draped around his neck, and scuffed, white leather Stan Smith Converse tennis shoes trimmed in green Naugahyde (fig. 3), he is a meticulous contrivance of contradictions, something between patrician gentility and American populism. This man has perpetrated intellectual, creative, and personal chaos in architecture like no other since his heroes Alberti and Piranesi. Conceived in South Orange, New Jersey, nearly coincidentally with his cousin Richard Meier, he was intellectually reared by Colin Rowe in art historical itinerancy via Tuscany, Cambridge, and Ithaca.

Fig. 3

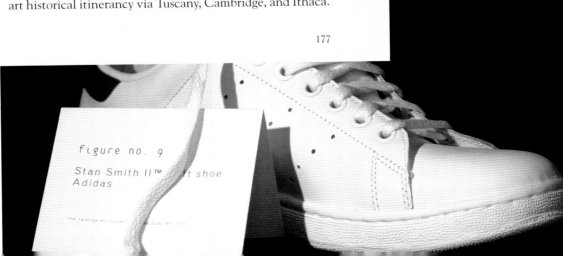

figure no. 9

Stan Smith II™ ft shoe
Adidas

A Journal for Ideas and
Criticism in Architecture

Published for The Institute
for Architecture and Urban Studies

By The MIT Press

Not only his appearance and behavior but also his psyche, resumé, and demeanor are rife with oppositions. Speaking of *Oppositions* (fig. 4), he is as adept at institution-building as he is at dismantling. Many of his crimes were committed under the cover of a blind that he referred to as The Institute for Architecture and Urban Studies, pitched amidst the forest of midtown high-rises in the city of New York, fifty-two miles northeast of the town of Princeton, New Jersey. From within this institution of his founding he managed to assassinate, without detection, those who would have been my heroic modern architecture grandfathers. Peter David Eisenman epitomizes the American intellectual whose voracious desire to occupy the center of a European canon is so propelling that the field is destroyed and transformed in the struggle. Eisenman is one of the great annihilators in our field. Infected by Rowe with a fever to synthesize British neo-Palladianism with modern academic formalism, he scorched the earth of the canonical architectural fathers that he so wanted to become someday. Sure, there are still those who keep trying to revive the corpses of Le Corbusier, Mies, Wright, Neutra, Terragni, Rietveld, even Stirling, the Smithsons, Kahn, and Rudolph. These figures are only known to me and mine as fallen ghosts in Eisenman's killing spree. Eisenman's ironic gift is that you have to study the traces of their murders even to discover that they have in fact been dead for thirty years. Of course, they had it coming. Funnily enough, they still do. People like Tom Wolfe claimed credit for finishing off the modernists a decade after they had already been smothered by the likes

178 TRACING EISENMAN

Fig. 4

anti-intellectualism at home, drove American academics to scurry around Tuscany in British-gentry drag, reading French *nouveau roman* literature while designing summer houses in Connecticut for one another.

When it comes to criminal acts of architecture perpetrated abroad by Americans, if you look on the surface, which is the only place to look for traces, there are only ever two kinds of architects: the first will leave you messages; the second will leave you traces. Michael Graves used to leave traces, as in the Hanselmann House (1967), but now he leaves us messages. Robert Venturi has always been a messenger. On the other hand, Bernard Tschumi leaves traces. And Peter is a tracer, as were those whose identities he assumed at various times: Adolf Loos and Giuseppe Terragni. The critical difference between a messenger and a tracer is not abstraction, as the Wexner Center [112] is less abstract and more historically referential than, say, the Library of San Juan Capistrano by Graves. The difference is also not the ability to sustain contradictions, as the Wexner Center is formally and materially riddled by the vocabularies of curtain wall, masonry and steel frame construction, and massing, as is the Library of San Juan Capistrano betwixt and between a Tuscan monastery and the Scandinavian early modernism of Erik Gunnar Asplund. If both Eisenman and Graves can sustain internal contradictions while fluctuating between formal abstraction and representational historicism, then what is the difference between a trace and a sign? Graves's clues can be found all over the shelves of Target. He is a populist, and more and more he came to assume that his audience was a collection of hapless idiots who needed bloated, well-resolved packages. Eisenman behaves as if, and invites us to believe that, he is on the run from some unthinkably astute investigator who tracks his every movement and is gradually building a criminal case against him.

The difference between a tracer and a messenger is the degree to which conflict is either perpetrated or resolved respectively. Graves's work after the Portland Public Services Building is abstract with suppressed complications that are smugly resolved compositionally and linguistically. Eisenman, being rife with contradictions himself, maintains an ambiguity and incompletion in his projects, and uses this instability as the compositional motor for the work. The projects remain unfinished and unresolved like giant cardboard models. Graves and Eisenman have been friends, collaborators, and colleagues for decades, since they were junior faculty together at Princeton in the mid-1960s (fig. 10). But the reason for their comparison is not simply biographical. Both Graves and Eisenman avoid construction, detailing, celebration of structure, or any other form of articulation that calls attention to materials, and especially to scale. When building in brick, as they both do regularly, the brick is stacked and bonded as a veneer, never to look load bearing. When structure is shown, it is most likely as a sign, performing no discernible structural function. Like Aldo Rossi and Le Corbusier before them, neither architect articulates the buildings as being built. Simple abstraction of scale and material does not explain this desire for the

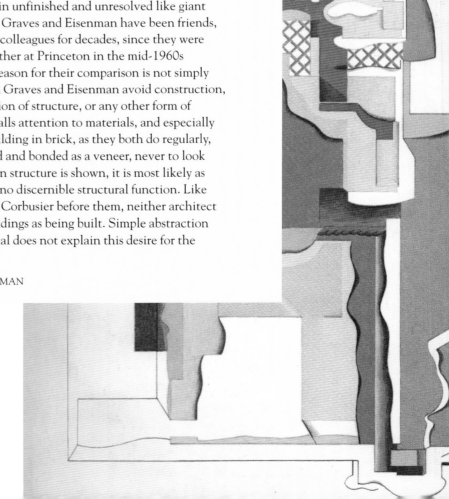

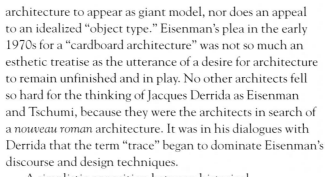

architecture to appear as giant model, nor does an appeal to an idealized "object type." Eisenman's plea in the early 1970s for a "cardboard architecture" was not so much an esthetic treatise as the utterance of a desire for architecture to remain unfinished and in play. No other architects fell so hard for the thinking of Jacques Derrida as Eisenman and Tschumi, because they were the architects in search of a *nouveau roman* architecture. It was in his dialogues with Derrida that the term "trace" began to dominate Eisenman's discourse and design techniques.

A simplistic opposition between historical postmodernists like Graves and so-called Corbusian modernists like Eisenman and Meier still clouds the field. We can thank Tom Wolfe and other architectural neophytes for a journalistic perspective on this opposition, but when the architects started to believe their press, they forgot that indeed they were more complicated oppositions themselves. It is difficult for me, at the intimate distance of both a former student and former employee, to even tell the difference between Graves's Library at San Juan Capistrano, Eisenman's Wexner Center, and Gehry's Schnabel Residence when it comes to style. They were all riddled with contradictions, from their massing to their architectural vocabulary. The significant difference between Peter Eisenman and Michael Graves, between a tracer and a messenger, is not the presence of historical quotation, high degrees of abstraction, or internal complexity; it is in the completion and stability of the compositions.

GREG LYNN   185

Fig. 10: Michael Graves, drawing for **Progressive Architecture** depicting his own and Eisenman's ideas as two sides of one coin.

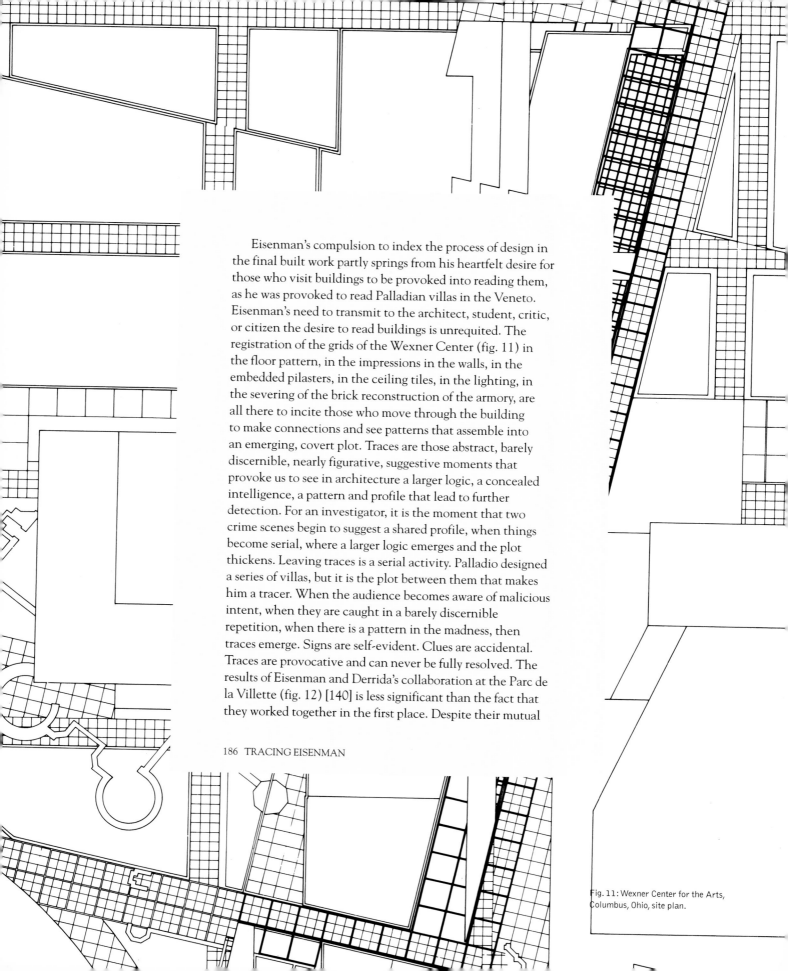

Eisenman's compulsion to index the process of design in
the final built work partly springs from his heartfelt desire for
those who visit buildings to be provoked into reading them,
as he was provoked to read Palladian villas in the Veneto.
Eisenman's need to transmit to the architect, student, critic,
or citizen the desire to read buildings is unrequited. The
registration of the grids of the Wexner Center (fig. 11) in
the floor pattern, in the impressions in the walls, in the
embedded pilasters, in the ceiling tiles, in the lighting, in
the severing of the brick reconstruction of the armory, are
all there to incite those who move through the building
to make connections and see patterns that assemble into
an emerging, covert plot. Traces are those abstract, barely
discernible, nearly figurative, suggestive moments that
provoke us to see in architecture a larger logic, a concealed
intelligence, a pattern and profile that lead to further
detection. For an investigator, it is the moment that two
crime scenes begin to suggest a shared profile, when things
become serial, where a larger logic emerges and the plot
thickens. Leaving traces is a serial activity. Palladio designed
a series of villas, but it is the plot between them that makes
him a tracer. When the audience becomes aware of malicious
intent, when they are caught in a barely discernible
repetition, when there is a pattern in the madness, then
traces emerge. Signs are self-evident. Clues are accidental.
Traces are provocative and can never be fully resolved. The
results of Eisenman and Derrida's collaboration at the Parc de
la Villette (fig. 12) [140] is less significant than the fact that
they worked together in the first place. Despite their mutual

186   TRACING EISENMAN

Fig. 11: Wexner Center for the Arts,
Columbus, Ohio, site plan.

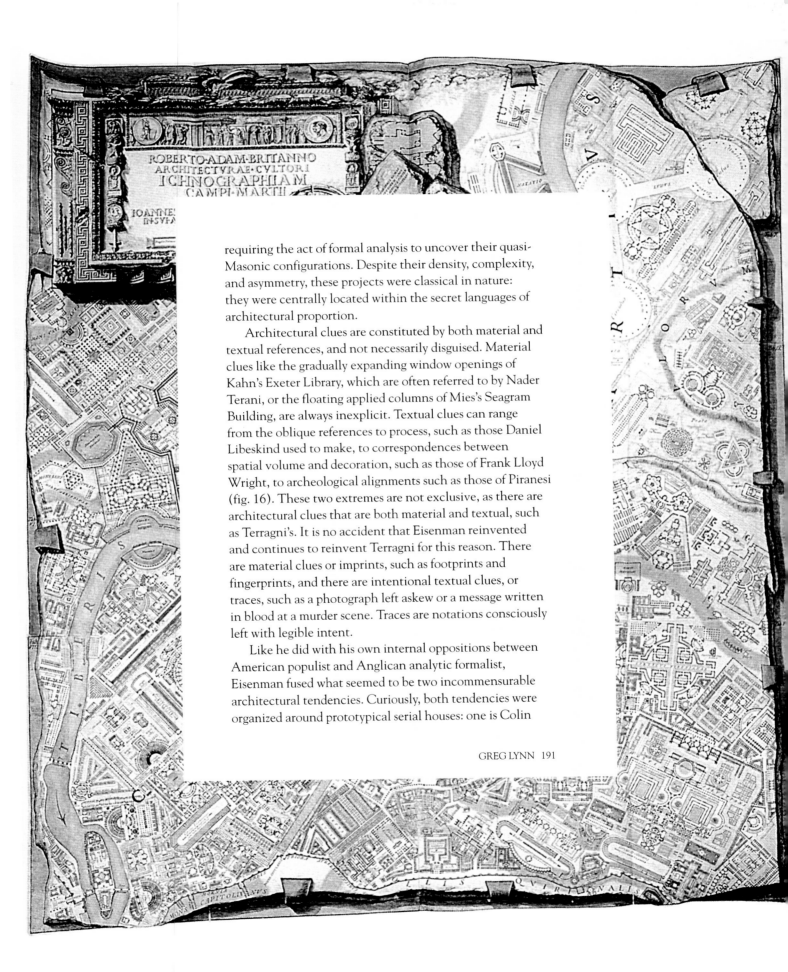

requiring the act of formal analysis to uncover their quasi-Masonic configurations. Despite their density, complexity, and asymmetry, these projects were classical in nature: they were centrally located within the secret languages of architectural proportion.

Architectural clues are constituted by both material and textual references, and not necessarily disguised. Material clues like the gradually expanding window openings of Kahn's Exeter Library, which are often referred to by Nader Terani, or the floating applied columns of Mies's Seagram Building, are always inexplicit. Textual clues can range from the oblique references to process, such as those Daniel Libeskind used to make, to correspondences between spatial volume and decoration, such as those of Frank Lloyd Wright, to archeological alignments such as those of Piranesi (fig. 16). These two extremes are not exclusive, as there are architectural clues that are both material and textual, such as Terragni's. It is no accident that Eisenman reinvented and continues to reinvent Terragni for this reason. There are material clues or imprints, such as footprints and fingerprints, and there are intentional textual clues, or traces, such as a photograph left askew or a message written in blood at a murder scene. Traces are notations consciously left with legible intent.

Like he did with his own internal oppositions between American populist and Anglican analytic formalist, Eisenman fused what seemed to be two incommensurable architectural tendencies. Curiously, both tendencies were organized around prototypical serial houses: one is Colin

Rowe's proposal of an ideal villa based on the averaging of geometric and proportional principles of Le Corbusier and Palladio, the other, the Case Study Houses of Eames, Neutra, and Schindler. The first traces in Eisenman's work were those of a transformational design process based on Rowe's methods and combined with the modernist vocabulary of the early Case Study Houses. The architectural vocabulary of these projects draws more heavily from Neutra and Schindler than from Le Corbusier and Mies, despite the New York Five's proclamations. With devolution turned into design technique, Eisenman was able to trace the sequential increase of complexity in the massing, fenestration, structure, and panelization of the Casa del Fascio. By reversing this process, he designed a series of numbered houses that proceeded from cubic primitives through shifting and, eventually, rotating operations to complex lattices of traces between grid frames and panels.

There are two continuities in Eisenman's tracing: the first is the perennial use of the term, the second is the continued technique of registering sequential design processes as spatial reveals and material reliefs. These continuities reveal a codependent evolution between technique and concept, a codependency that at different moments has bifurcated and fractured. At these moments, the difference between an architecture of signs and an architecture of traces becomes most apparent. It is also at these moments that the architect must privilege either theory or technique. In several projects we can see the consequences of alternative decisions for technique or theory. For example, in the

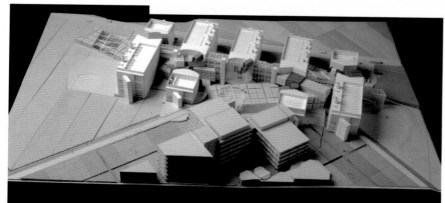

Fig. 17: Biocenter, Frankfurt am Main, Germany, competition model.

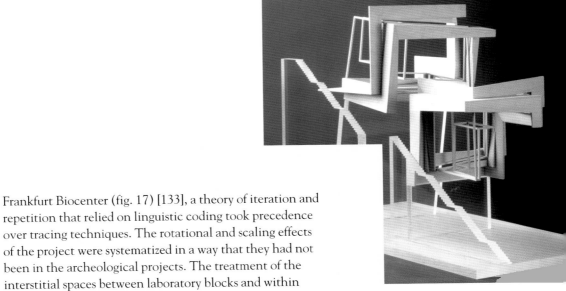

Fig. 18: Guardiola House, Cadiz, Spain.

Frankfurt Biocenter (fig. 17) [133], a theory of iteration and repetition that relied on linguistic coding took precedence over tracing techniques. The rotational and scaling effects of the project were systematized in a way that they had not been in the archeological projects. The treatment of the interstitial spaces between laboratory blocks and within the spatial canyon of the project was less developed than, say, at the Wexner Center, because the linguistic structure was so dogmatic there was no friction in the parti. A similar situation could be seen in another rigorously coded project of that period, the Carnegie Mellon Research Institute (fig. 19) [144]. These two projects were the most procedurally driven, and not coincidentally they were also the first to have a computer model running parallel to their design development. Compared with the Guardiola House (fig. 18) [148], the Banyoles Olympic Hotel [170], and Koizumi Sangyo headquarters [163], which were all being designed at the same time as the Biocenter and Carnegie Mellon, these latter projects were rather rigid in their reliance on coded processes and lacking in the tracery of notation. They are formally the most monolithic projects and the most rigorously generated since the early houses. The fusion of these rigorous, monolithic procedural processes with the sophisticated two-and-a-half dimensional techniques of registration that emerged in the Guardiola House resulted in the addition to the Aronoff Center for Design and Art at the University of Cincinnati (fig. 20) [154]. A series of repeated cubic volumes was put through sequential rotation in three axes, and each rotation left an imprint on the previous

GREG LYNN 193

Fig. 19 (below): Carnegie Mellon Research Institute, Pittsburgh, Pennsylvania, presentation model.

volume. The rippling and cascading massing reverberates across the skin of the building as relief traces impressed into the volumes, and as gaps between elements that appear as skylights and apertures.

In literal terms, traces in Eisenman's work have been either the negative gaps that emerged between elements once a geometric operation was performed, or even better, the two-and-a-half dimensional impressions that formed a relief pattern on surfaces. The first negative gaps, which at the time Eisenman often referred to as traces, were the classical modernist reveals favored by the New York Five. These were derived from the Miesian grid operations being used by Hedjuk, Meier, and Graves, which became the core of the "9-square grid problem," which they all used as a pedagogical tool, along with Rowe, Fred Koetter, and other so-called postmodernists. The relief work was often referred to as imprints, which Eisenman drew not from Mies or the modernists but from architects of the Italian Renaissance, primarily Giulio Romano. In a project such as Eisenman's House VI [66], the difference between the trace and imprint is initially a difference of notation. Both are records of transformational formal operations. These traces of the genesis, and therefore the genetics, of design were left for the detectives, who, as Eisenman did for Terragni, would unravel the crimes of the design. Yet the deepest insight into Peter's work, I believe, is that of Harry Cobb, who claimed that it was not Michael Graves or Robert Venturi but Peter Eisenman who invented contemporary ornament, not in printed facades but in the ubiquitous contemporary

Fig. 20: Aronoff Center for Design and Art, Cincinnati, Ohio, 1996.

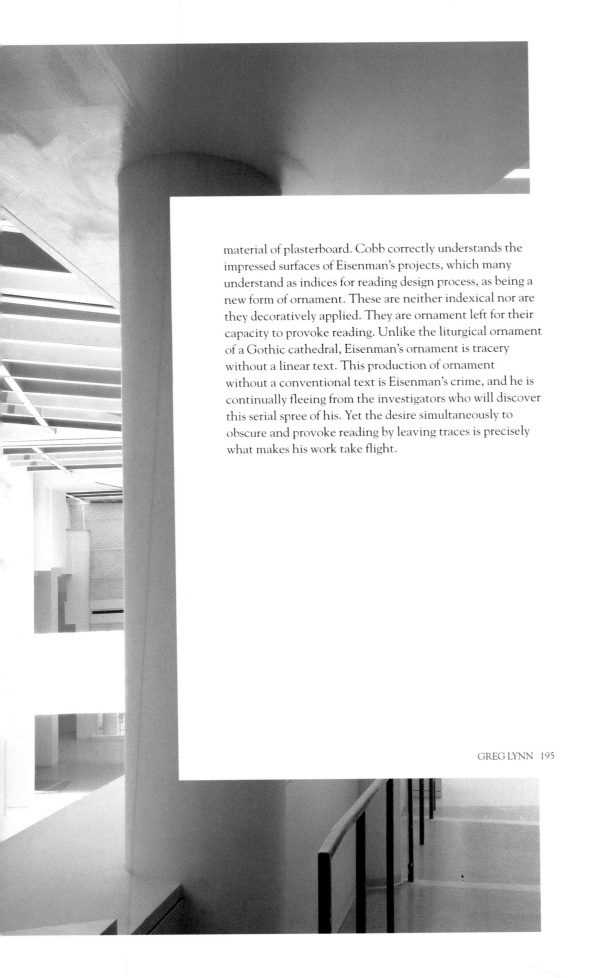

material of plasterboard. Cobb correctly understands the
impressed surfaces of Eisenman's projects, which many
understand as indices for reading design process, as being a
new form of ornament. These are neither indexical nor are
they decoratively applied. They are ornament left for their
capacity to provoke reading. Unlike the liturgical ornament
of a Gothic cathedral, Eisenman's ornament is tracery
without a linear text. This production of ornament
without a conventional text is Eisenman's crime, and he is
continually fleeing from the investigators who will discover
this serial spree of his. Yet the desire simultaneously to
obscure and provoke reading by leaving traces is precisely
what makes his work take flight.

Groningen Music-Video Pavilion
1990
Groningen, The Netherlands

This pavilion, a museum satellite for the 1990 Groningen City Festival, considers the idea that new video technology, nurtured by the growing home video industry, is revolutionizing the notion of the moving image, or, more precisely, the very perception of the world.

The design is based on an analysis of the way a video image is produced. An electron beam sweeps across a screen, from left to right, filling in an image point by point. Beginning at the top, the beam first scans the odd-numbered lines (horizontal trace). It then flies back to the upper part of the screen in a chevron figure (the vertical retrace), and draws in the even-numbered lines (horizontal retrace). When the beam reaches the right edge, it turns off as it moves to the starting point of the next line. During this "horizontal retrace," it is not visible. The beam passes over the screen twice to produce a single full image, yet a complete image is never on the screen because the first lines disappear as the alternate lines are filled in.

The figure produced by the beam's movement is that of two identical chevron lines running in parallel – horizontal trace and retrace – overlaid by a third, larger zigzagging line, the vertical retrace. Our project is based on this pattern, and focuses on the points (lines) of interference occurring between the three basic chevron figures.

A visitor to the pavilion follows a path analogous to that of the beam. Moving along the chevron path, one is constantly repositioned in the space. The visitor becomes part of the medium itself, passing in front of screens and crossing through images, shifting position to form images in different ways, and running interference.

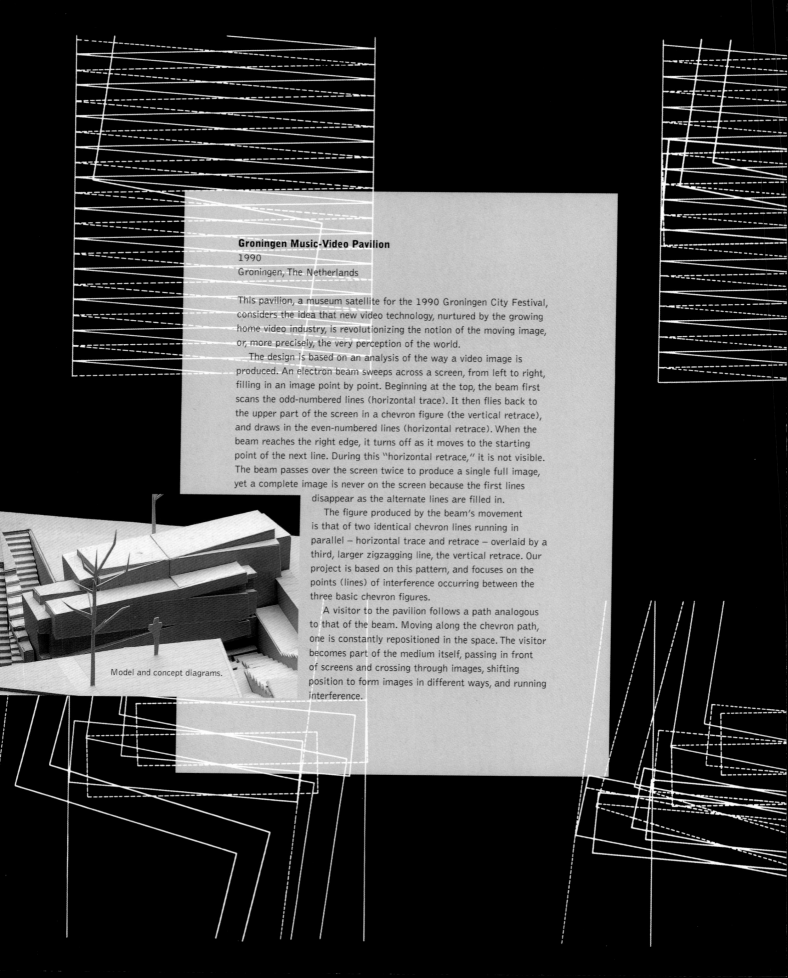

Model and concept diagrams.

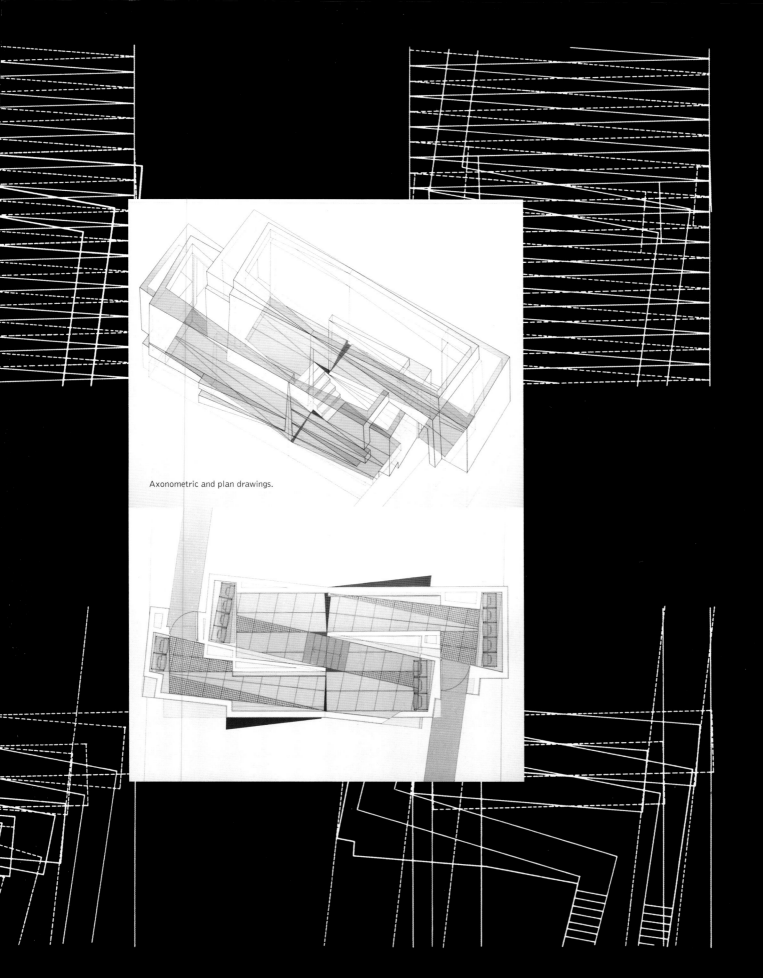

Axonometric and plan drawings.

Entrance to temporary pavilion.

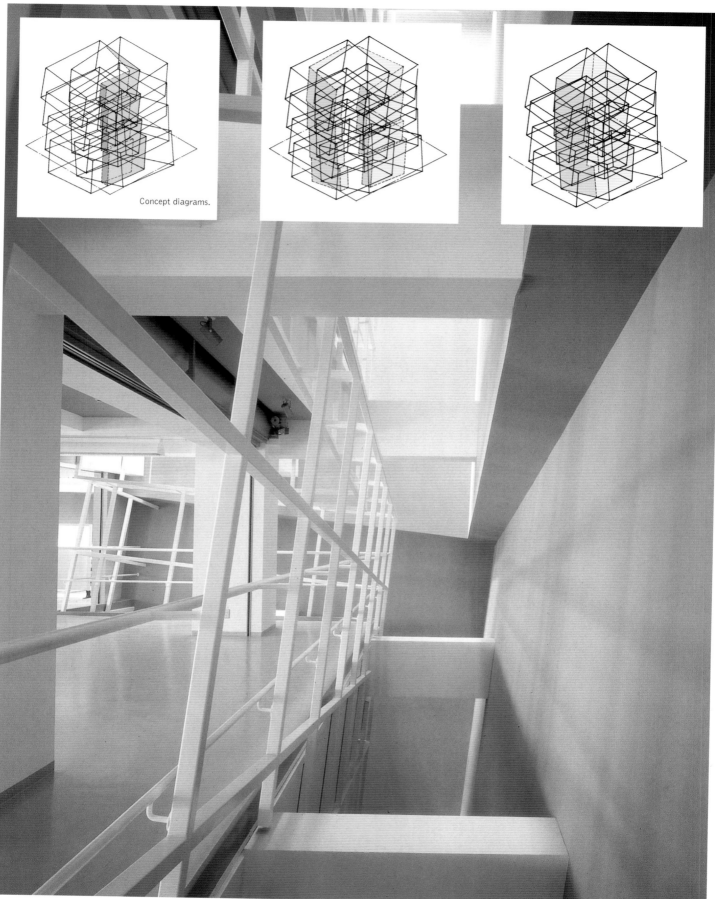

Concept diagrams.

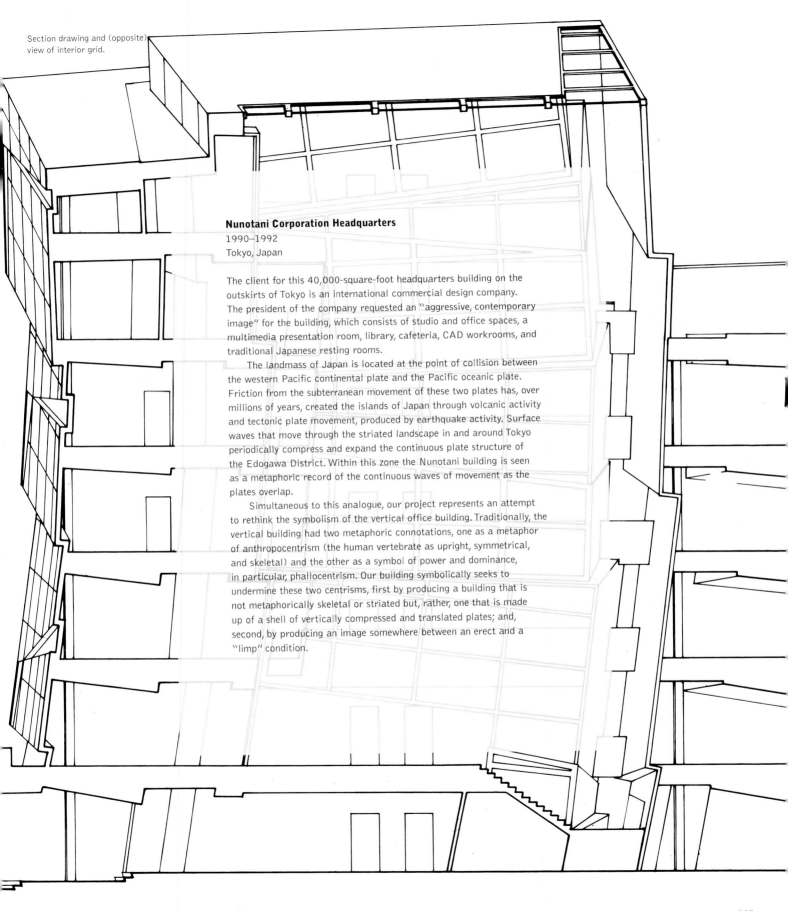

Section drawing and (opposite) view of interior grid.

Nunotani Corporation Headquarters

1990–1992
Tokyo, Japan

The client for this 40,000-square-foot headquarters building on the outskirts of Tokyo is an international commercial design company. The president of the company requested an "aggressive, contemporary image" for the building, which consists of studio and office spaces, a multimedia presentation room, library, cafeteria, CAD workrooms, and traditional Japanese resting rooms.

The landmass of Japan is located at the point of collision between the western Pacific continental plate and the Pacific oceanic plate. Friction from the subterranean movement of these two plates has, over millions of years, created the islands of Japan through volcanic activity and tectonic plate movement, produced by earthquake activity. Surface waves that move through the striated landscape in and around Tokyo periodically compress and expand the continuous plate structure of the Edogawa District. Within this zone the Nunotani building is seen as a metaphoric record of the continuous waves of movement as the plates overlap.

Simultaneous to this analogue, our project represents an attempt to rethink the symbolism of the vertical office building. Traditionally, the vertical building had two metaphoric connotations, one as a metaphor of anthropocentrism (the human vertebrate as upright, symmetrical, and skeletal) and the other as a symbol of power and dominance, in particular, phallocentrism. Our building symbolically seeks to undermine these two centrisms, first by producing a building that is not metaphorically skeletal or striated but, rather, one that is made up of a shell of vertically compressed and translated plates; and, second, by producing an image somewhere between an erect and a "limp" condition.

Above: study models and final presentation model (far right).

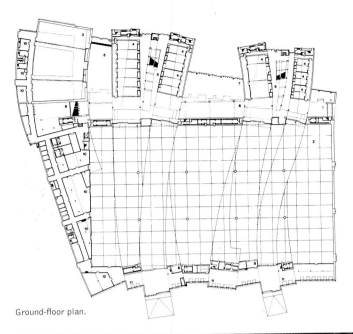

Ground-floor plan.

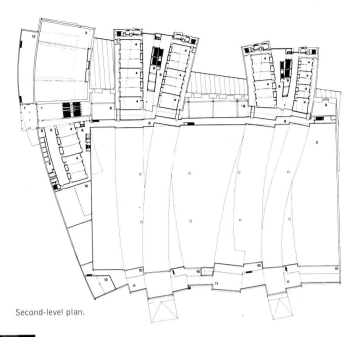

Second-level plan.

Left: Aerial view.
Below: High Street façade.
Opposite: Skylit concourse looking north.

Loading docks.

Aerial view looking southeast.

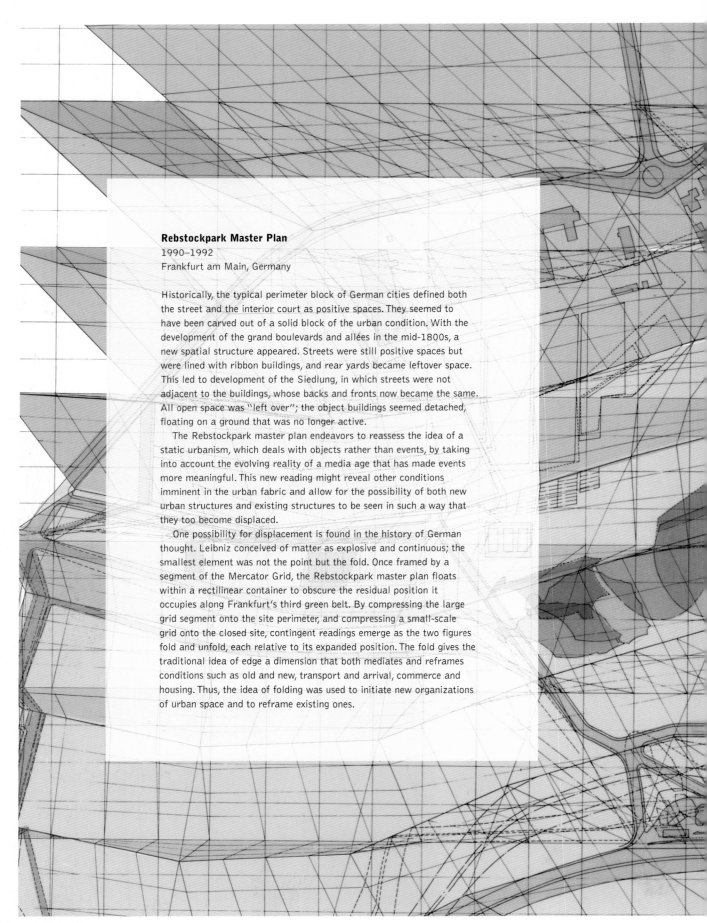

Rebstockpark Master Plan
1990–1992
Frankfurt am Main, Germany

Historically, the typical perimeter block of German cities defined both the street and the interior court as positive spaces. They seemed to have been carved out of a solid block of the urban condition. With the development of the grand boulevards and allées in the mid-1800s, a new spatial structure appeared. Streets were still positive spaces but were lined with ribbon buildings, and rear yards became leftover space. This led to development of the Siedlung, in which streets were not adjacent to the buildings, whose backs and fronts now became the same. All open space was "left over"; the object buildings seemed detached, floating on a ground that was no longer active.

The Rebstockpark master plan endeavors to reassess the idea of a static urbanism, which deals with objects rather than events, by taking into account the evolving reality of a media age that has made events more meaningful. This new reading might reveal other conditions imminent in the urban fabric and allow for the possibility of both new urban structures and existing structures to be seen in such a way that they too become displaced.

One possibility for displacement is found in the history of German thought. Leibniz conceived of matter as explosive and continuous; the smallest element was not the point but the fold. Once framed by a segment of the Mercator Grid, the Rebstockpark master plan floats within a rectilinear container to obscure the residual position it occupies along Frankfurt's third green belt. By compressing the large grid segment onto the site perimeter, and compressing a small-scale grid onto the closed site, contingent readings emerge as the two figures fold and unfold, each relative to its expanded position. The fold gives the traditional idea of edge a dimension that both mediates and reframes conditions such as old and new, transport and arrival, commerce and housing. Thus, the idea of folding was used to initiate new organizations of urban space and to reframe existing ones.

Perspective rendering
(below).

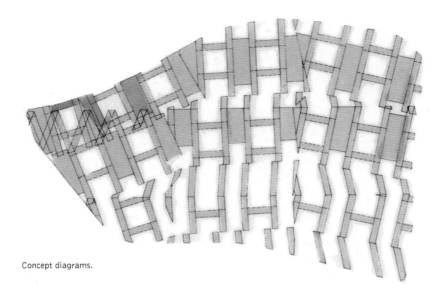

Concept diagrams.

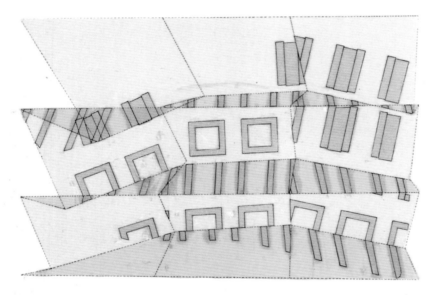

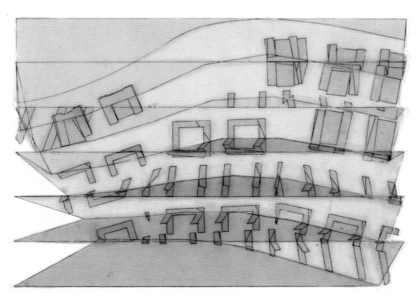

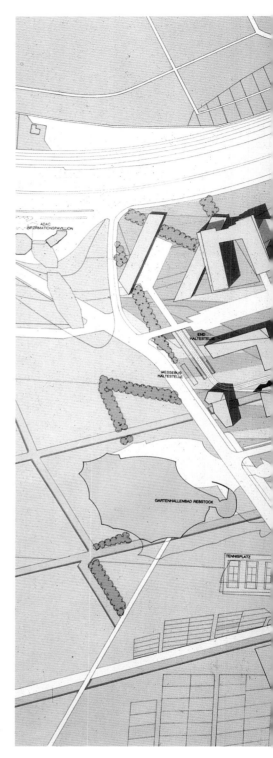

Site plan.

Competition model.

Alteka Office Building

1991

Tokyo, Japan

A paradigmatic city of accumulation, juxtaposition, and compression, Tokyo is an index of contingent, tentative relations and new, complex urban realities. Enfolded within the evolving reality of a mediated age, every Tokyo site is a nexus of activity that each building tries to stabilize and repress.

This project suggests another relationship to the city. Caught between the traditional city fabric and the Jigamae, a new large avenue, our folded tower suggests that an object is no longer defined by a standard of maintaining the appearance, or imposing a law, of constancy, but by a situation in which the fluctuation of the norm replaces the permanence of law, with the object taking place in a continuum. Thus, the object no longer corresponds to a spatial mold but rather to a temporal modulation that implies a continual variation as much as a perpetual development of the form. The object becomes an event, opening up, unfolding. The building evades a purely Cartesian definition by not representing an essential form. Instead, it is a form "becoming."

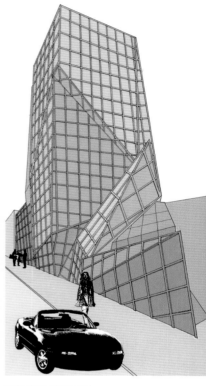

Wide-angle perspective.

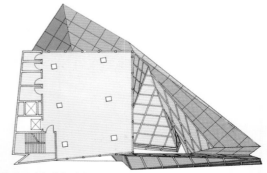

Second-level plan.

Eighth- through tenth-level plan.

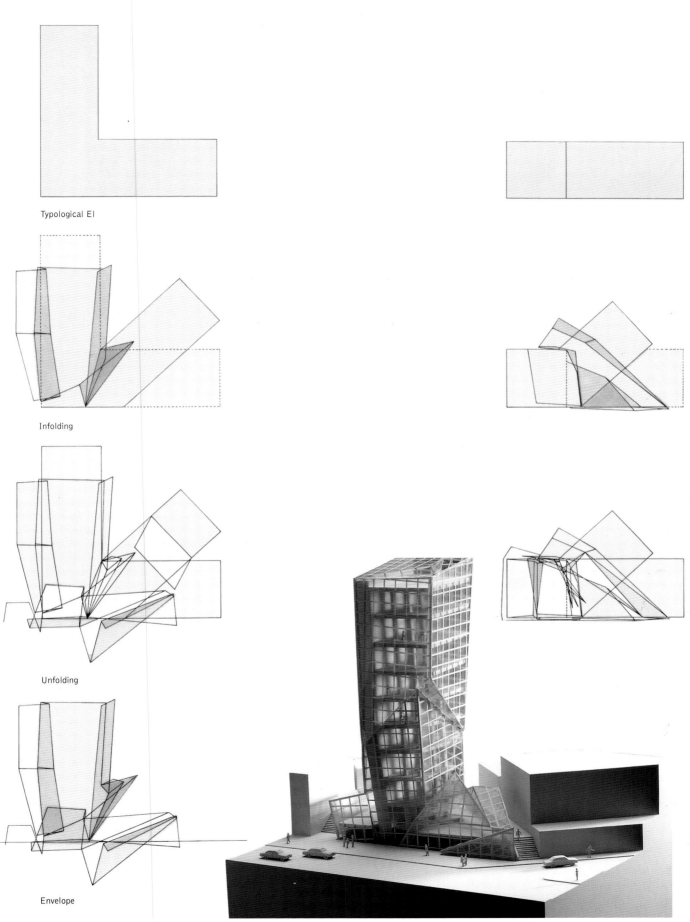

Typological El

Infolding

Unfolding

Envelope

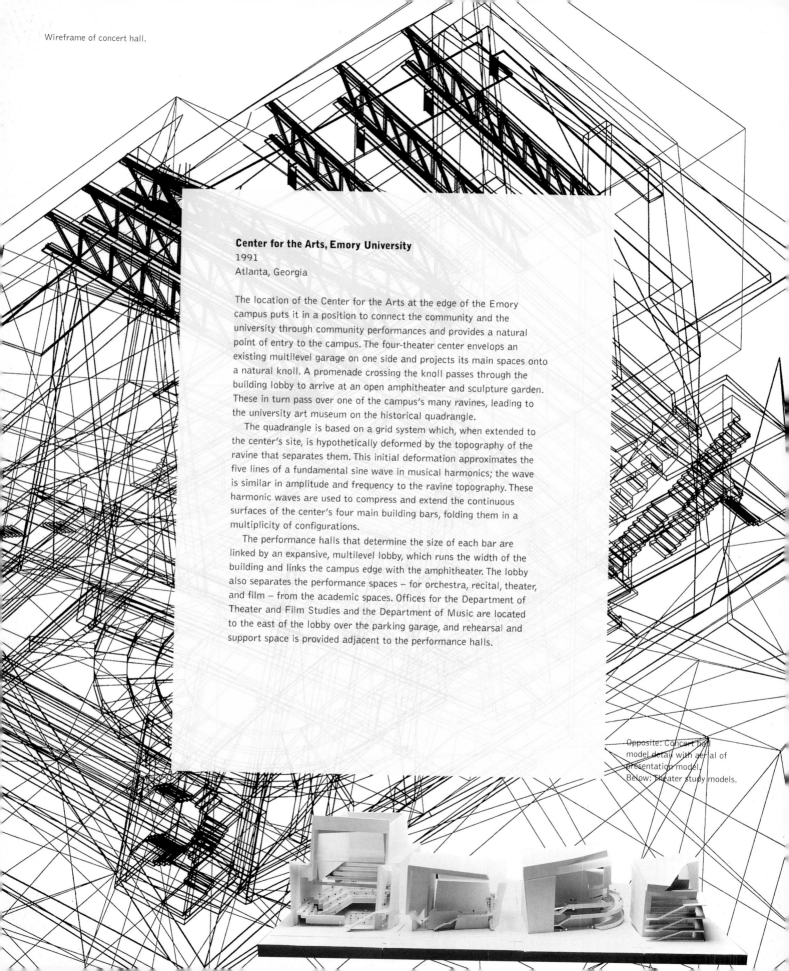

Center for the Arts, Emory University
1991
Atlanta, Georgia

The location of the Center for the Arts at the edge of the Emory campus puts it in a position to connect the community and the university through community performances and provides a natural point of entry to the campus. The four-theater center envelops an existing multilevel garage on one side and projects its main spaces onto a natural knoll. A promenade crossing the knoll passes through the building lobby to arrive at an open amphitheater and sculpture garden. These in turn pass over one of the campus's many ravines, leading to the university art museum on the historical quadrangle.

The quadrangle is based on a grid system which, when extended to the center's site, is hypothetically deformed by the topography of the ravine that separates them. This initial deformation approximates the five lines of a fundamental sine wave in musical harmonics; the wave is similar in amplitude and frequency to the ravine topography. These harmonic waves are used to compress and extend the continuous surfaces of the center's four main building bars, folding them in a multiplicity of configurations.

The performance halls that determine the size of each bar are linked by an expansive, multilevel lobby, which runs the width of the building and links the campus edge with the amphitheater. The lobby also separates the performance spaces – for orchestra, recital, theater, and film – from the academic spaces. Offices for the Department of Theater and Film Studies and the Department of Music are located to the east of the lobby over the parking garage, and rehearsal and support space is provided adjacent to the performance halls.

Opposite: Concert hall model detail with aerial of presentation model.
Below: Theater study models.

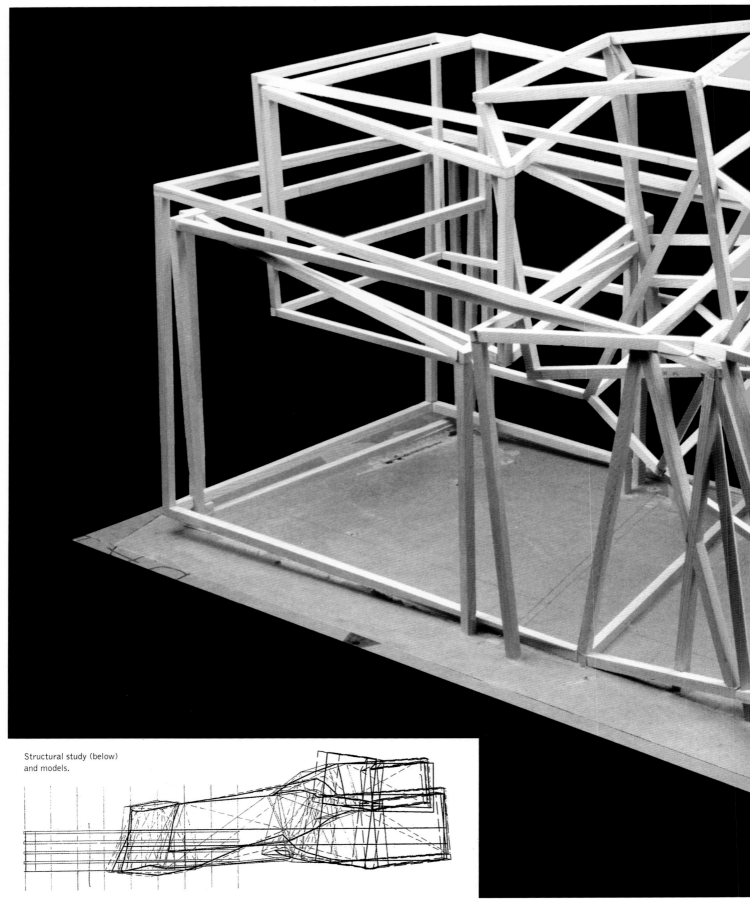

Structural study (below)
and models.

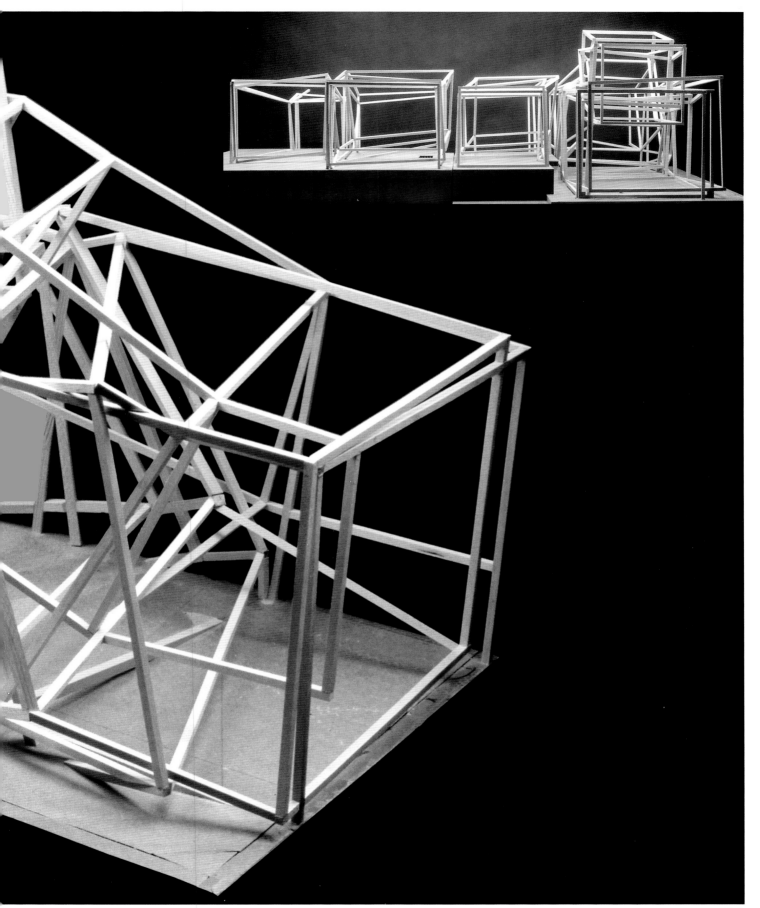

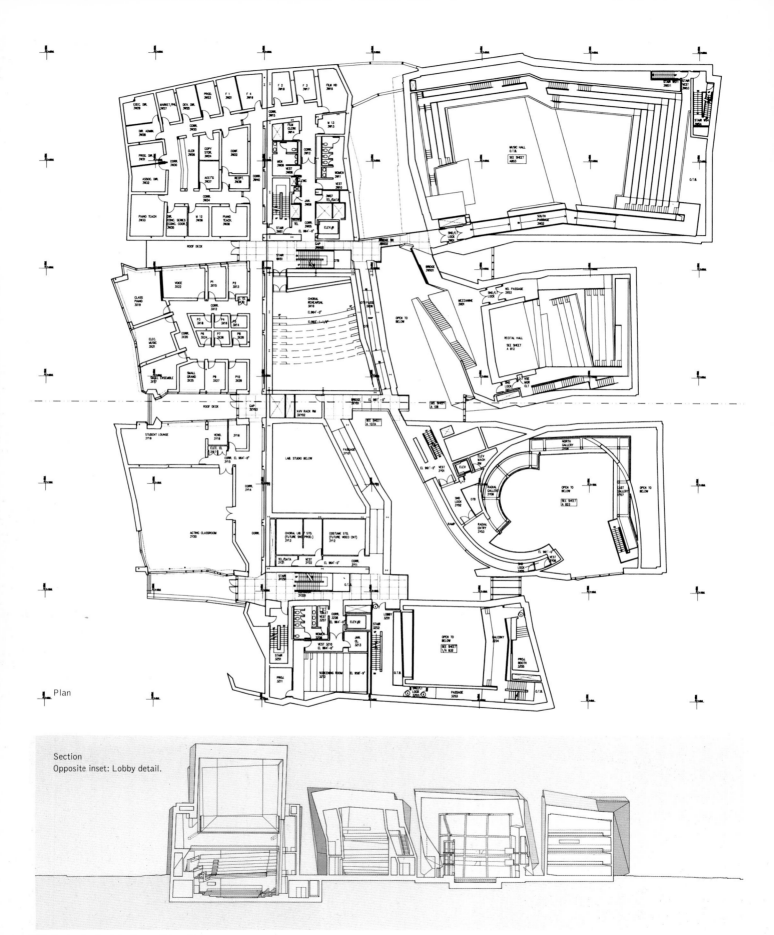

Plan

Section
Opposite inset: Lobby detail.

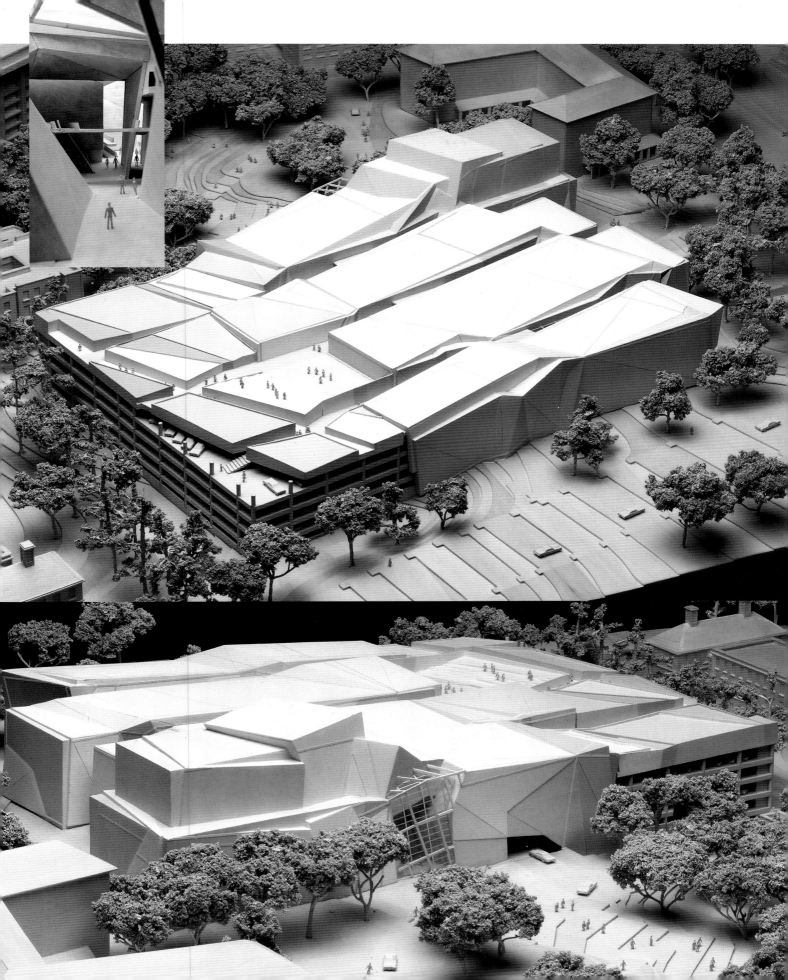

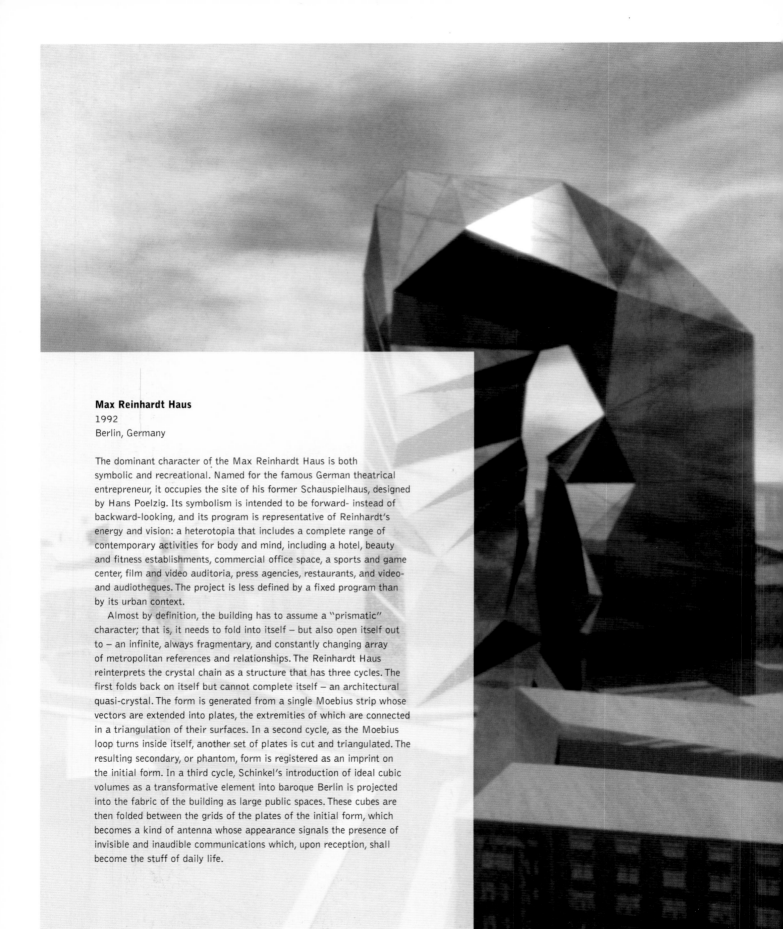

Max Reinhardt Haus
1992
Berlin, Germany

The dominant character of the Max Reinhardt Haus is both symbolic and recreational. Named for the famous German theatrical entrepreneur, it occupies the site of his former Schauspielhaus, designed by Hans Poelzig. Its symbolism is intended to be forward- instead of backward-looking, and its program is representative of Reinhardt's energy and vision: a heterotopia that includes a complete range of contemporary activities for body and mind, including a hotel, beauty and fitness establishments, commercial office space, a sports and game center, film and video auditoria, press agencies, restaurants, and video- and audiotheques. The project is less defined by a fixed program than by its urban context.

Almost by definition, the building has to assume a "prismatic" character; that is, it needs to fold into itself — but also open itself out to — an infinite, always fragmentary, and constantly changing array of metropolitan references and relationships. The Reinhardt Haus reinterprets the crystal chain as a structure that has three cycles. The first folds back on itself but cannot complete itself — an architectural quasi-crystal. The form is generated from a single Moebius strip whose vectors are extended into plates, the extremities of which are connected in a triangulation of their surfaces. In a second cycle, as the Moebius loop turns inside itself, another set of plates is cut and triangulated. The resulting secondary, or phantom, form is registered as an imprint on the initial form. In a third cycle, Schinkel's introduction of ideal cubic volumes as a transformative element into baroque Berlin is projected into the fabric of the building as large public spaces. These cubes are then folded between the grids of the plates of the initial form, which becomes a kind of antenna whose appearance signals the presence of invisible and inaudible communications which, upon reception, shall become the stuff of daily life.

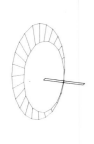

First revolution
Attaching panels

Transparent diagram
Slicing of panels

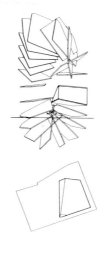

Volumetric realization
Panel surfaces

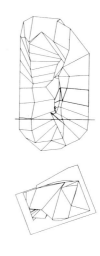

Form of first revolution
Almost crystallized

Second revolution
Panel separation

Transparent diagram
Splitting of panels

Separation of surface along
panel edges

Phantom impression on the
almost crystallized form

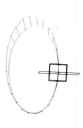

Third revolution
Cubic volume

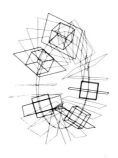

Attached cubic volumes

Misfolding of plates on the cube

Almost realized with
crystallized deformation

Section drawing and selected floor plans.
Opposite: Structural study model.

Nördliches Derendorf Master Plan Competition
1992
Düsseldorf, Germany

Our proposal recognizes that we are living in a new era of the electronic, which has replaced the mechanical one. Architectural elements once determined by and symbolic of mechanical means now reflect the influences of electronic communication: media, the computer, lasers. In this new era, order can emerge out of seeming chaos only at certain critical points in the flow of matter and energy.

In Düsseldorf, one of these specific limits is the system of radar and radio which, because of the site's proximity to the flight path of the airport, causes a certain height restriction to be mapped onto this project. This mapping derives from the intersection of the radar pattern with the radio pattern, which produces a third interference pattern that becomes one of the form-generators on the site.

A moiré pattern derived from the mathematical representation of the superposition of radar and radio signals provides an idea of limit for physical design. This new mapping is overlaid on the site as a topological structure. Instead of the grid, there is a matrix, which is produced by the stretching of the interference pattern in section over the site.

This is not a utopian idea that spreads as a growth all over Düsseldorf. It is an attempt to deal with a specific urban condition of boundary and how we deal with boundaries that relate to what people who live there understand, because now, through computers and video networks, their boundaries extend to Tokyo and Hong Kong as much as to Hamburg and Berlin. Our project expresses these connections, while at the same time making an urban living place for people – a place that enables them to understand both their specific place and their connection to the larger world.

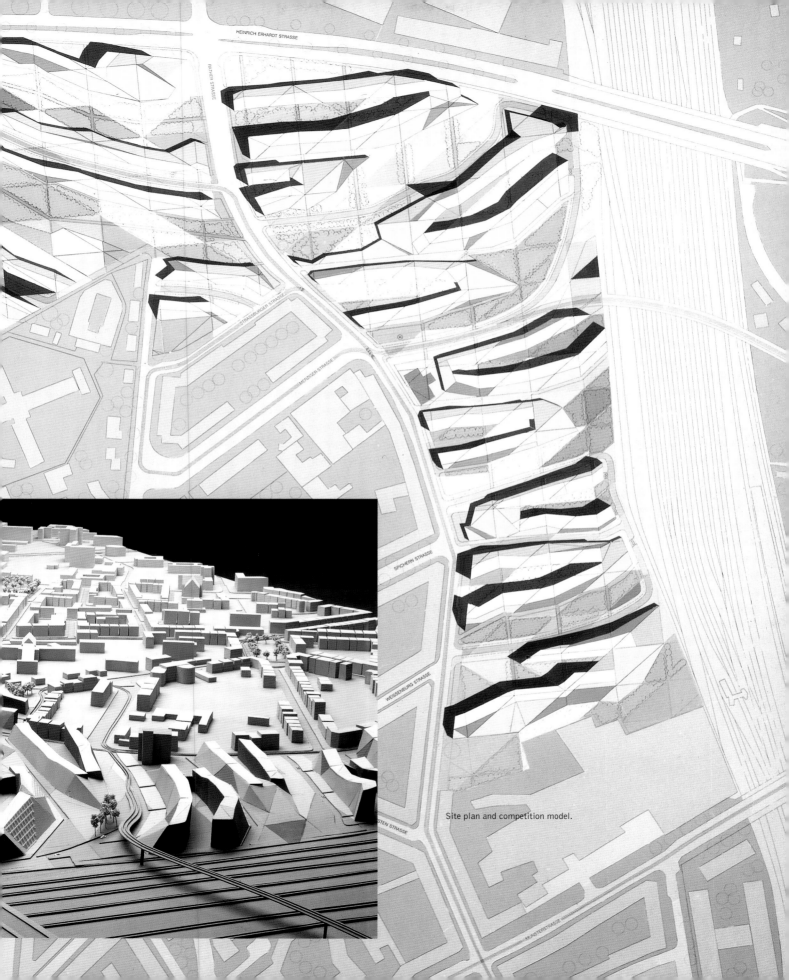

Site plan and competition model.

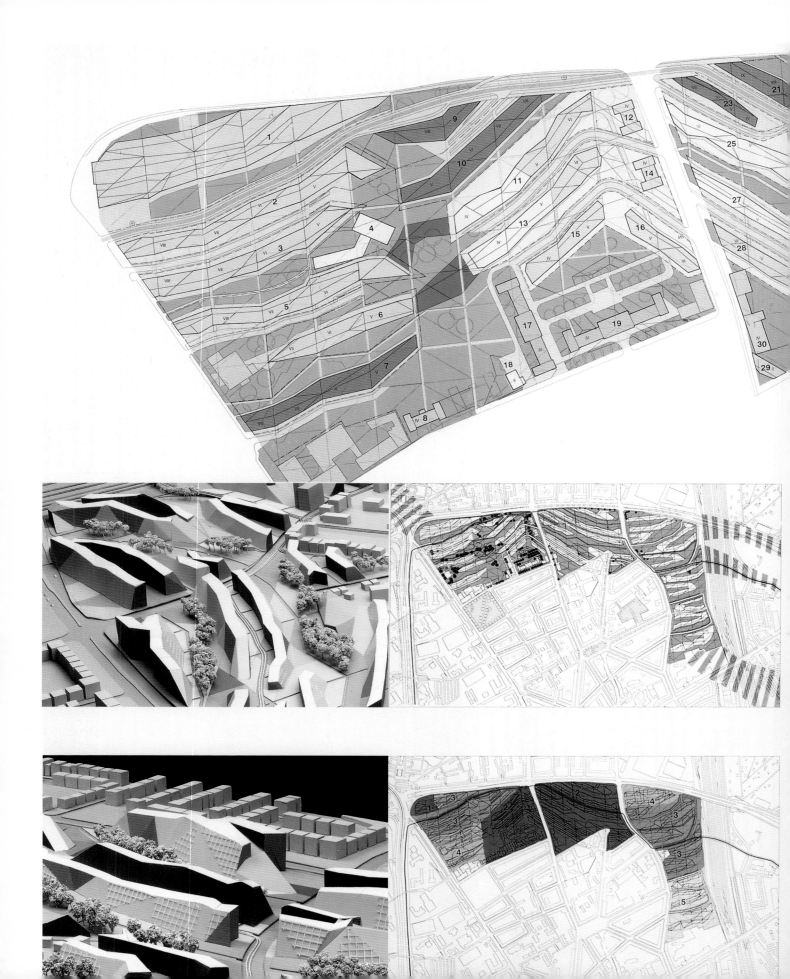

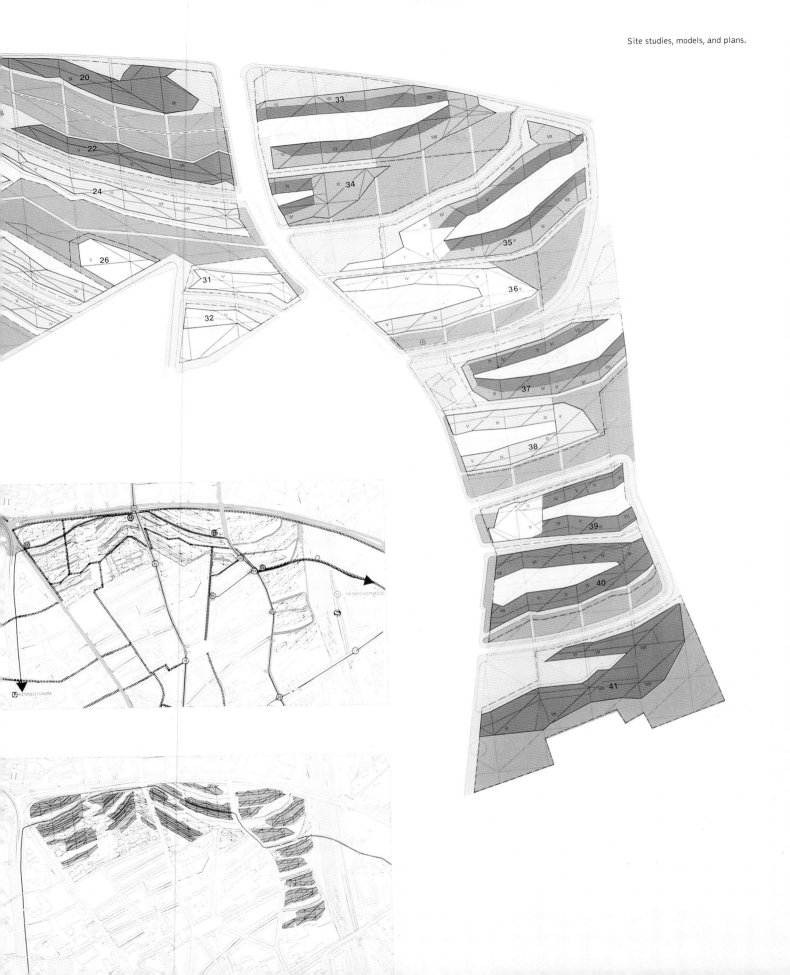

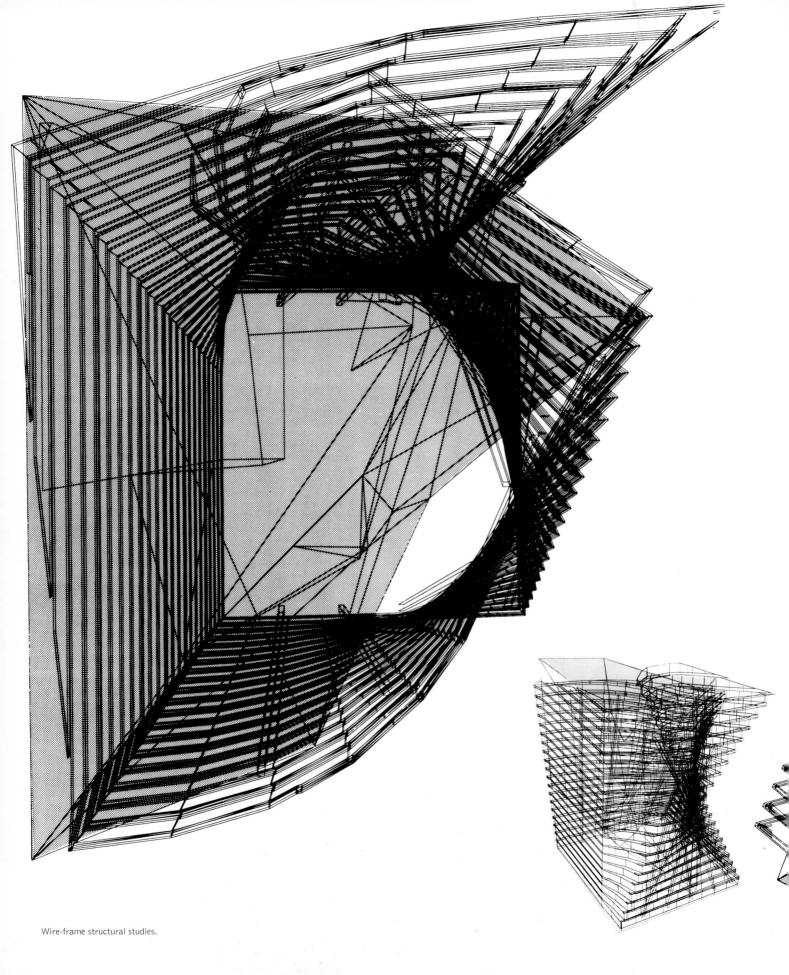

Wire-frame structural studies.

Haus Immendorff
1993
Düsseldorf, Germany

For Haus Immendorff, we looked at analogies that could be brought
to architecture from other, more dynamic, unpredictable systems of
organization. Two possible spatial organizations seemed to elude
traditional architectural construction. One was the modeling of voids,
rather than solids, in the sense of figure-figure. The second was the
possibility of modeling a figure-figure relationship to create contingent
or interstitial spatial relationships that were neither poché nor residual
functions. This required a system that was doubled from its inception.
One such system is the soliton wave. Solitons are pulses of energy that
move through solids, liquids, or gases and form nonlinear interactions
binding individual sine waves together. At critical moments, these
interactions produce spontaneous self-organizing, or emergent, systems.

In such systems, the role of the author is questioned, as well as
how we read. The possibility of reading blurred or disrupted figures
and figure-figure relationships initially depends on the possibility of
destabilizing the traditional state of the architectural integer (columns,
openings, etc.). Given their unique instrumentality (to provide shelter
that resists gravity), architectural integers usually refuse to lose
their presence. Thus, the profile of the figure is a dominant aspect of
reading. To displace profile would perhaps begin to destabilize reading.

The blurred external profile that began to emerge at Haus
Immendorff – which from any static point of view could be seen as
twisting and changing – was from such a haptic and unauthored
process. The project is composed of an inner volume and an outer
volume whose oblique surfaces intersect as they twist vertically, forming
a vortexlike cone rising to the top of the building. The exterior volume
is a stepped "skin" of glass windows alternating with louvers set back
at various widths from the glass. The inner volume is a solid wall with
glazed cuts, to be used as a painting surface; viewed from outside the
glass volume, it becomes a six-story showcase for the client's artwork.

Plan and section drawings.

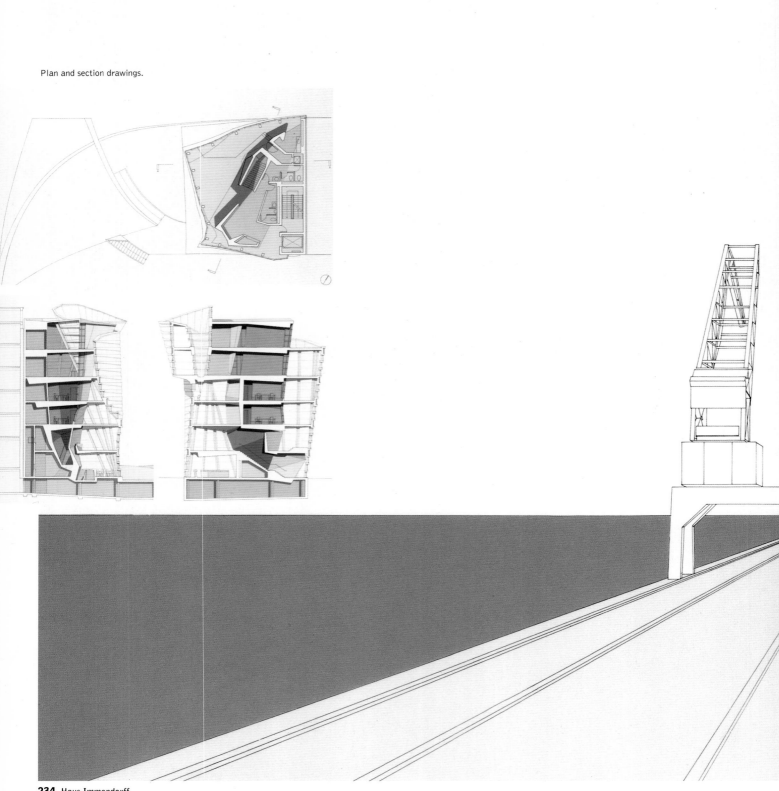

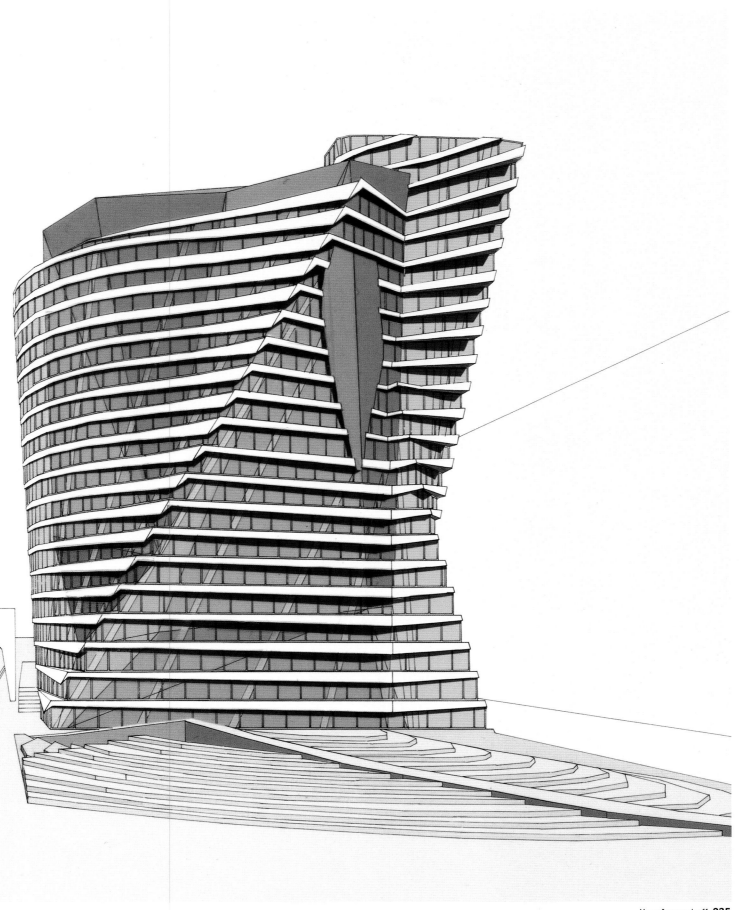

Regional Music Conservatory and Contemporary Arts Center
1993–1994
Tours, France

Rather than ask what form a contemporary cultural center should take, we asked how a contemporary cultural center should be given form. Thus, rather than design autonomous forms for a space between two existing buildings, we designed a complex of buildings that borrows from yet transforms the design vocabulary of the existing buildings, and respects yet modifies an alignment with the grid of the city's major boulevard and the grid on which the buildings sit. The project provides a new kind of dynamic space between the existing structures. This de-emphasizes any hierarchy in the relationship of building to open space and renders both equally important. Through a strategy of striation, space is woven through the buildings, as much as buildings are woven through the spaces.

The specific form was derived with a morphing software typically used in film and video to achieve the transformation of one figure or form into another. In the methodological development of the project, this allowed for the space between the two buildings to be the site of a series of transformations, registered along the lines and forms of striation. The plan outlines and roof contours of the buildings were morphed, or transformed, in order to arrive at new plan and section configurations, which are both an alteration and residue of the existing references. The spaces created in this way are equally deliberate and incidental; the outside is contingent on the inside and vice versa.

Transverse and longitudinal sections.

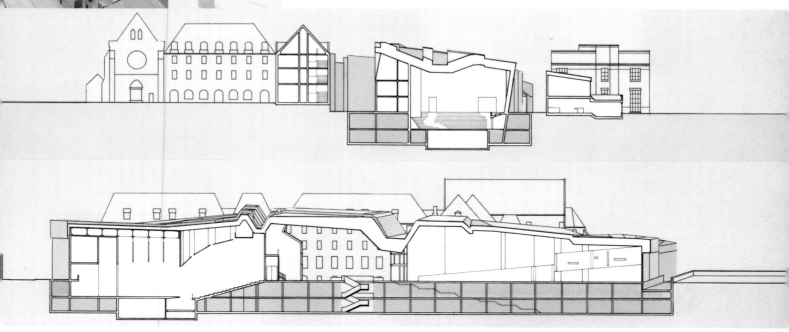

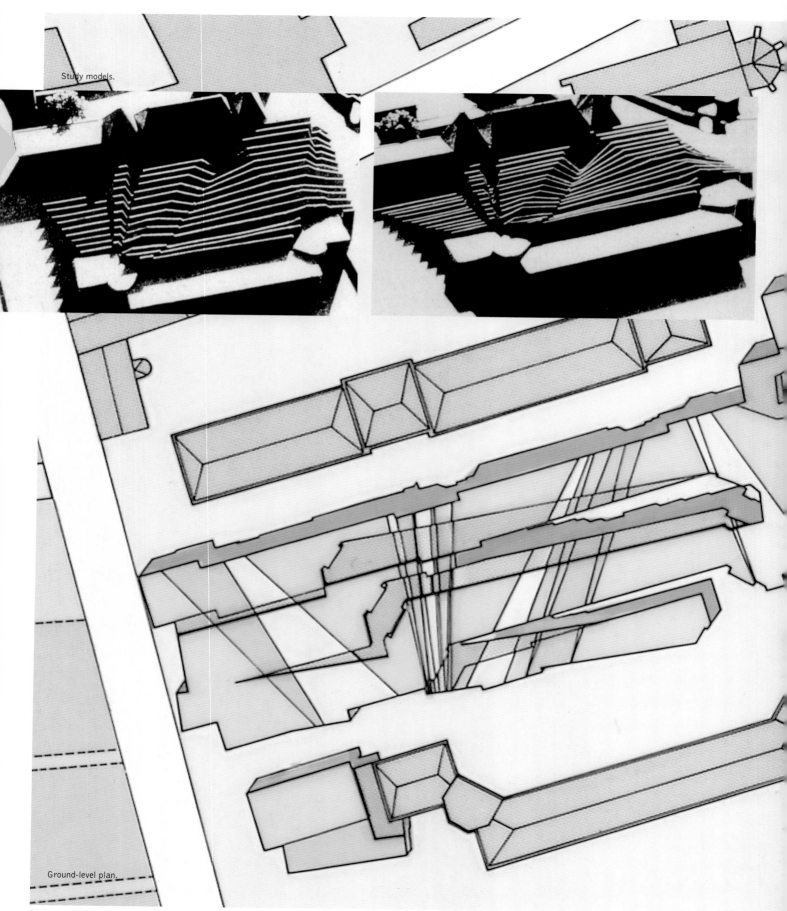

Study models.

Ground-level plan.

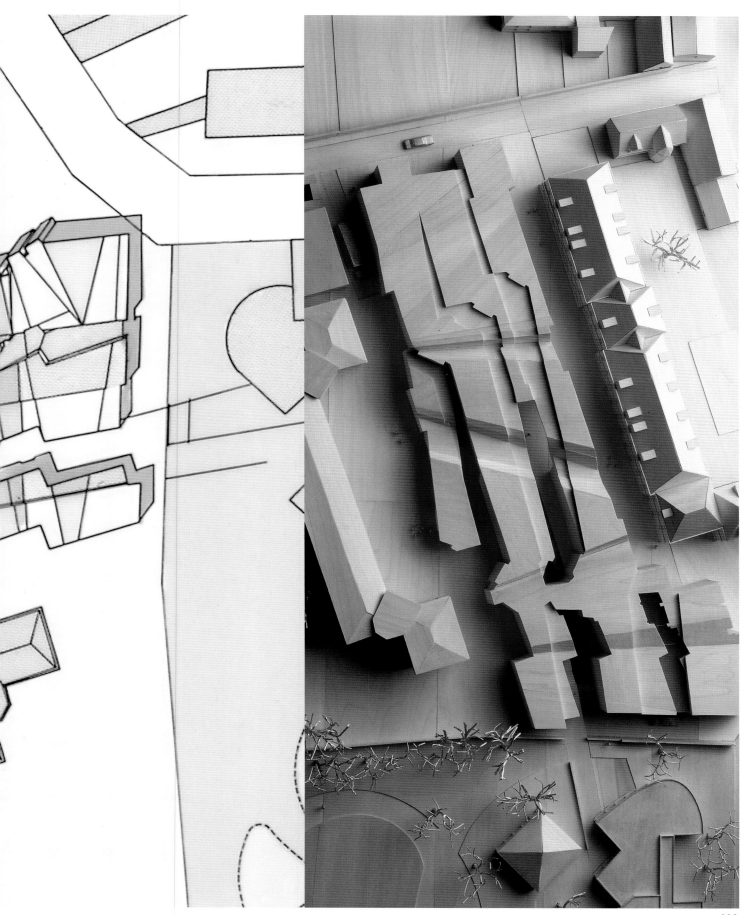

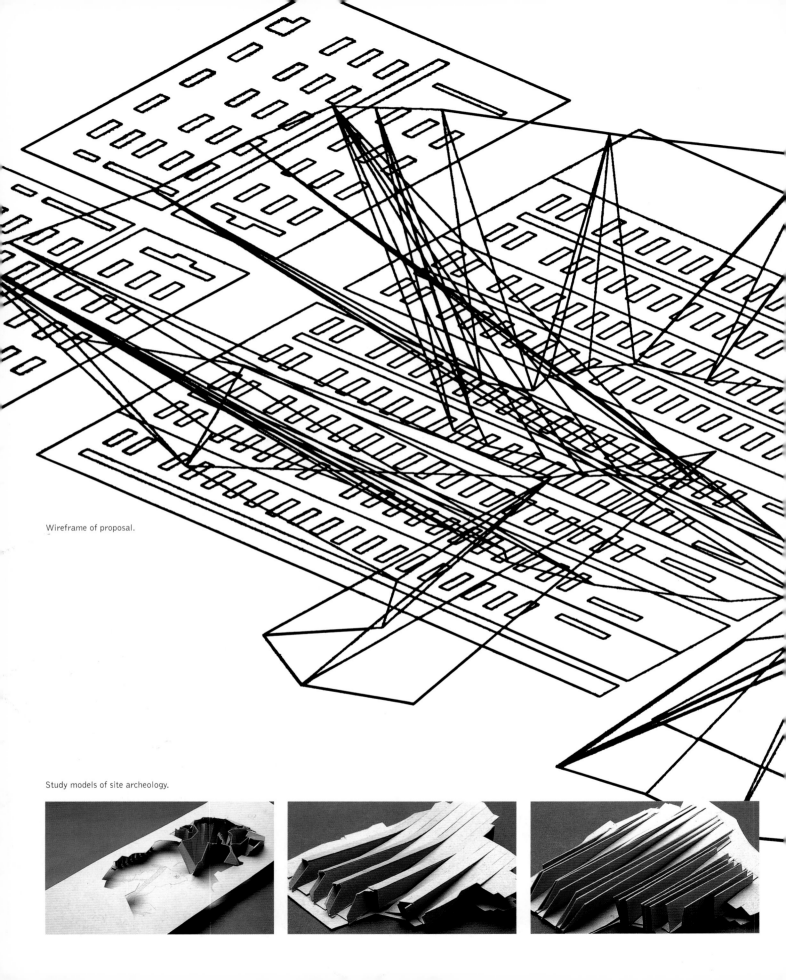

Wireframe of proposal.

Study models of site archeology.

**Monument and Memorial Site Dedicated to the Jewish Victims
of the Nazi Regime in Austria, 1938–1945**
1995–1996
Vienna, Austria

This memorial project challenges the premises of the two poles of
Western thought, reason and expression. The site is inscribed through
the interrelationships of specific historical maps that bear on this
question. These maps engender a series of forms that question not
only the ways in which history is remembered but also the meaning
of the forms themselves.

   The three elements of our proposal are deployed in three
different, layered positions on the site. The first layer is three
meters below grade. It consists of two different maps of Viennese
ghettos (destroyed in 1421 and 1678), which are scaled to occupy
the Judenplatz site. The second layer is three meters above grade and
is a rescaled map of Germany and Austria following the Anschluss in
1938. The contours of the maps, which represent changing territorial
boundaries and their consequences, are joined to rupture the ground
of the Judenplatz, forever changing it and marking its new boundaries.
This rupture is enclosed by a series of vertical steel plates. One enters
this enclosure at ground level, the ground of the everyday, the ground
of the ordinary, of the reasonable. Third, a series of lights inscribed into
this ground follow a reduced plan of Auschwitz. This plan represents the
extreme of reason, of rationality gone mad. The intersections of reason
and expression and their results are inscribed in the ground-level
surfaces inside the rupture.

   It has been said that the Talmud, the spirit of Jewish culture and
thought, provides a question for every answer rather than an answer
for every question. The Talmud can be thought of as a catalog of
debate. Instead of producing a memorial that embodies meaning, we
propose a process whereby the meaning of the memorial questions the
premises and conditions of the Holocaust and the means through which
a cultural form may represent these conditions.

Competition model.

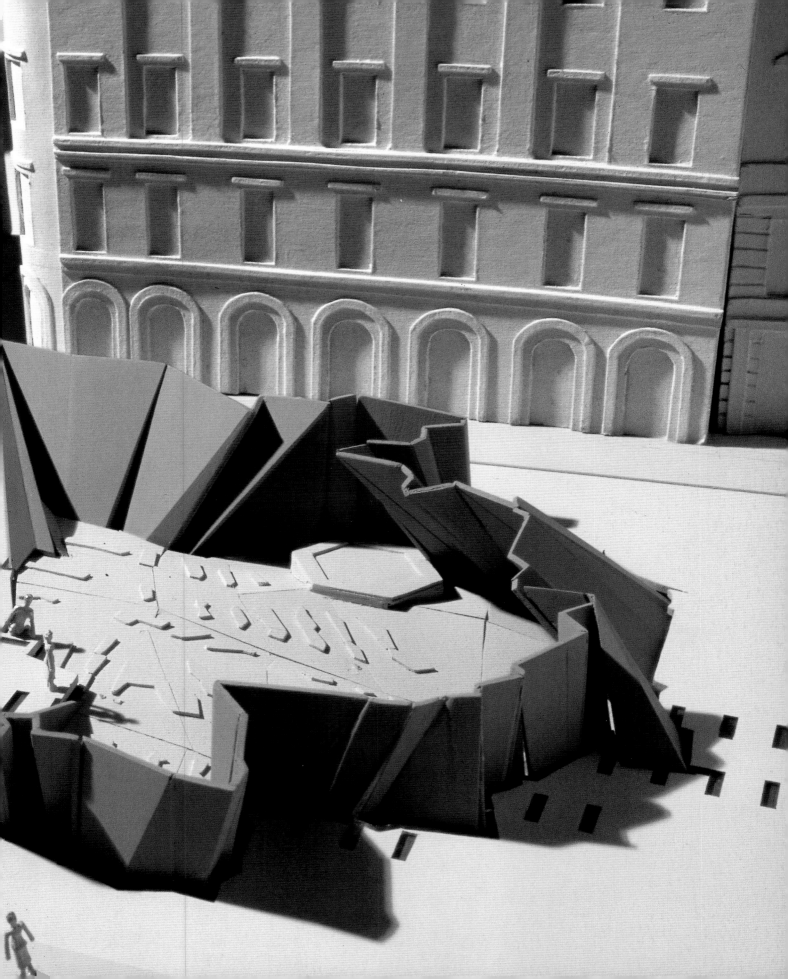

Church of the Year 2000
1996
Rome, Italy

The pilgrimage church occupies a special place in the development
of ecclesiastical space. The pilgrimage was a therapy through space.
The idea of distance symbolized needs which were unsatisfied; the
pilgrimage expressed a yearning for intimacy. The architectural effect
of these inverted desires and conditions was found in many pilgrimage
churches, which sharpened the sense of desire and fulfillment by playing
out the pilgrimage in miniature, within the body of the church itself.

Today, air travel and media have collapsed the distance of the
pilgrimage and created universal access to its experience. The church
itself must provide the pilgrim's experience of distance and proximity. In
our project the nave becomes symbolic of proximity and distance with
its two side aisles, or two routes, providing passage as in a pilgrimage
space of communion. These passages, on either side of the roofless
central nave, are enclosed, heightening the contrasts of light and
shadow, space and mass to express the distant mystery of the sacrament.
Thus, the church becomes two routes, one secular and the other the
ecclesiastical route through the space of communion.

From the Middle Ages to the Gothic cathedral, the church mediated
between the celebrant of the Mass and the congregant. Today we are
seeing a cultural shift from a world in which technology and its
mechanisms were the mediators to one in which information is
becoming the new mediator between God, man, and nature. How does
the church sort through this information to relay its religious message?

In the Gothic cathedrals stained glass was a major form of media.
Our church introduces a contemporary form of "stained glass": a media
wall in each side aisle that can be seen from the aisles and the outdoor
nave. The media walls allow light and image to penetrate the body of
the church and allow everyone to witness the sacraments during large
assemblies. The media wall is made up of panels of liquid crystals,
which are also the iconography of the church.

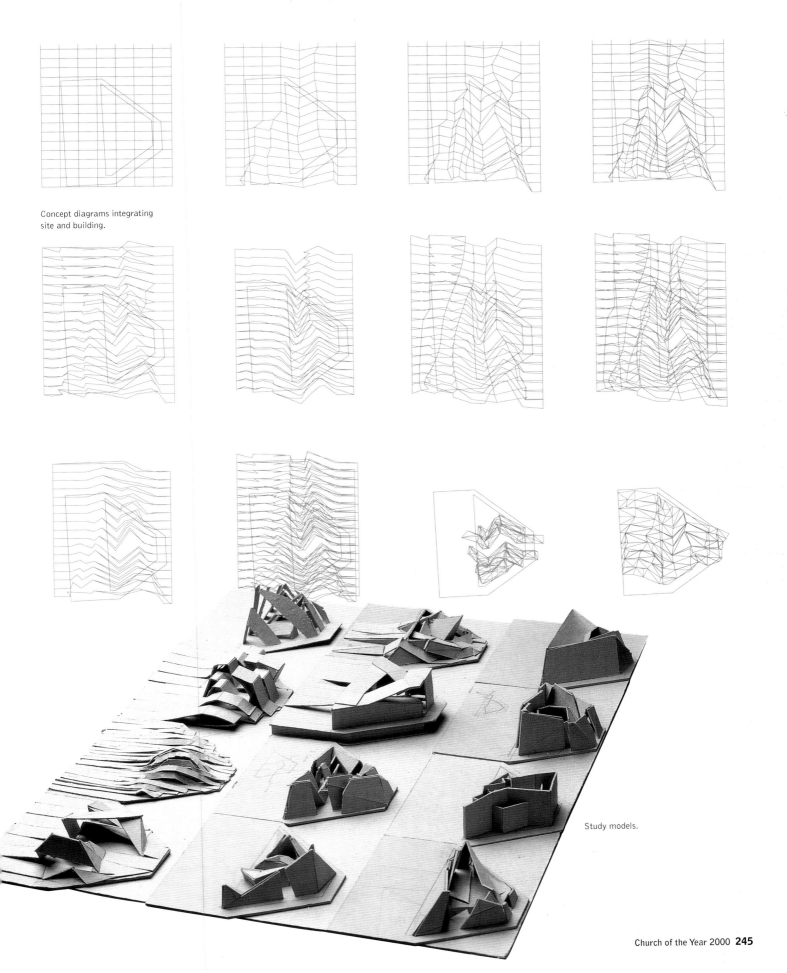

Concept diagrams integrating
site and building.

Study models.

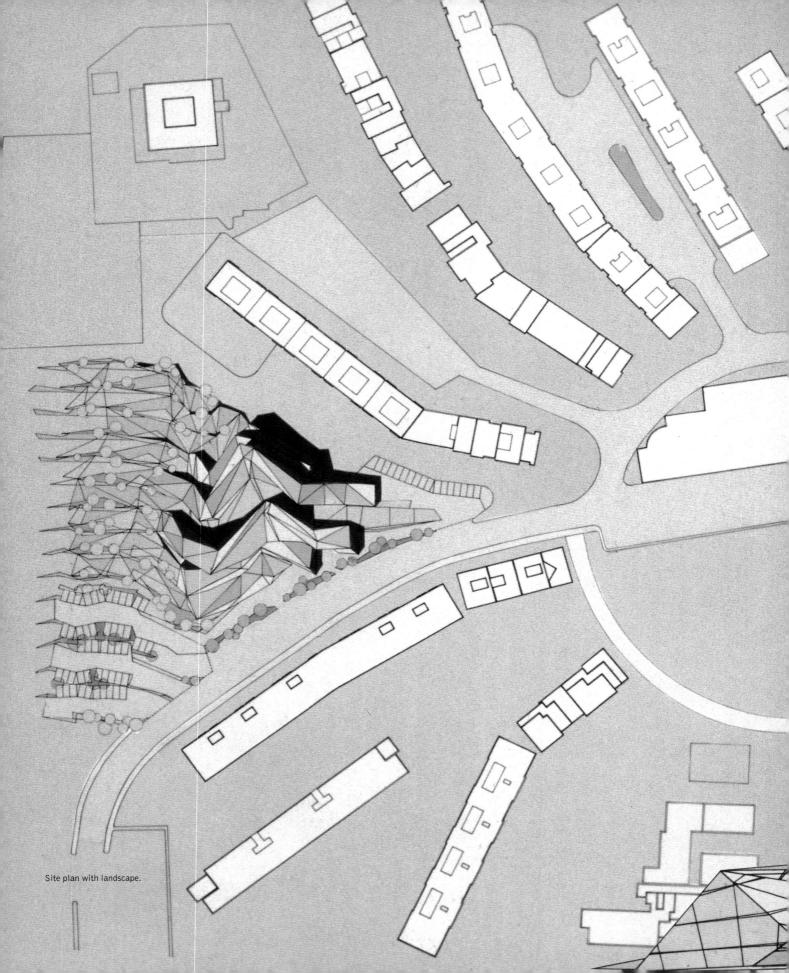

Site plan with landscape.

Model and perspective drawing (below).

Presentation model with detail of
a side chapel (opposite).

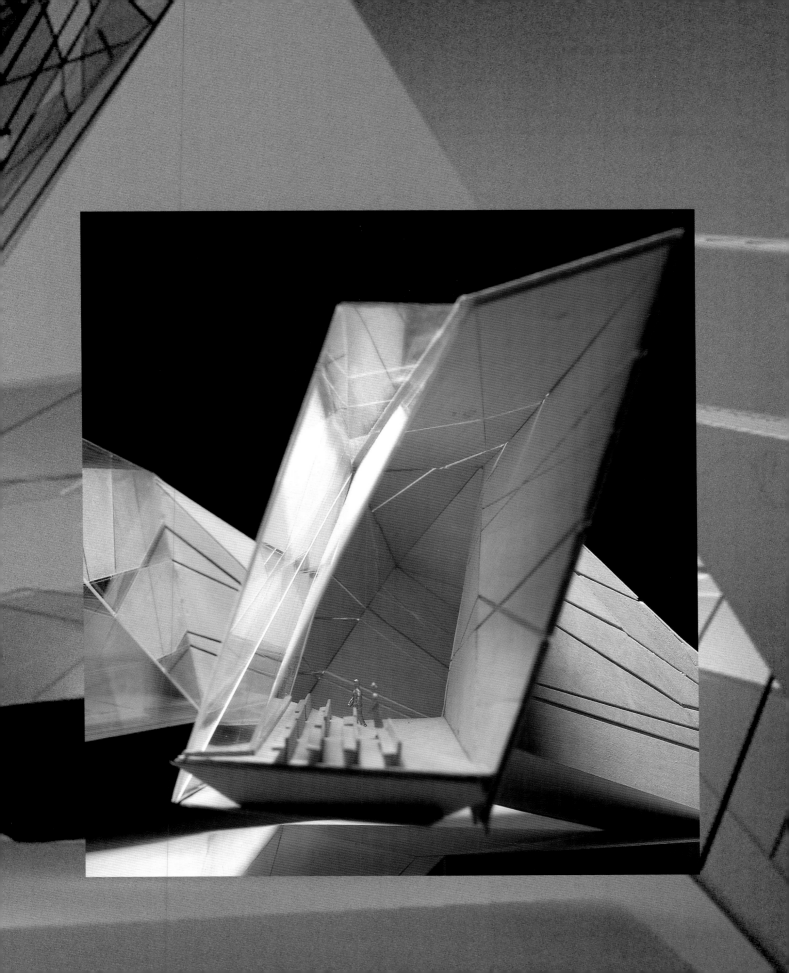

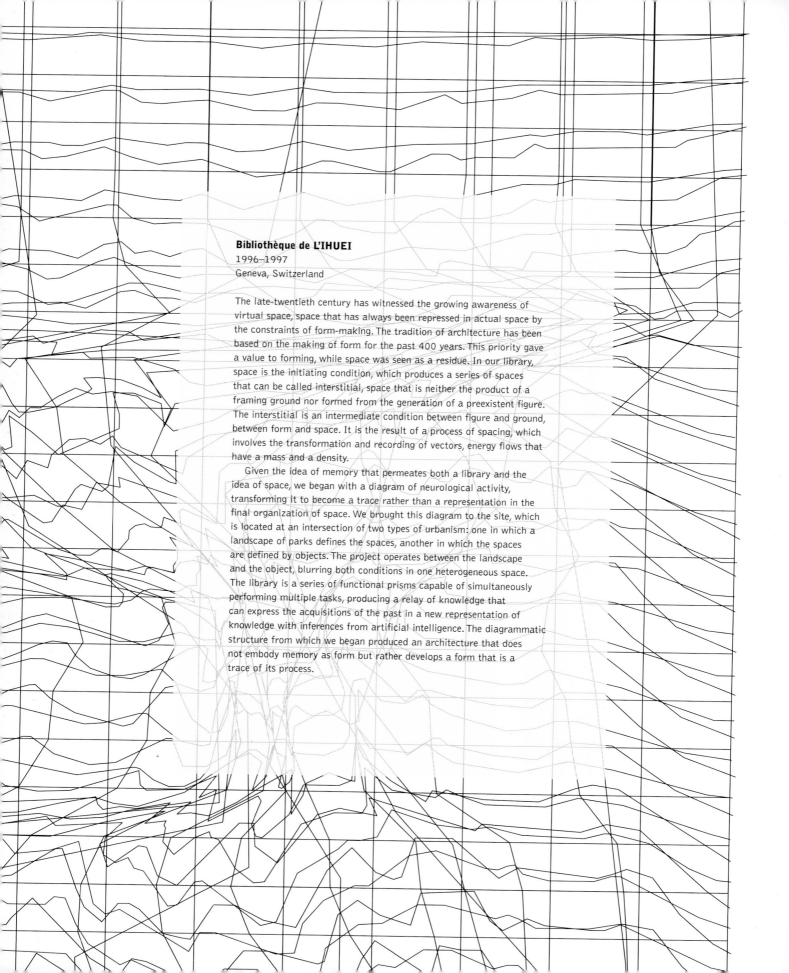

Bibliothèque de L'IHUEI

1996–1997
Geneva, Switzerland

The late-twentieth century has witnessed the growing awareness of virtual space, space that has always been repressed in actual space by the constraints of form-making. The tradition of architecture has been based on the making of form for the past 400 years. This priority gave a value to forming, while space was seen as a residue. In our library, space is the initiating condition, which produces a series of spaces that can be called interstitial, space that is neither the product of a framing ground nor formed from the generation of a preexistent figure. The interstitial is an intermediate condition between figure and ground, between form and space. It is the result of a process of spacing, which involves the transformation and recording of vectors, energy flows that have a mass and a density.

Given the idea of memory that permeates both a library and the idea of space, we began with a diagram of neurological activity, transforming it to become a trace rather than a representation in the final organization of space. We brought this diagram to the site, which is located at an intersection of two types of urbanism: one in which a landscape of parks defines the spaces, another in which the spaces are defined by objects. The project operates between the landscape and the object, blurring both conditions in one heterogeneous space. The library is a series of functional prisms capable of simultaneously performing multiple tasks, producing a relay of knowledge that can express the acquisitions of the past in a new representation of knowledge with inferences from artificial intelligence. The diagrammatic structure from which we began produced an architecture that does not embody memory as form but rather develops a form that is a trace of its process.

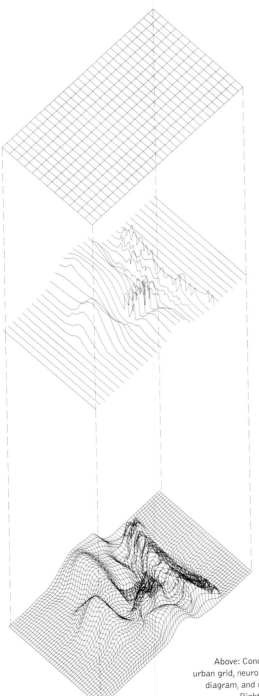

Above: Concept diagram –
urban grid, neurological activity
diagram, and new landscape.
Right: Study model.

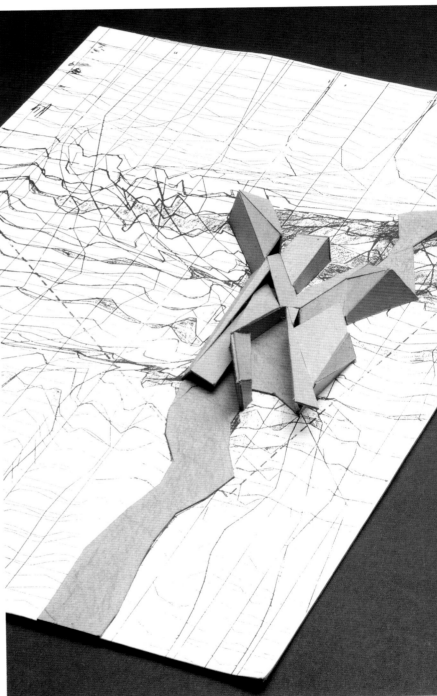

Structural study models.

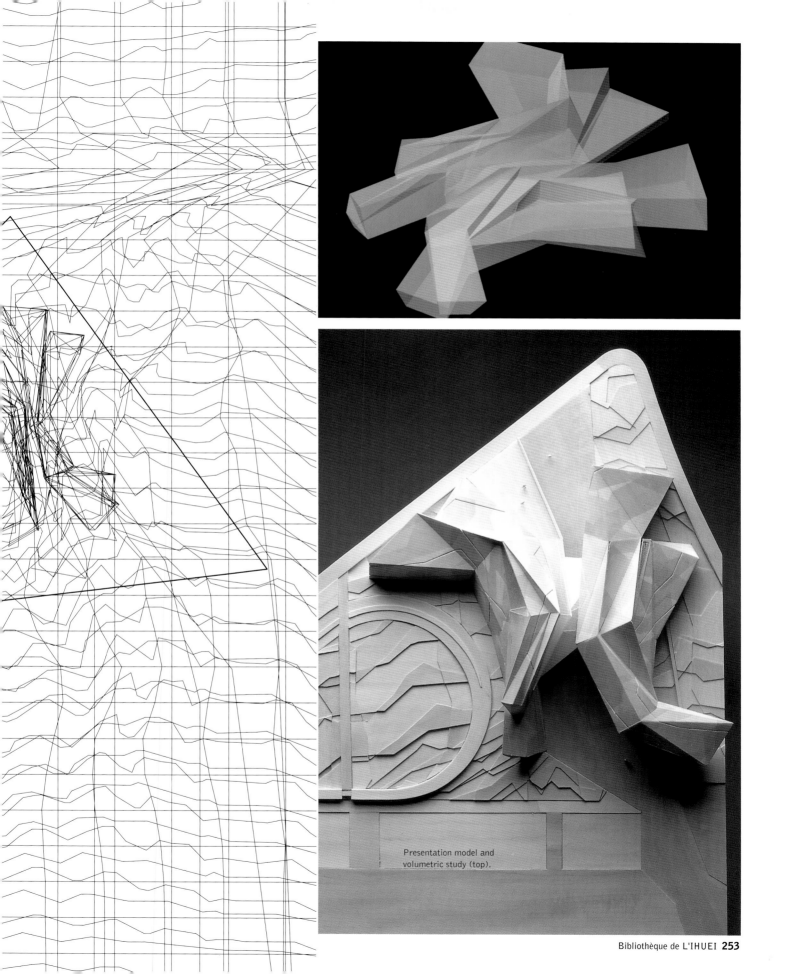

Presentation model and
volumetric study (top).

JC Decaux Bus Shelter
1996
Aachen, Germany

Street furniture prototypes for the French company JC Decaux were based on the idea of folding to create unique yet mass-produceable forms. The bus shelter installed on Elisenbrunnenplatz in central Aachen consists of two parts. The first is a folded towerlike structure with an electronic display for announcements and potential advertising. The second is the shelter itself, a legged "creature" made of steel. Two intertwining steel "plates," one gray and one deep gold, are folded and unfolded to establish a non-Cartesian space. The gray plates also fold into projecting benches to provide seating for waiting bus passengers. Though the openings appear regular and repetitive, in fact each "leg" of the creature is different.

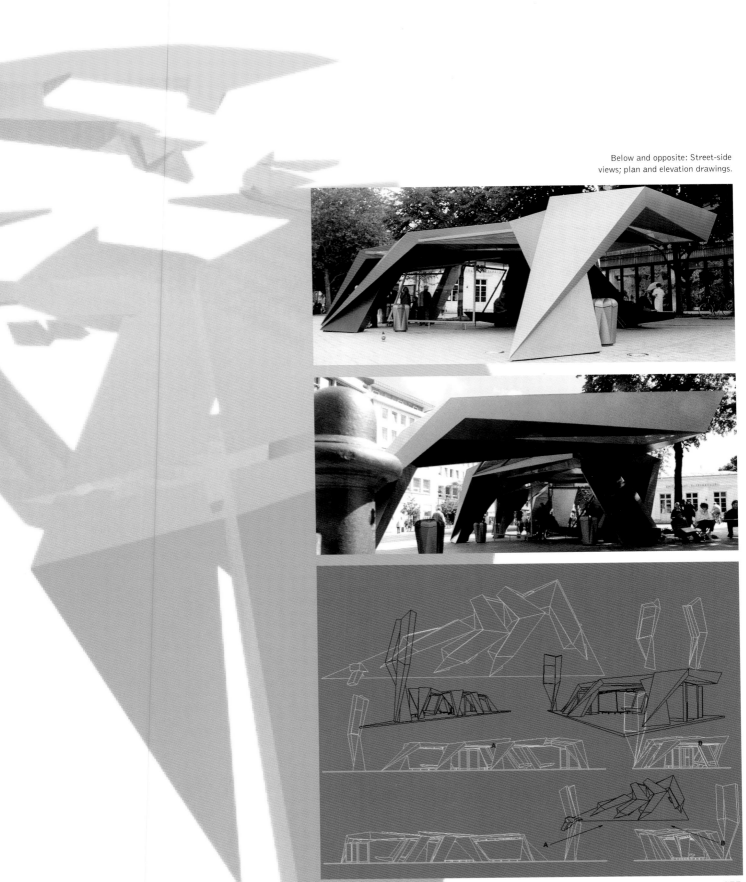

Below and opposite: Street-side views; plan and elevation drawings.

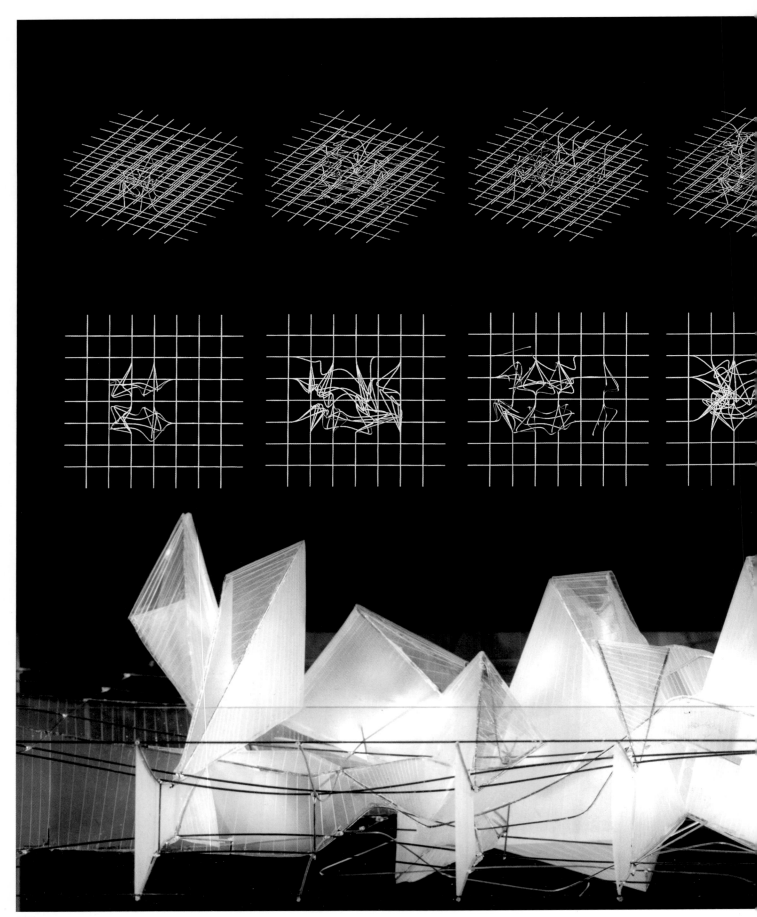

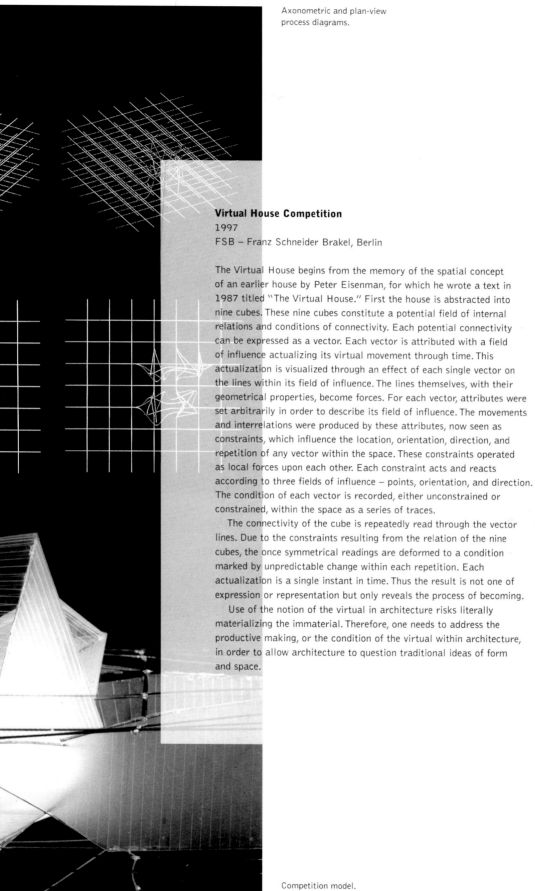

Virtual House Competition
1997
FSB – Franz Schneider Brakel, Berlin

The Virtual House begins from the memory of the spatial concept
of an earlier house by Peter Eisenman, for which he wrote a text in
1987 titled "The Virtual House." First the house is abstracted into
nine cubes. These nine cubes constitute a potential field of internal
relations and conditions of connectivity. Each potential connectivity
can be expressed as a vector. Each vector is attributed with a field
of influence actualizing its virtual movement through time. This
actualization is visualized through an effect of each single vector on
the lines within its field of influence. The lines themselves, with their
geometrical properties, become forces. For each vector, attributes were
set arbitrarily in order to describe its field of influence. The movements
and interrelations were produced by these attributes, now seen as
constraints, which influence the location, orientation, direction, and
repetition of any vector within the space. These constraints operated
as local forces upon each other. Each constraint acts and reacts
according to three fields of influence – points, orientation, and direction.
The condition of each vector is recorded, either unconstrained or
constrained, within the space as a series of traces.

The connectivity of the cube is repeatedly read through the vector
lines. Due to the constraints resulting from the relation of the nine
cubes, the once symmetrical readings are deformed to a condition
marked by unpredictable change within each repetition. Each
actualization is a single instant in time. Thus the result is not one of
expression or representation but only reveals the process of becoming.

Use of the notion of the virtual in architecture risks literally
materializing the immaterial. Therefore, one needs to address the
productive making, or the condition of the virtual within architecture,
in order to allow architecture to question traditional ideas of form
and space.

Competition model.
Overleaf: Plan-view perspective.

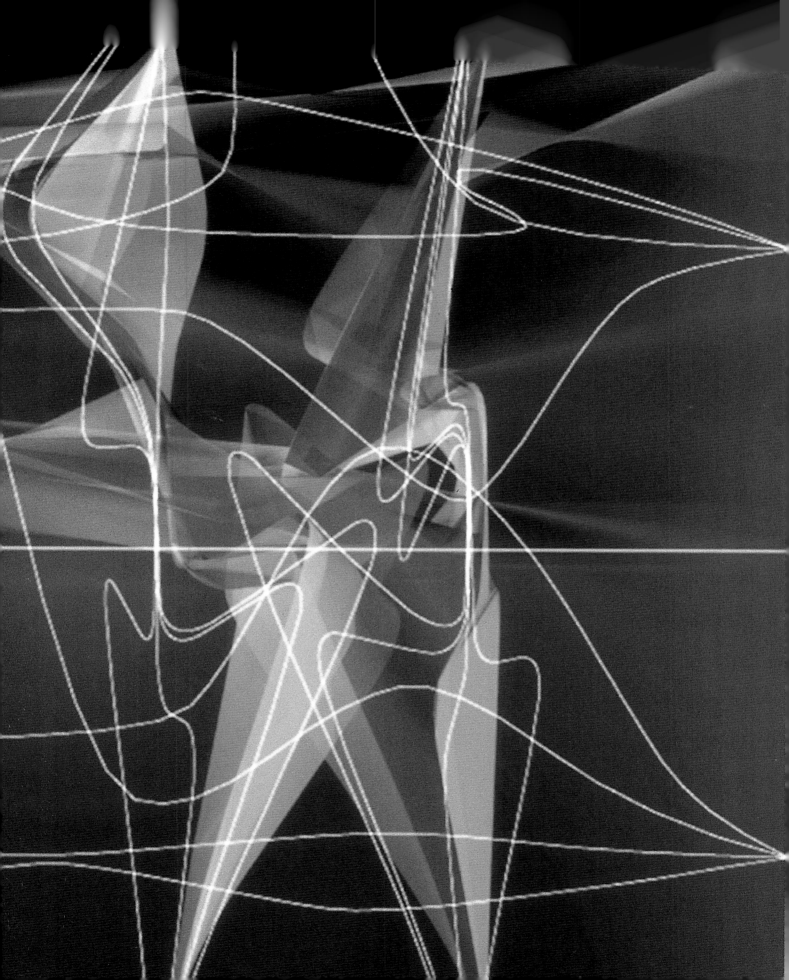

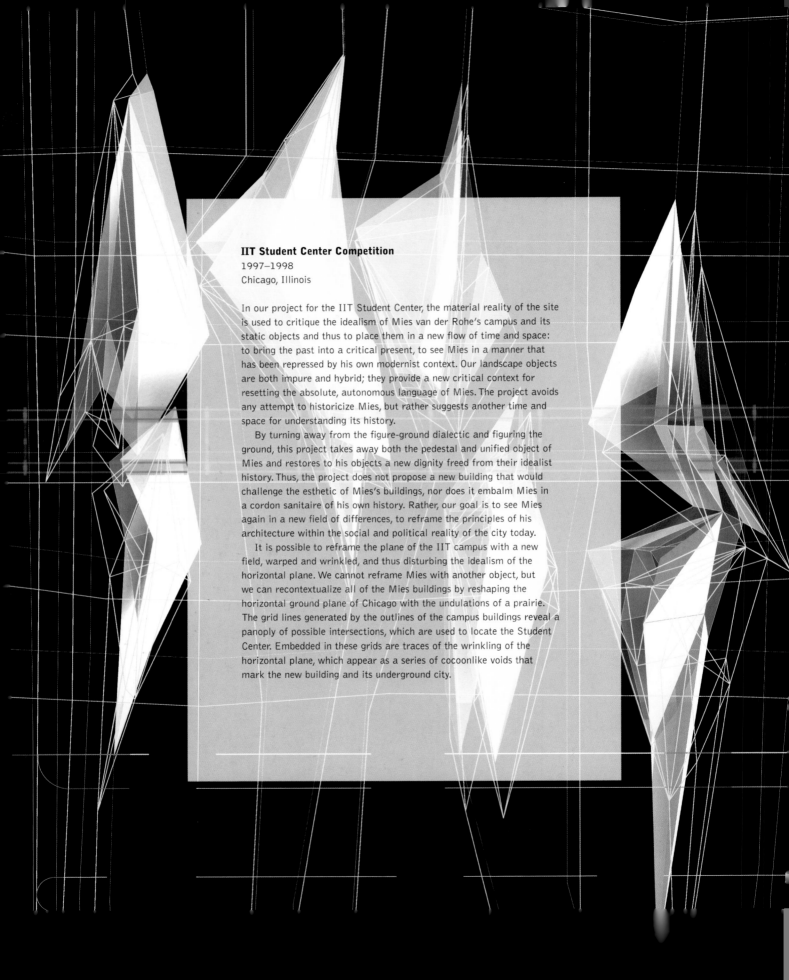

IIT Student Center Competition
1997–1998
Chicago, Illinois

In our project for the IIT Student Center, the material reality of the site is used to critique the idealism of Mies van der Rohe's campus and its static objects and thus to place them in a new flow of time and space: to bring the past into a critical present, to see Mies in a manner that has been repressed by his own modernist context. Our landscape objects are both impure and hybrid; they provide a new critical context for resetting the absolute, autonomous language of Mies. The project avoids any attempt to historicize Mies, but rather suggests another time and space for understanding its history.

By turning away from the figure-ground dialectic and figuring the ground, this project takes away both the pedestal and unified object of Mies and restores to his objects a new dignity freed from their idealist history. Thus, the project does not propose a new building that would challenge the esthetic of Mies's buildings, nor does it embalm Mies in a cordon sanitaire of his own history. Rather, our goal is to see Mies again in a new field of differences, to reframe the principles of his architecture within the social and political reality of the city today.

It is possible to reframe the plane of the IIT campus with a new field, warped and wrinkled, and thus disturbing the idealism of the horizontal plane. We cannot reframe Mies with another object, but we can recontextualize all of the Mies buildings by reshaping the horizontal ground plane of Chicago with the undulations of a prairie. The grid lines generated by the outlines of the campus buildings reveal a panoply of possible intersections, which are used to locate the Student Center. Embedded in these grids are traces of the wrinkling of the horizontal plane, which appear as a series of cocoonlike voids that mark the new building and its underground city.

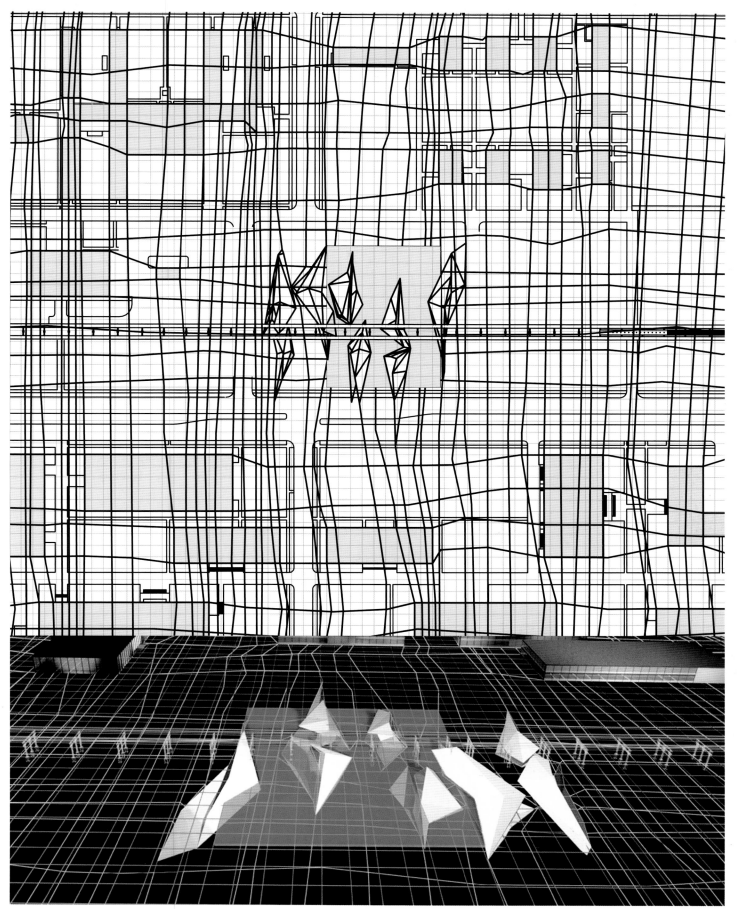

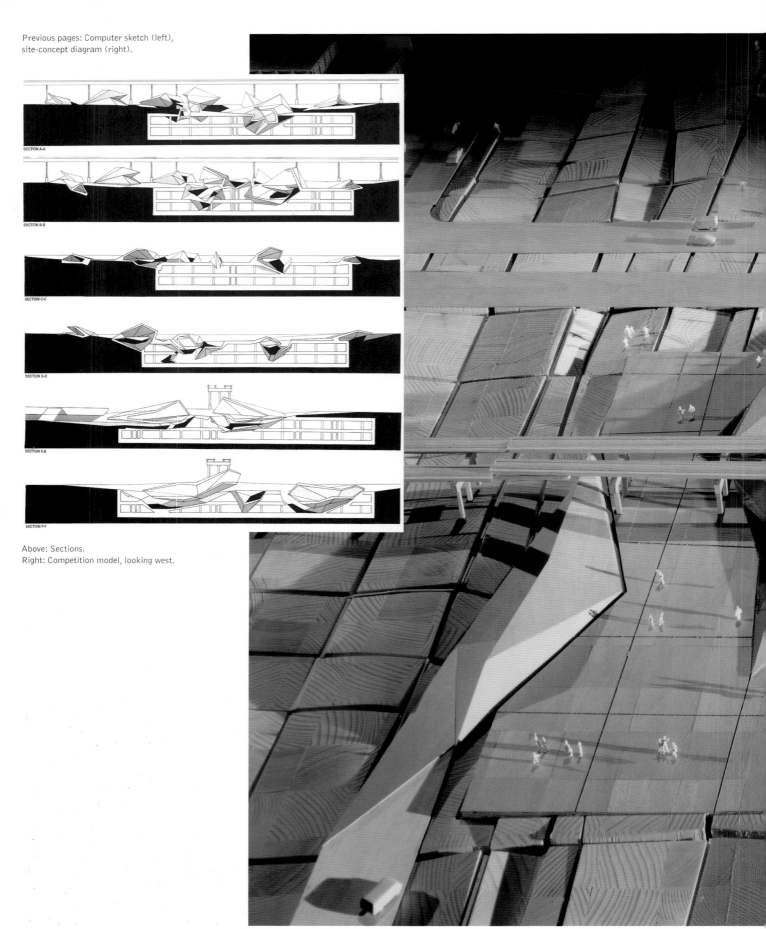

Previous pages: Computer sketch (left),
site-concept diagram (right).

SECTION A-A

SECTION B-B

SECTION C-C

SECTION D-D

SECTION E-E

SECTION F-F

Above: Sections.
Right: Competition model, looking west.

Staten Island Institute for Arts and Sciences
1997–2001
St. George, Staten Island, New York

A primary gateway to Staten Island is the St. George Ferry Terminal,
a principal hub of intermodal transportation and an unprecedented
opportunity to enhance the physical, cultural, economic, and technical
fabric of New York City. As the terminal undergoes restoration and
renovation, this natural tourist destination becomes a magnet for
cultural development. The new museum for the Staten Island Institute
for Arts and Sciences, located beside the terminal, not only takes
advantage of the potential audience of an annual twenty million
commuters passing through the terminal, but also provides a real
reason for tourists to disembark from the ferry and spend time on
Staten Island.

The swirled form of the new museum is derived from the linear axes
typical of museums, which, through a process of warping and striation,
become torqued into a centroidal mass. This seemingly centroidal nature
is deceptive, however, for while the striations twist into a centroid
structure, that structure differs in essential ways from the centroid
spaces of Frank Lloyd Wright's New York Guggenheim and Frank
Gehry's Guggenheim in Bilbao.

The Staten Island Institute for Arts and Sciences appears to be
similar in organization to both Guggenheims because it seems massed
toward a center, but the visitor in fact moves across the warped
striations and is denied any continuous spiral. If anything, these striated
forms owe their pedigree to Robert Morris's "Hanging Felt Pieces" or
John Hejduk's fishtail forms in his Berlin Masque. Here, the smooth
nature of the space is striated by deep, V-shaped sections that begin
to define a series of interlocking layers of space. The spatial experience
becomes an incomplete narrative, a destination without a proscribed end.

Opposite: Perspective looking
northeast, toward Lower Manhattan.
Overleaf: Concept diagrams.

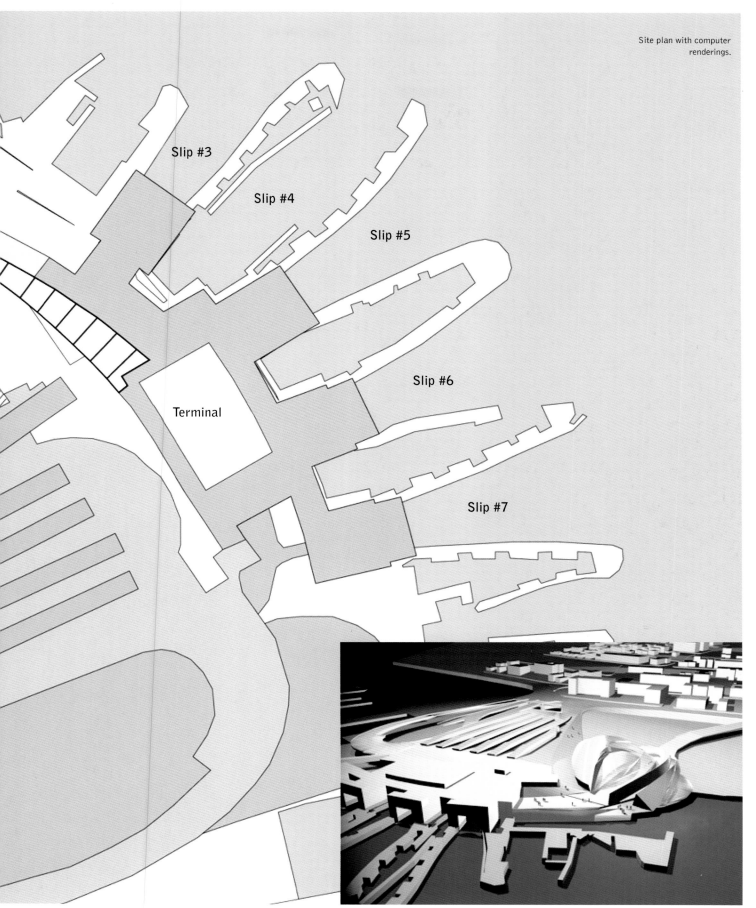

Site plan with computer renderings.

Slip #3

Slip #4

Slip #5

Slip #6

Terminal

Slip #7

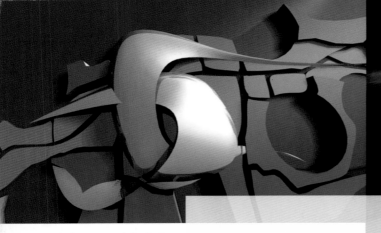

Preliminary proposal sketch of stadium with landscape.

Cardinals Stadium

1997–2006
Glendale, Arizona

In an era when theme parks and the media typically package their activities and productions to create a controlled, universal experience, sport has surged in value as a source of the unexpected and unpredictable. The public desire for uncertainty is evident in the phenomenal success of "reality" television programs, which essentially stage confrontations and conflicts that amount to a sport with an unpredictable outcome. As the primary locus of the unexpected, the sports stadium has emerged as the new civic icon and attained a symbolic resonance that was historically once held in America only by town halls, libraries, and museums.

The Cardinals Stadium is a 68,000-seat National Football League stadium for the Arizona Cardinals, which expands to accommodate 73,000 spectators for the Super Bowl and other extravaganzas. By integrating the stadium with the facilities required for a convention center, this multipurpose venue is equally effective for hosting exhibitions and sporting events. In addition to providing innovative suites and concourse accommodations, the stadium features a retractable roof and a movable field of natural grass that is rolled into the arena on game days.

The stadium is clad in alternating sections of metal panels and recessed vertical glass bands that allow views out from the circulation concourses. The shiny, metallic panels will reflect shifting desert light patterns to mimic the ever-changing colors of the Arizona sky, as well as throw off the desert heat. The translucent fabric roof admits daylight and creates the feeling of being outdoors, yet protects spectators and players from the direct heat of the sun.

Rendering of night game with roof open.

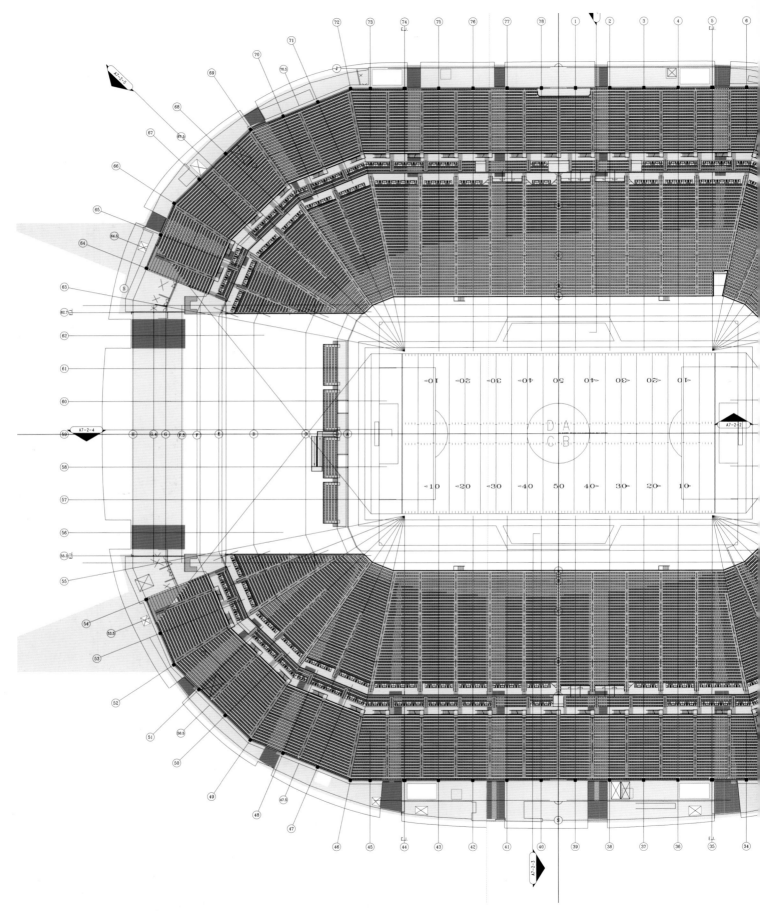

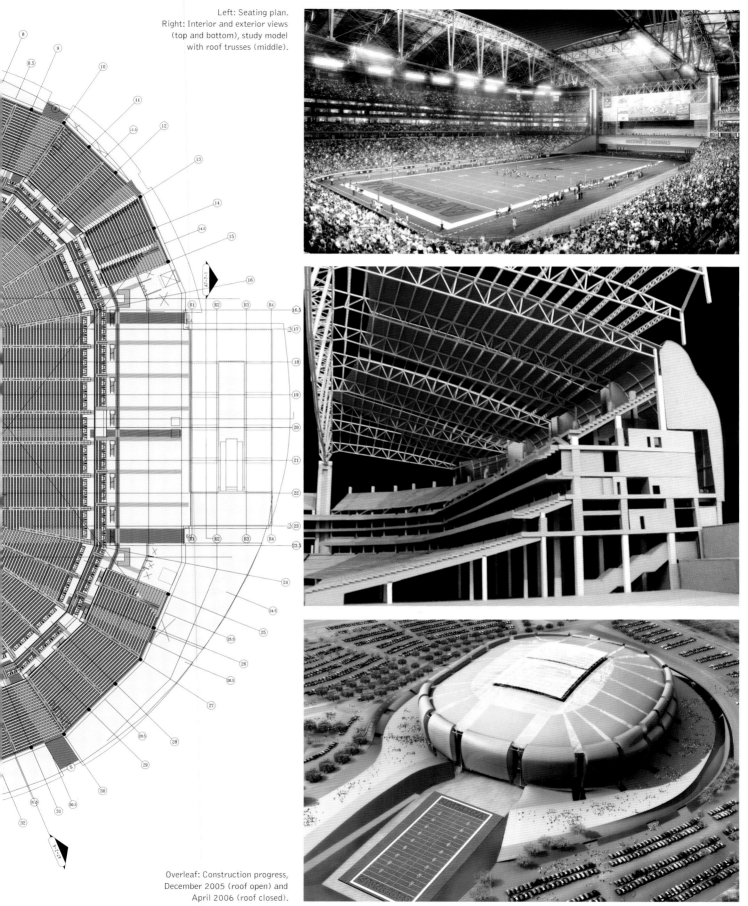

Left: Seating plan.
Right: Interior and exterior views
(top and bottom), study model
with roof trusses (middle).

Overleaf: Construction progress,
December 2005 (roof open) and
April 2006 (roof closed).

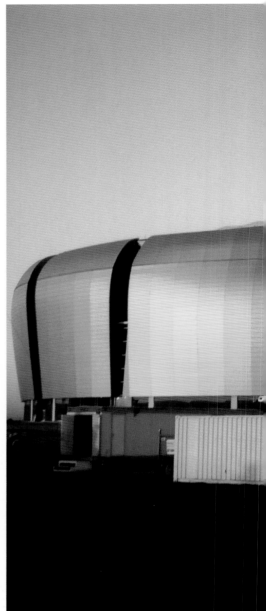

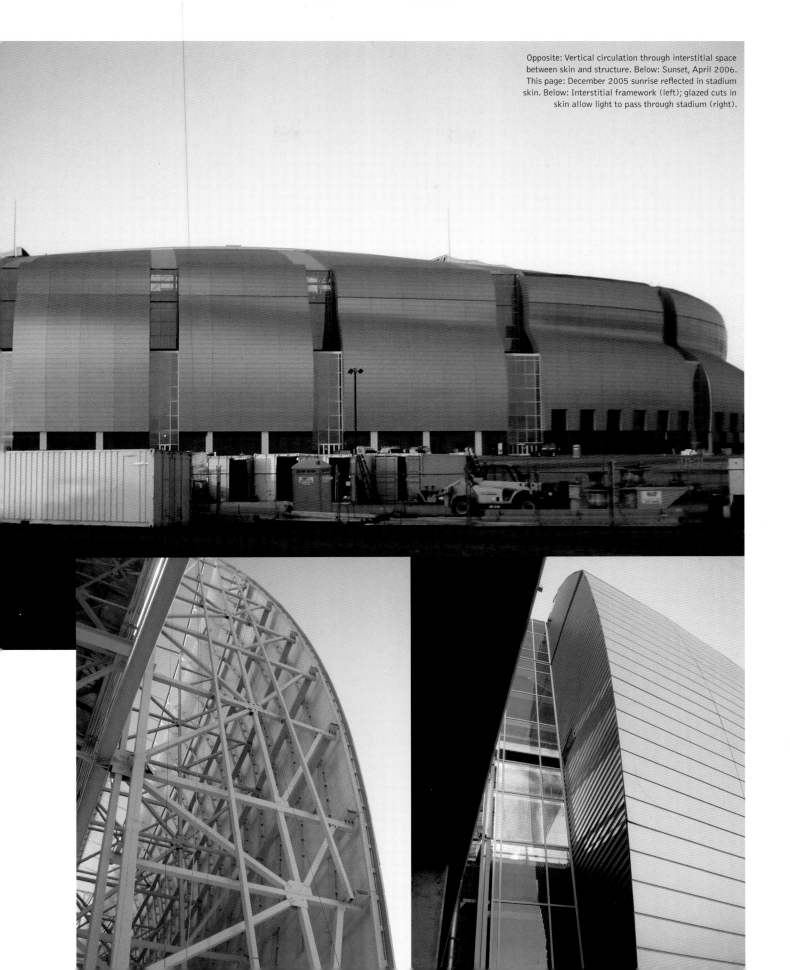

Opposite: Vertical circulation through interstitial space between skin and structure. Below: Sunset, April 2006. This page: December 2005 sunrise reflected in stadium skin. Below: Interstitial framework (left); glazed cuts in skin allow light to pass through stadium (right).

Two trusses, 700 feet long and 87 feet tall, support the roof structure. Built on the ground, the trusses were jacked into place in February 2005.

Interior construction progress,
December 2005, with roof open.

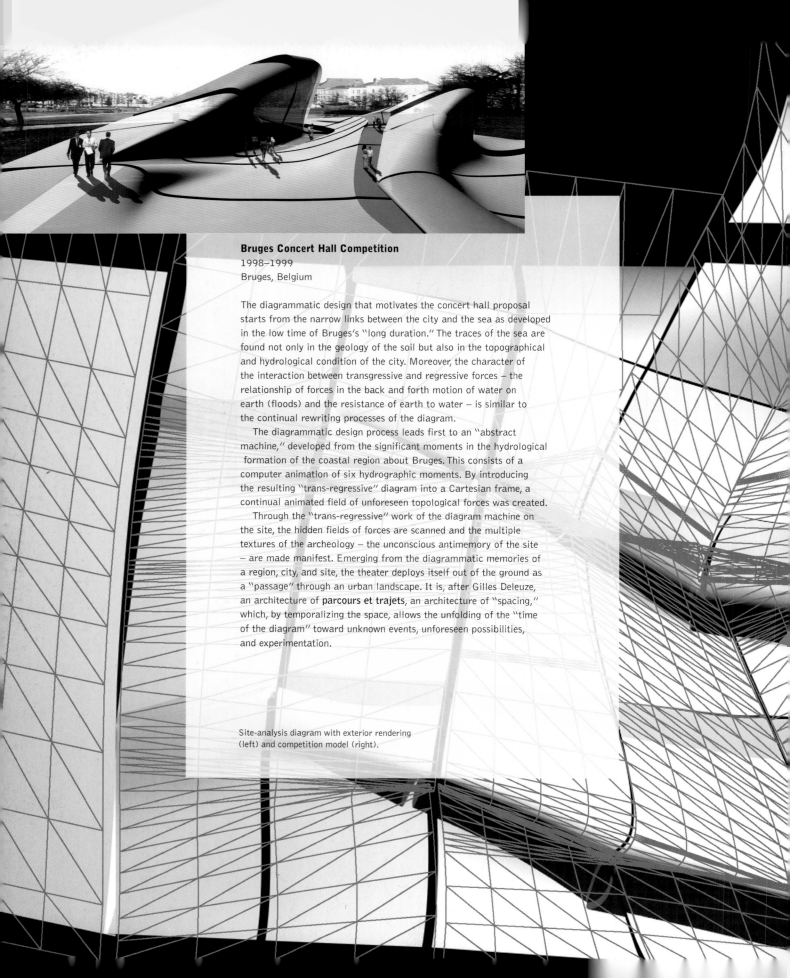

Bruges Concert Hall Competition
1998–1999
Bruges, Belgium

The diagrammatic design that motivates the concert hall proposal starts from the narrow links between the city and the sea as developed in the low time of Bruges's "long duration." The traces of the sea are found not only in the geology of the soil but also in the topographical and hydrological condition of the city. Moreover, the character of the interaction between transgressive and regressive forces – the relationship of forces in the back and forth motion of water on earth (floods) and the resistance of earth to water – is similar to the continual rewriting processes of the diagram.

The diagrammatic design process leads first to an "abstract machine," developed from the significant moments in the hydrological formation of the coastal region about Bruges. This consists of a computer animation of six hydrographic moments. By introducing the resulting "trans-regressive" diagram into a Cartesian frame, a continual animated field of unforeseen topological forces was created.

Through the "trans-regressive" work of the diagram machine on the site, the hidden fields of forces are scanned and the multiple textures of the archeology – the unconscious antimemory of the site – are made manifest. Emerging from the diagrammatic memories of a region, city, and site, the theater deploys itself out of the ground as a "passage" through an urban landscape. It is, after Gilles Deleuze, an architecture of **parcours et trajets**, an architecture of "spacing," which, by temporalizing the space, allows the unfolding of the "time of the diagram" toward unknown events, unforeseen possibilities, and experimentation.

Site-analysis diagram with exterior rendering (left) and competition model (right).

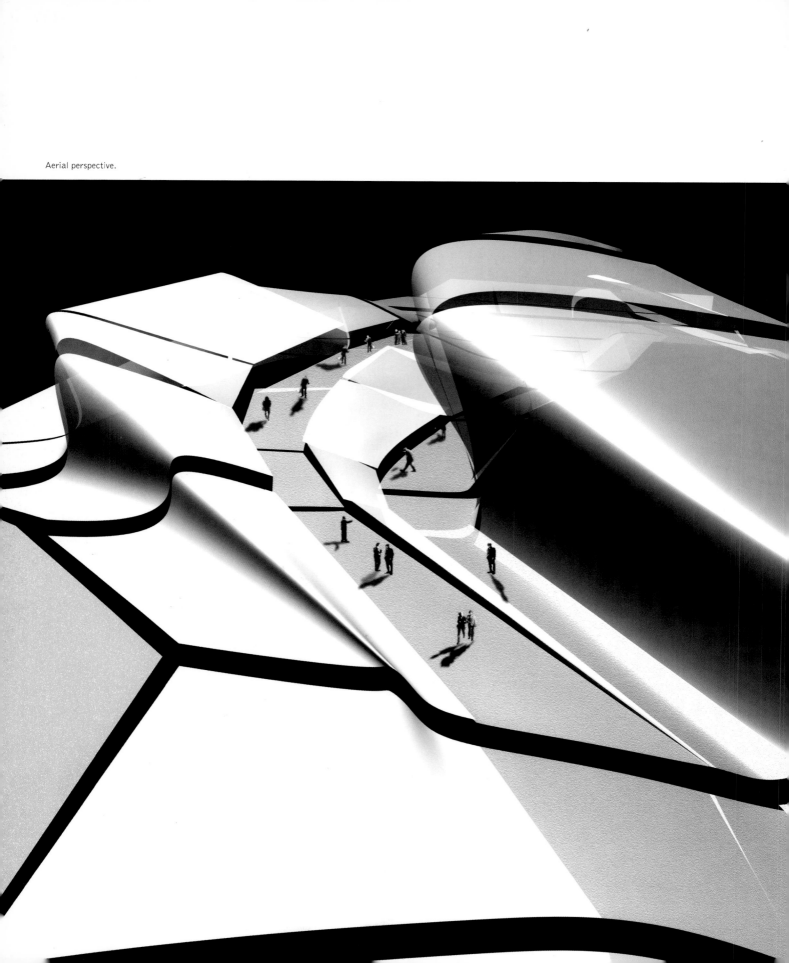

Aerial perspective.

Analytic diagram.

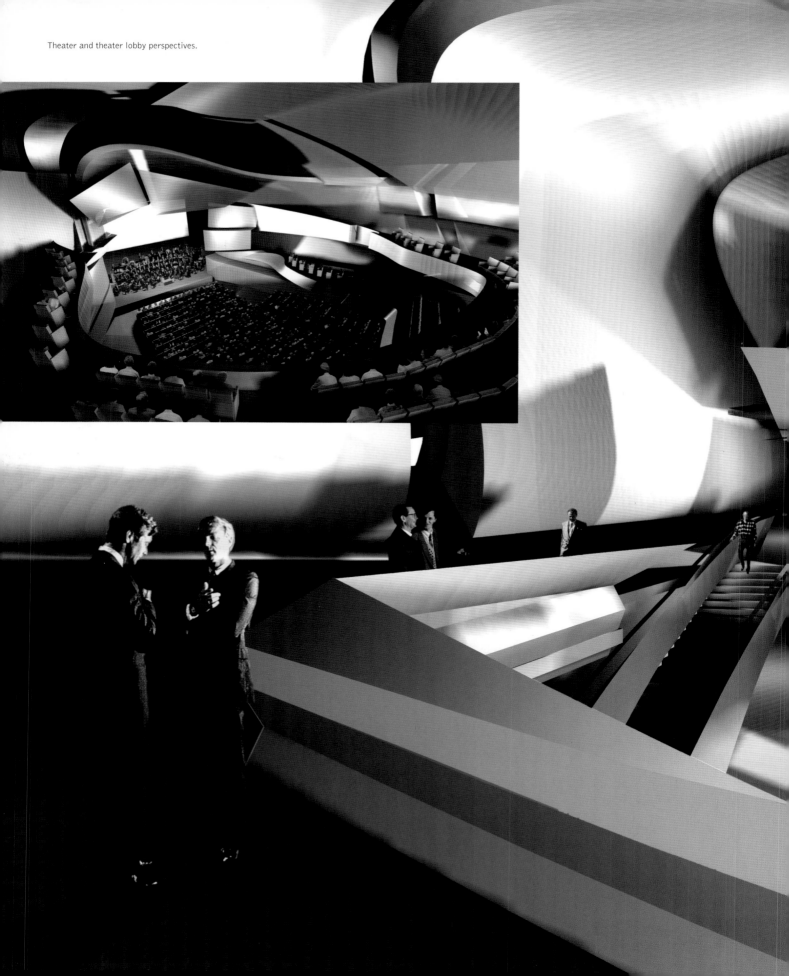

Theater and theater lobby perspectives.

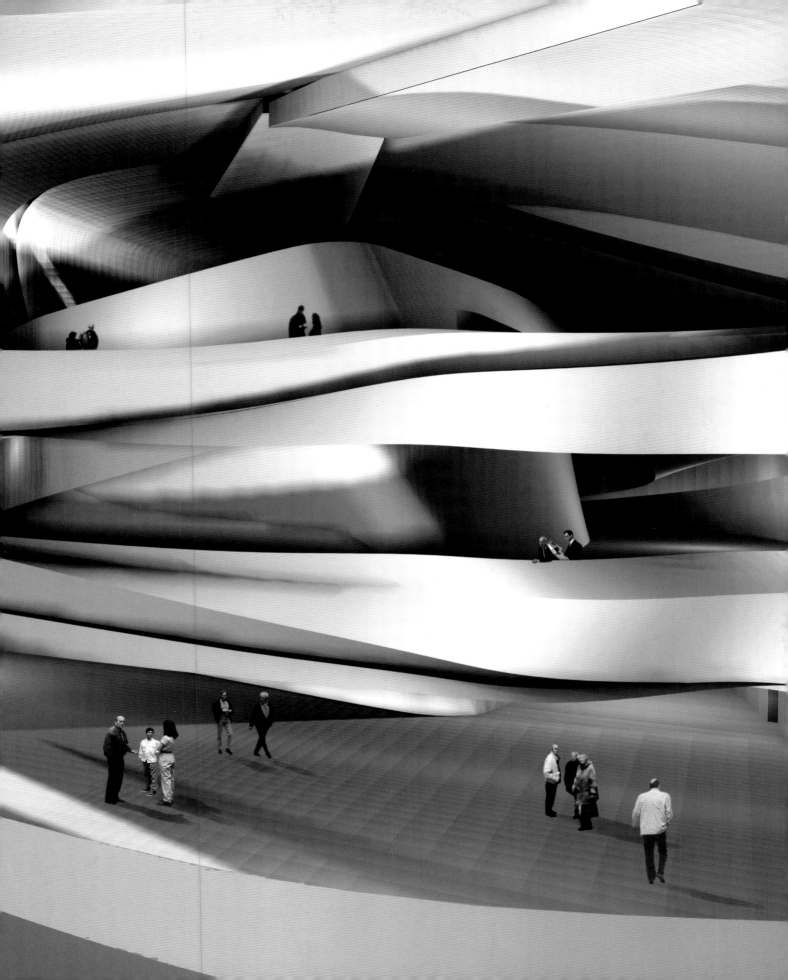

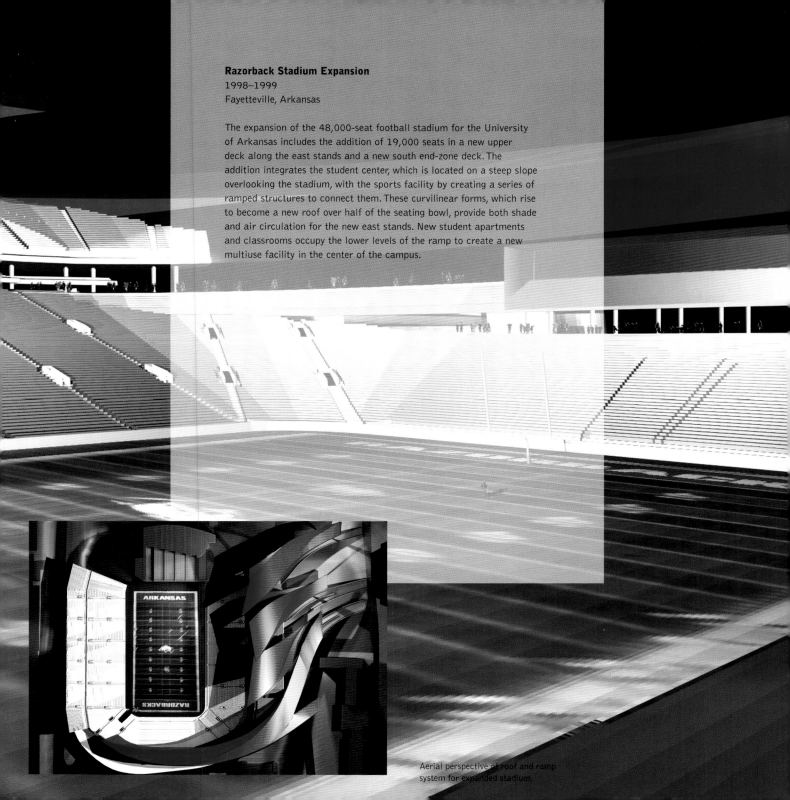

Razorback Stadium Expansion
1998–1999
Fayetteville, Arkansas

The expansion of the 48,000-seat football stadium for the University of Arkansas includes the addition of 19,000 seats in a new upper deck along the east stands and a new south end-zone deck. The addition integrates the student center, which is located on a steep slope overlooking the stadium, with the sports facility by creating a series of ramped structures to connect them. These curvilinear forms, which rise to become a new roof over half of the seating bowl, provide both shade and air circulation for the new east stands. New student apartments and classrooms occupy the lower levels of the ramp to create a new multiuse facility in the center of the campus.

Aerial perspective of roof and ramp system for expanded stadium.

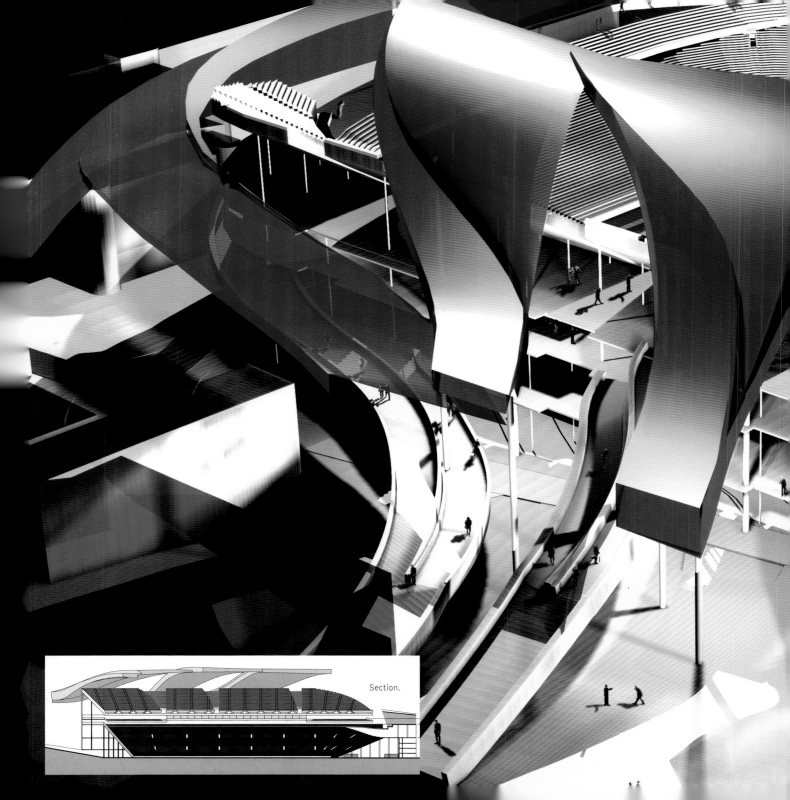

Section.

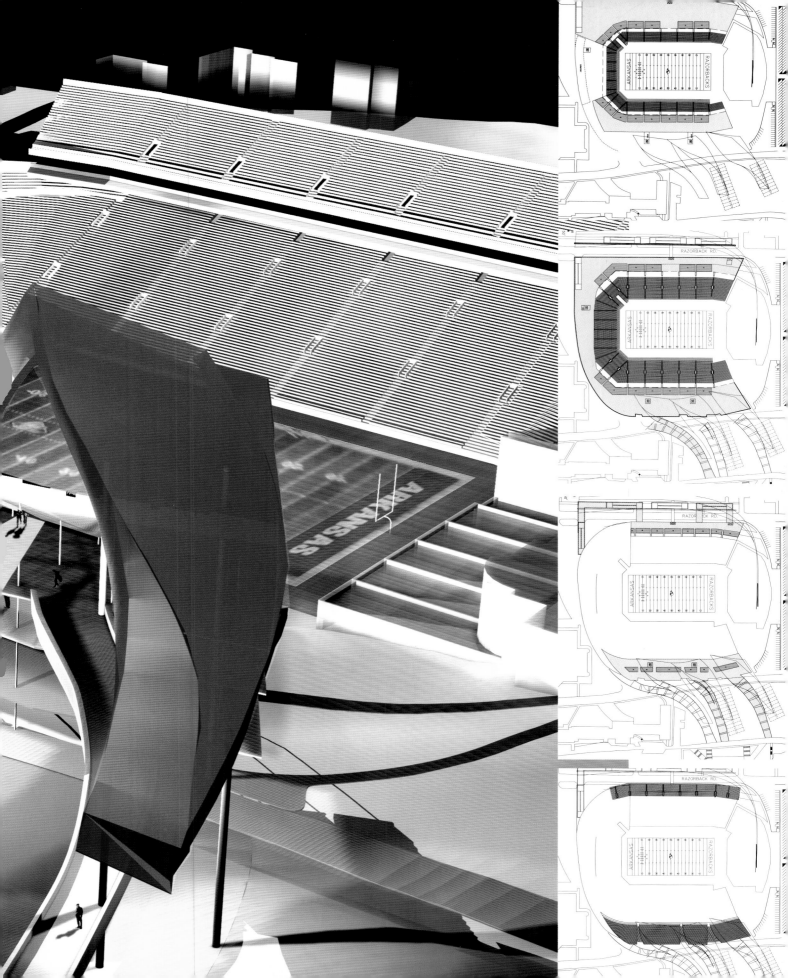

Memorial to the Murdered Jews of Europe
1998–2005
Berlin, Germany

This project manifests the instability inherent in what seems to be a system, here a rational grid, and its potential for dissolution in time. It suggests that when a supposedly rational and ordered system grows too large and out of proportion to its intended purpose, it loses touch with human reason. It then begins to reveal the innate disturbances and potential for chaos in all systems of apparent order.

The design begins from a rigid grid structure composed of 2,711 concrete pillars, or stelae, each 95 centimeters wide and 2.375 meters long, with heights varying from zero to 4 meters. The pillars are spaced 95 centimeters apart to allow only for individual passage through the grid. Each plane is determined by the intersections of the voids of the pillar grid and the gridlines of the larger context of Berlin. A slippage in the grid structure occurs, causing indeterminate spaces to develop. These spaces condense, narrow, and deepen to provide a multilayered experience from any point.

Remaining intact, however, is the idea that the pillars extend between two undulating grids. The way these two systems interact describes a zone of instability between them. These instabilities, or irregularities, are superimposed on both the topography of the site and on the top plane of the field of concrete pillars. A perceptual and conceptual divergence between the topography of the ground and the top plane of the stelae is thus created. It denotes a difference in time. The monument's registration of this difference makes for a place of loss and contemplation, elements of memory.

In this monument there is no goal, no end, no working one's way in or out. The duration of an individual's experience of it grants no further understanding, since understanding the Holocaust is impossible. The time of the monument, its duration from top surface to ground, is disjoined from the time of experience. In this context, there is no nostalgia, no memory of the past, only the living memory of the individual experience.

Study models of ground plane and pillars.

Aerial view of memorial from
northeast with details of the field of
stones (below and opposite).

Looking northwest from within the field.

Section.

One of four exhibition rooms in the below-grade Ort.

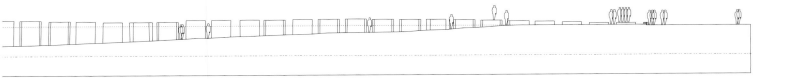

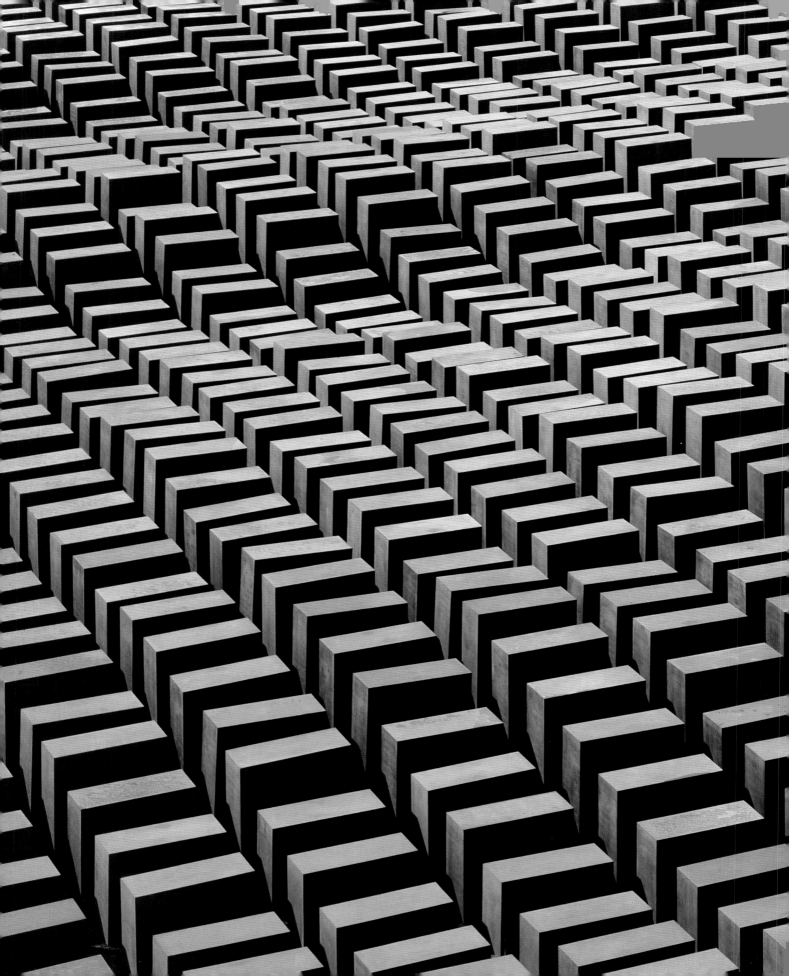

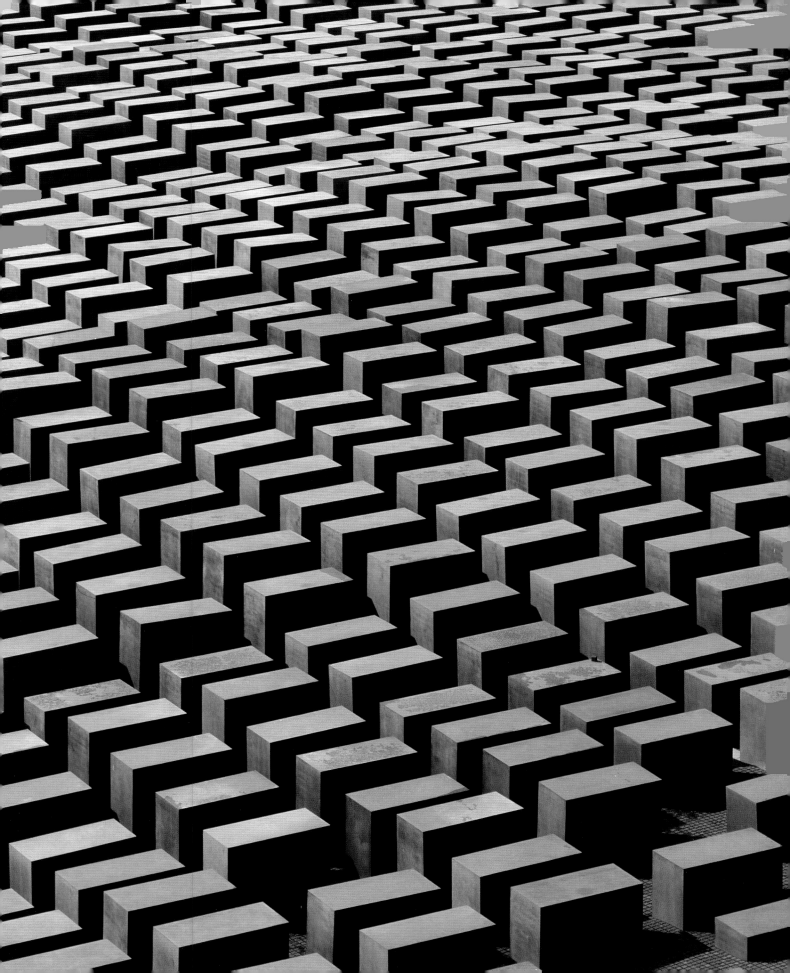

IFCCA Prize Competition For the Design of Cities
1999
New York, New York

One of the paradoxes of our time is that the new nature of the computer and its speed of computation can reinstate "the natural" in opposition to the alienated mechanisms of the machine age, which opposed nature. For example, the folding and warping of surfaces made possible by the computer appear to us as natural conditions. At the same time, computation can restore the unpredictable and unforeseeable to human intentionality and thus to architecture. This paradox occurs because the digital computational processes, which are essentially on/off (+/-), can be speeded up to introduce such a level of complexity that what was striated space, such as the urban grid, can be made to appear smooth.

In the world of digital information there is also a different space/time condition that resides between the former classical dialectic of reality and appearance: the virtual, a condition in real space that contains the oscillation between past and present time, between figure and ground, between smooth and striated space. Our project is an amalgam of striated (existing gridded) space and a new smooth space that blurs the traditional figure-ground (+/-) distinction between building and context. This strategy can be seen in the way three "buildings" — a stadium, a convention center, and a new Madison Square Garden arena — are integrated into a continuous fabric of public space.

The architectural idea for the West Side project is twofold. The first idea is to warp the ground — formerly a flat datum of gridded space — in order to make it figural. The warping process leads to a figure-figure ground condition. The second architectural idea activates the section of the figure-figure condition in different but complementary ways. The sectional space between the building objects meets the new ground, which is now a positive surface. The intersection of these two figures creates an interstitial space that is generally seen as residual, or between. Here, however, this residual space is activated for program.

Concept sketches.

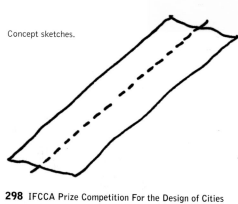
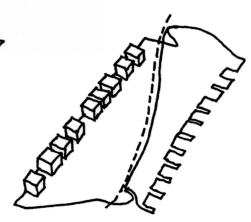

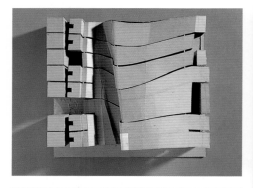

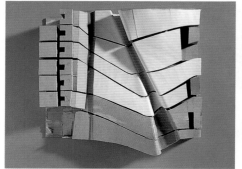

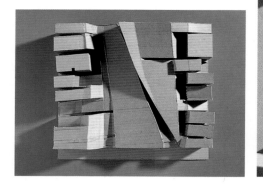

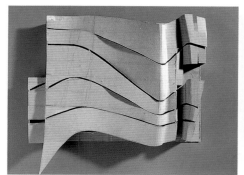

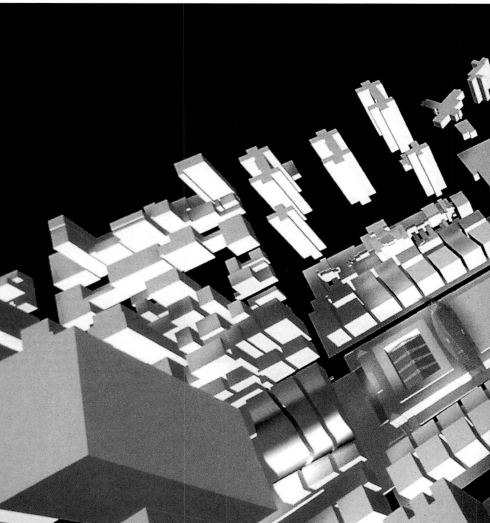

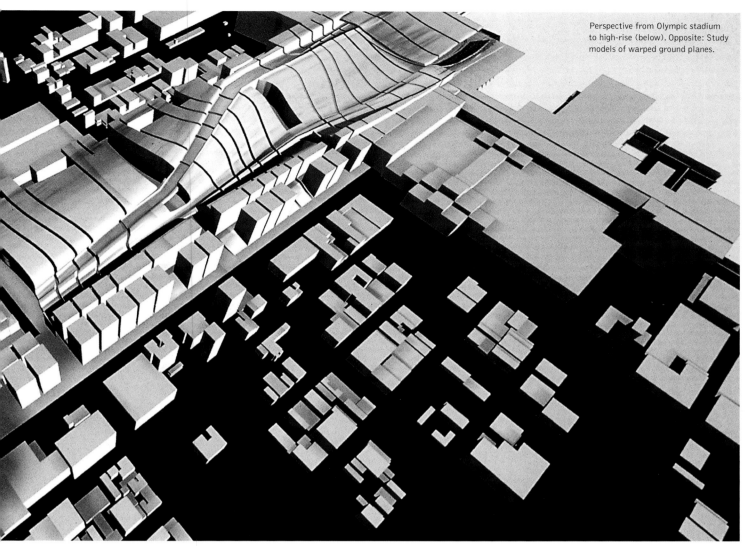

Perspective from Olympic stadium to high-rise (below). Opposite: Study models of warped ground planes.

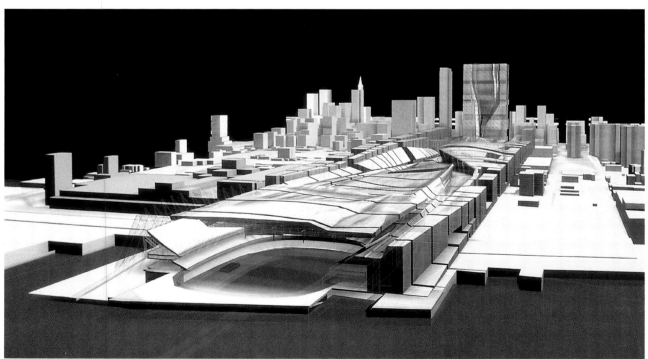

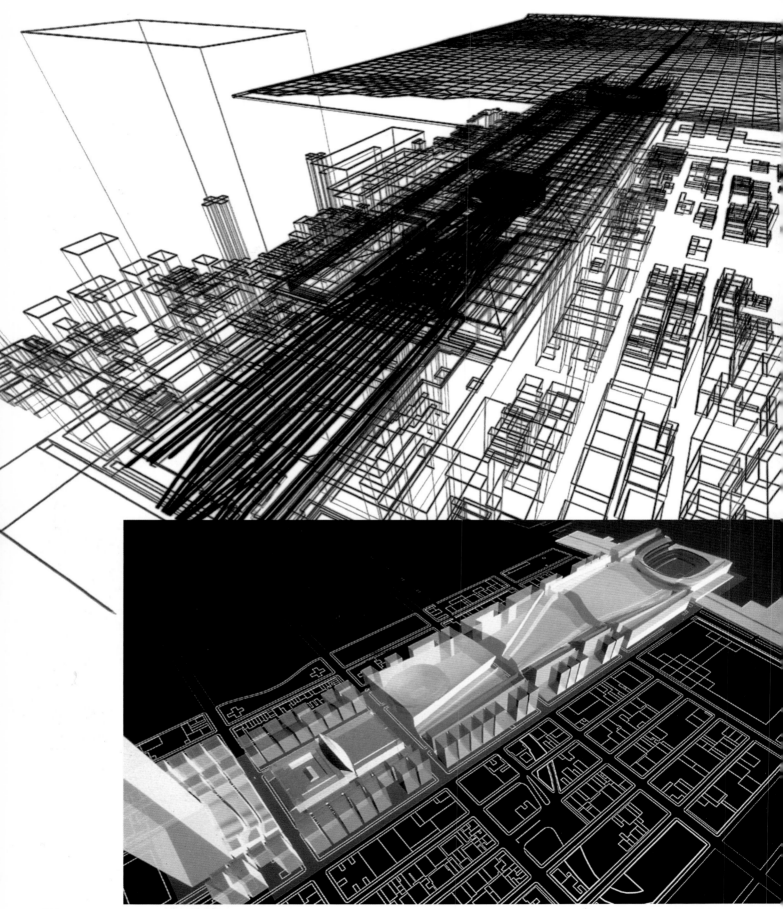

Wire-frame rendering with
programmatic diagram (inset) and
competition model.

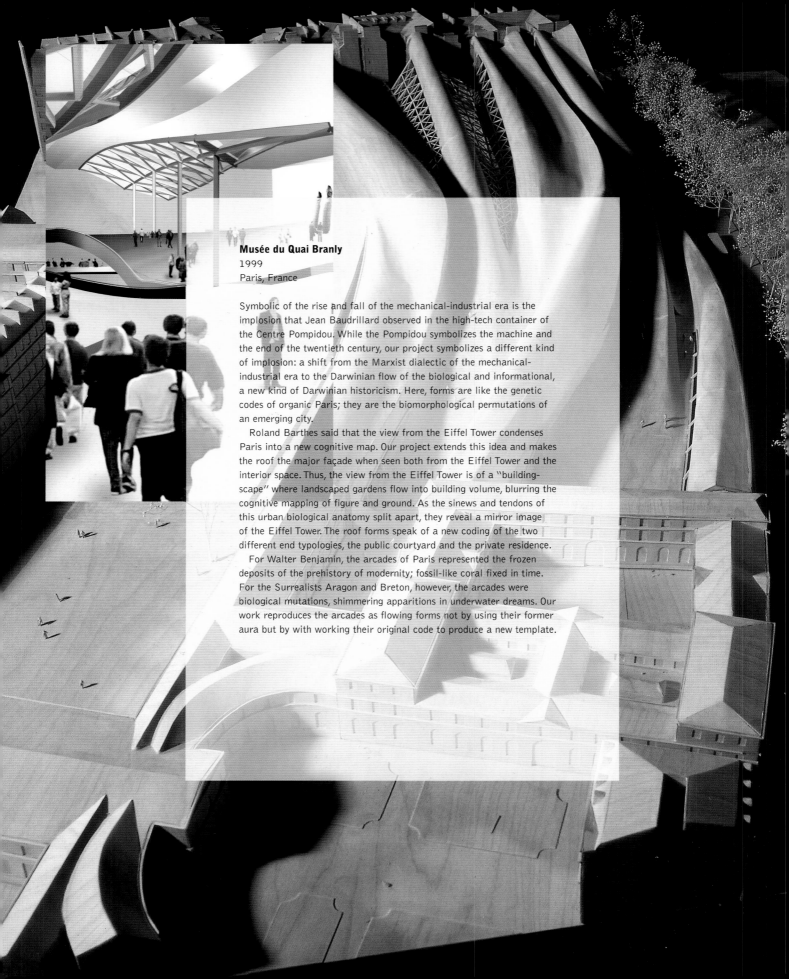

Musée du Quai Branly
1999
Paris, France

Symbolic of the rise and fall of the mechanical-industrial era is the implosion that Jean Baudrillard observed in the high-tech container of the Centre Pompidou. While the Pompidou symbolizes the machine and the end of the twentieth century, our project symbolizes a different kind of implosion: a shift from the Marxist dialectic of the mechanical-industrial era to the Darwinian flow of the biological and informational, a new kind of Darwinian historicism. Here, forms are like the genetic codes of organic Paris; they are the biomorphological permutations of an emerging city.

Roland Barthes said that the view from the Eiffel Tower condenses Paris into a new cognitive map. Our project extends this idea and makes the roof the major façade when seen both from the Eiffel Tower and the interior space. Thus, the view from the Eiffel Tower is of a "building-scape" where landscaped gardens flow into building volume, blurring the cognitive mapping of figure and ground. As the sinews and tendons of this urban biological anatomy split apart, they reveal a mirror image of the Eiffel Tower. The roof forms speak of a new coding of the two different end typologies, the public courtyard and the private residence.

For Walter Benjamin, the arcades of Paris represented the frozen deposits of the prehistory of modernity; fossil-like coral fixed in time. For the Surrealists Aragon and Breton, however, the arcades were biological mutations, shimmering apparitions in underwater dreams. Our work reproduces the arcades as flowing forms not by using their former aura but by with working their original code to produce a new template.

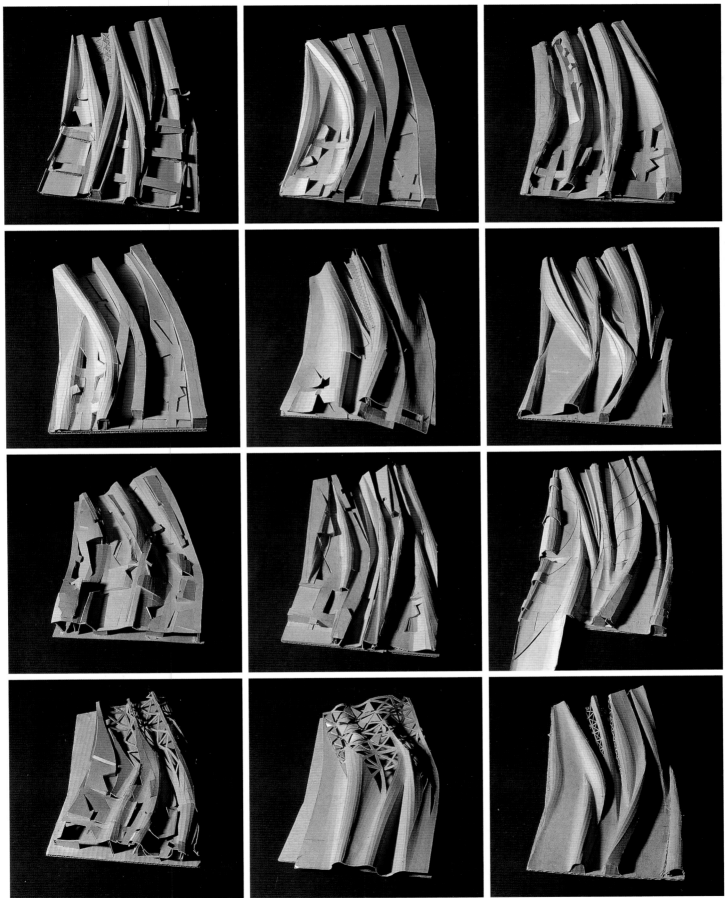

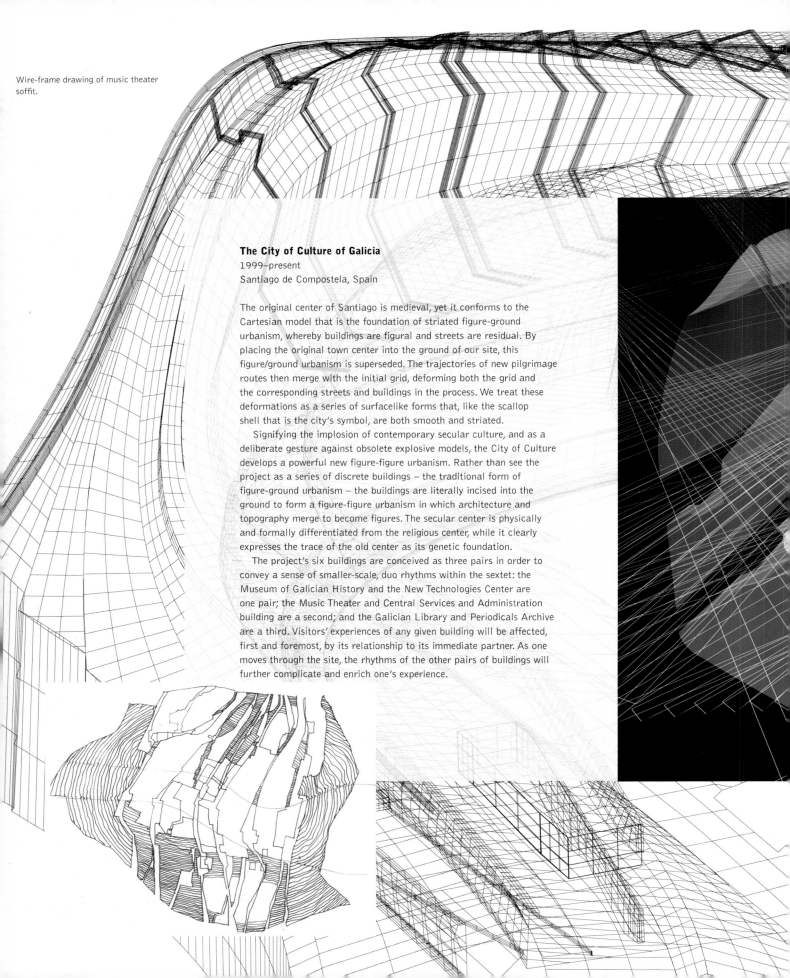

Wire-frame drawing of music theater soffit.

The City of Culture of Galicia
1999–present
Santiago de Compostela, Spain

The original center of Santiago is medieval, yet it conforms to the Cartesian model that is the foundation of striated figure-ground urbanism, whereby buildings are figural and streets are residual. By placing the original town center into the ground of our site, this figure/ground urbanism is superseded. The trajectories of new pilgrimage routes then merge with the initial grid, deforming both the grid and the corresponding streets and buildings in the process. We treat these deformations as a series of surfacelike forms that, like the scallop shell that is the city's symbol, are both smooth and striated.

Signifying the implosion of contemporary secular culture, and as a deliberate gesture against obsolete explosive models, the City of Culture develops a powerful new figure-figure urbanism. Rather than see the project as a series of discrete buildings – the traditional form of figure-ground urbanism – the buildings are literally incised into the ground to form a figure-figure urbanism in which architecture and topography merge to become figures. The secular center is physically and formally differentiated from the religious center, while it clearly expresses the trace of the old center as its genetic foundation.

The project's six buildings are conceived as three pairs in order to convey a sense of smaller-scale, duo rhythms within the sextet: the Museum of Galician History and the New Technologies Center are one pair; the Music Theater and Central Services and Administration building are a second; and the Galician Library and Periodicals Archive are a third. Visitors' experiences of any given building will be affected, first and foremost, by its relationship to its immediate partner. As one moves through the site, the rhythms of the other pairs of buildings will further complicate and enrich one's experience.

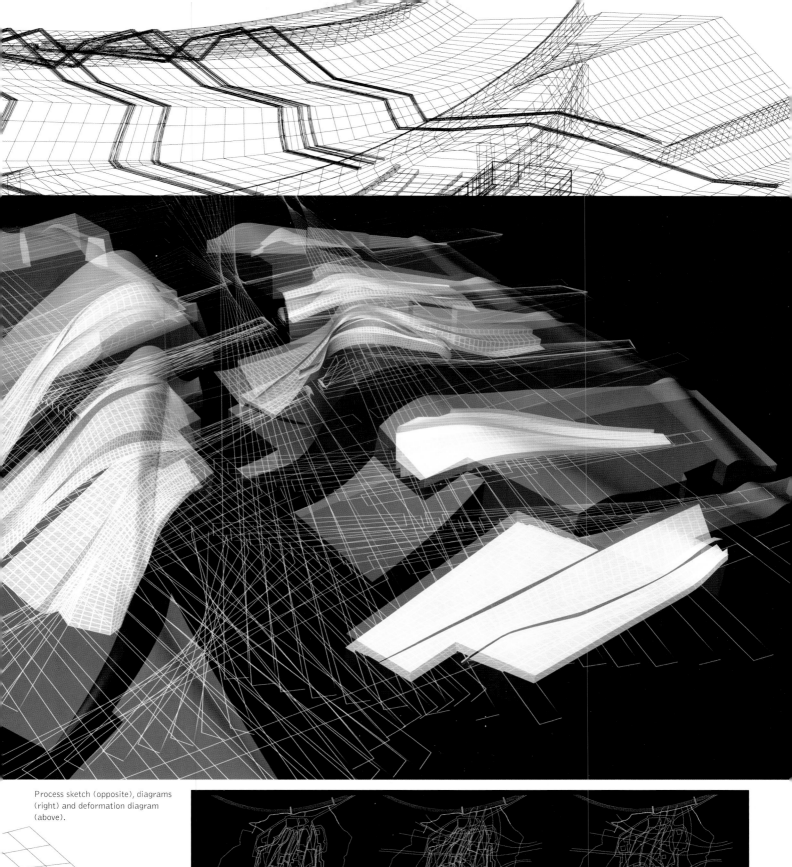

Process sketch (opposite), diagrams
(right) and deformation diagram
(above).

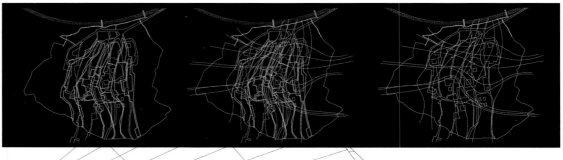

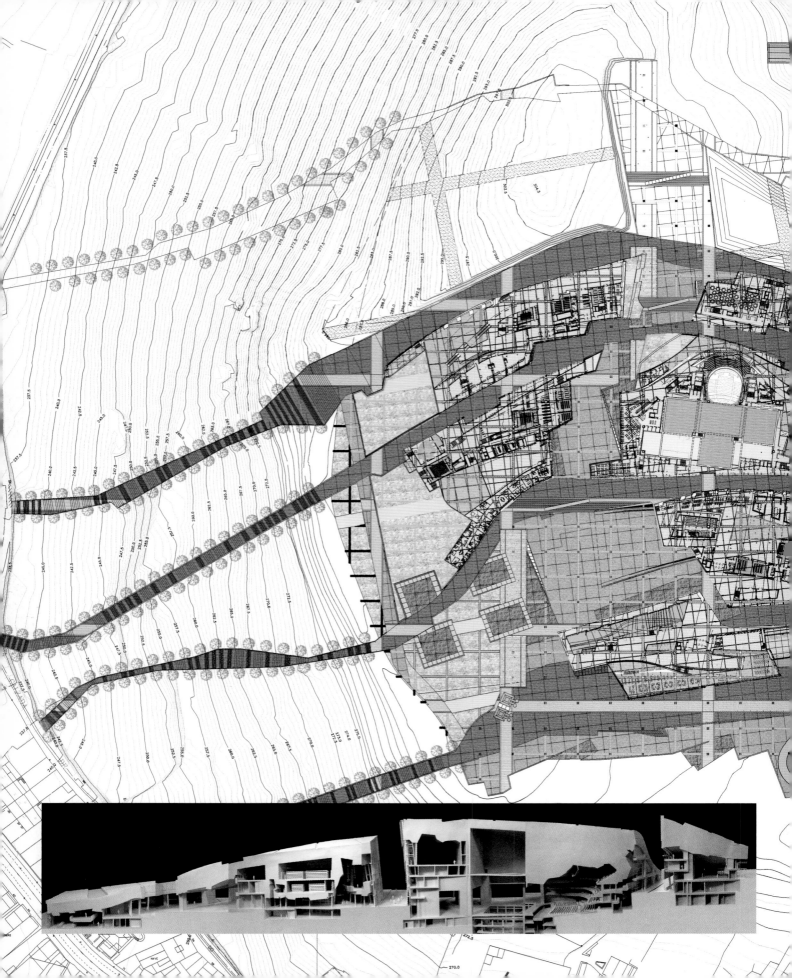

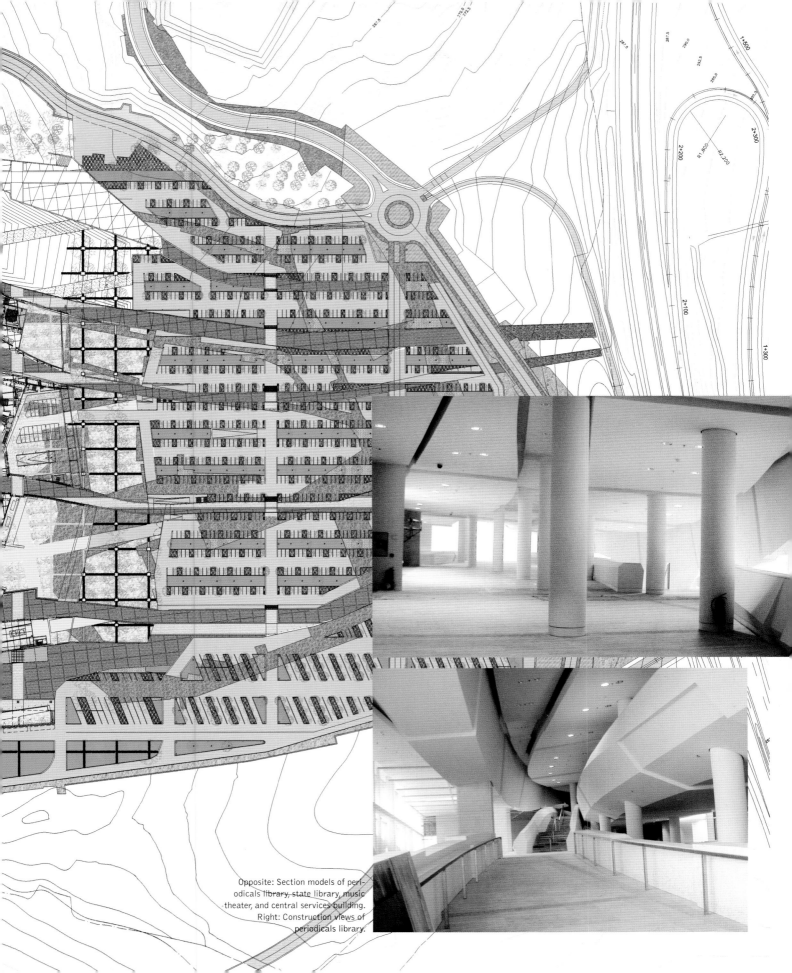

Opposite: Section models of periodicals library, state library, music theater, and central services building.
Right: Construction views of periodicals library.

Periodicals library roof.

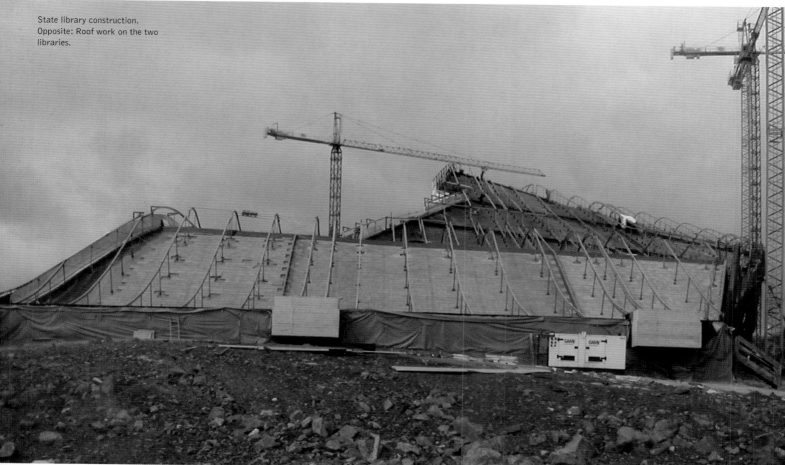

State library construction.
Opposite: Roof work on the two
libraries.

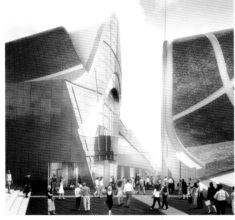

Construction of central services building with rendering.
Opposite: Central services (top) and construction of history museum.

Above: The "camino" between the two libraries.
Right: Four of the six buildings of the City of Culture under construction in spring 2006.

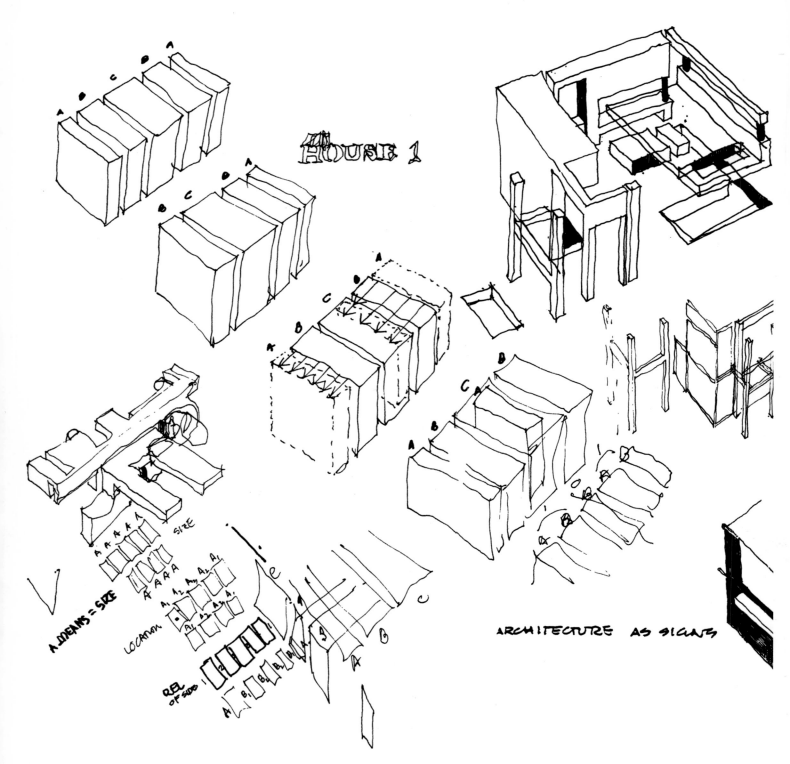

House 1

A MEANS = SIZE

SIZE

LOCATION

REL OF SIDES

ARCHITECTURE AS SIGNS

Peter Eisenman, sketch for House I,
Princeton, New Jersey.

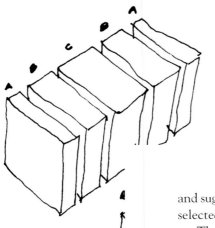

and suggests a specific value for the material the author selected for the book.

The drawing's significance in an inquiry into Eisenman's work is its content, an incongruity if not the clear staging of the coexistence of the two extremes of an antinomy: the presence of a written annotation that refers to an idea external to the graphic images. In this way, the drawing differs from all of Eisenman's other published drawings, in which writing functions solely to caption the graphics. It is only in this drawing that the writing, the syntagma placed at the lower-center of the page – architecture as signs – inscribes, projects, and ultimately identifies the entire discipline of architecture as a system within another system, the semiotic system, which is inexorably tied to and subsumed within the signifier-signified relationship. On the other hand, the graphic image moves in a cinematographic fashion, mimicking the movement of a zoom lens, from very generic diagrams at the lower left to some geometric constructive details on the right, which suggest diagrams that would later become the ordering systems of projects such as House VI.[10] The diagrams seem to fold in on themselves, exploring rather than finding possible internal rules for the self-referential articulation of the geometric material. In the drawing this self-referential presentation of architecture is constantly confirmed by the consistent nature of the operations undertaken at different scales. It is the emptying of all possible symbolic content (for example, the diagrams present no "original" but look like part of a sequence of iterations of primary integers), functional

10. See Peter Eisenman, *Houses of Cards* (New York: Oxford University Press, 1987).

GUIDO ZULIANI 323

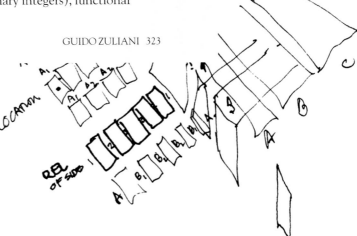

House I, axonometric diagram.

meaning (the sheltering architectural volume is voided, emptied, fragmented, and opened up), and technological content (the definition of the element to the right seems to respond more to a syntactic requirement than to a specific technical one) that radically contrasts with the written notation that architecture belongs to the regime of signs structured by the relationship between signifier and signified. Thus a radical interiority that is independent of any external signification is postulated with its opposite, the declared semiotic nature of the discipline, and its dependence on a structured relation with a radical exteriority: even in a more hermetic and difficult to decipher state, like a simple mark or scratch, an index, a sign is always the sign of something else, and always has a referent, its signified.

How does one begin to understand this bifurcation, this *mis à nu* conflict, without reducing architecture to the banal pragmatic dialectic of sign and signified? Is it possible to reconstruct a genealogy for this juxtaposition that would shed light on the nature of this split manifesto? The volumetric diagram at the top left of the drawing gives us a clue that may offer a way out of the impasse that the drawing presents, and allow us to construct a possible genesis for what is formalized in this odd assemblage.

The first part of the sequence of diagrams at the lower left of the drawing is a purely quantitative ordering of elemental formal integers in terms of size, location, and relations. The second part, just above, is a set of permutations and iterations of those same integers drawn in possible volumetric forms and differentiated in size.[11] The diagram at the top left seems

11. These formal procedures are in debt to the asemantic work of minimalists of the time, like Sol LeWitt and Donald Judd. Eisenman's essays on conceptual architecture testify to his interest in their work. See his "Notes on Conceptual Architecture: Towards a Definition," *Casabella* 359/360 (1971) and "Conceptual Architecture II: Double Deep Structure I," *A+U* 39 (1974), among others.

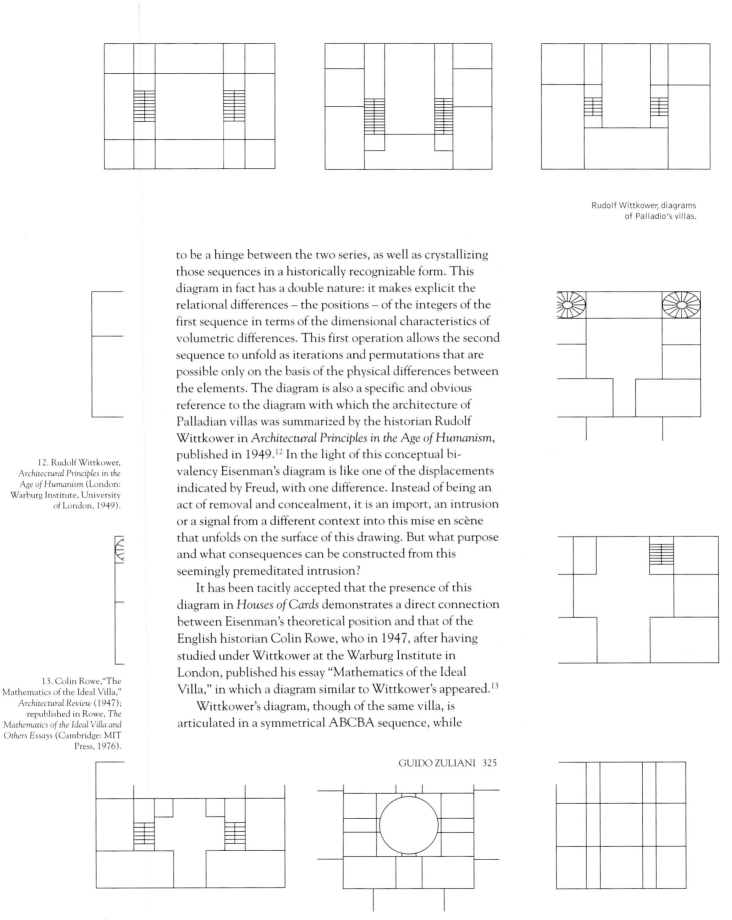

Rudolf Wittkower, diagrams
of Palladio's villas.

to be a hinge between the two series, as well as crystallizing
those sequences in a historically recognizable form. This
diagram in fact has a double nature: it makes explicit the
relational differences – the positions – of the integers of the
first sequence in terms of the dimensional characteristics of
volumetric differences. This first operation allows the second
sequence to unfold as iterations and permutations that are
possible only on the basis of the physical differences between
the elements. The diagram is also a specific and obvious
reference to the diagram with which the architecture of
Palladian villas was summarized by the historian Rudolf
Wittkower in *Architectural Principles in the Age of Humanism*,
published in 1949.[12] In the light of this conceptual bi-
valency Eisenman's diagram is like one of the displacements
indicated by Freud, with one difference. Instead of being an
act of removal and concealment, it is an import, an intrusion
or a signal from a different context into this mise en scène
that unfolds on the surface of this drawing. But what purpose
and what consequences can be constructed from this
seemingly premeditated intrusion?

It has been tacitly accepted that the presence of this
diagram in *Houses of Cards* demonstrates a direct connection
between Eisenman's theoretical position and that of the
English historian Colin Rowe, who in 1947, after having
studied under Wittkower at the Warburg Institute in
London, published his essay "Mathematics of the Ideal
Villa," in which a diagram similar to Wittkower's appeared.[13]

Wittkower's diagram, though of the same villa, is
articulated in a symmetrical ABCBA sequence, while

12. Rudolf Wittkower,
*Architectural Principles in the
Age of Humanism* (London:
Warburg Institute, University
of London, 1949).

13. Colin Rowe, "The
Mathematics of the Ideal Villa,"
Architectural Review (1947);
republished in Rowe, *The
Mathematics of the Ideal Villa and
Others Essays* (Cambridge: MIT
Press, 1976).

GUIDO ZULIANI 325

Rowe's is articulated in an iterative ABABA sequence. More significantly, Wittkower's diagram describes the structure of internal relations that, for him, constitute the signifying content of Palladian villas, whereas Rowe's diagram is a paradigmatic configuration, a guarantor of structure, in his view, of the correct relations and hierarchies against which to evaluate the proper and improper nature of specific design choices. Wittkower's diagram is the instrumental result of the analytic effort of a structuralist historian to comprehend a single historical phenomenon; Rowe's diagram is the normative idealization of the critic's preferences. Both diagrams articulate analytic methodologies for architecture that at first seem similar but in fact are substantially different. This difference is important, for the diagrams represent two different kinds of what can be generically called structuralism, and these differences have consequences for reading Eisenman's House I drawing. Before this distinction can be articulated, however, a supplemental investigation is needed. Look again at Eisenman's second sequence of diagrams: the volumetric integers undergo a series of operations, in a Palladian manner, that consist of lateral movements parallel to the frontal plane. But rather than obeying, as Palladio would, the axial structure of the diagram and its contingent symmetry, Eisenman's diagrams respond to a sort of lateral polarized pull, which results in a figure similar to a half-plan vis-à-vis the frontal symmetry.[14]

For my argument, it is important to note that the object of these displacements is volumes rather than wall-

14. See the examples of Venetian palaces that Eisenman illustrated in his "La Futilità degli Oggetti" ("The Futility of Objects: Decomposition and the Processes of Difference"), *Lotus International* 42 (February 1984).

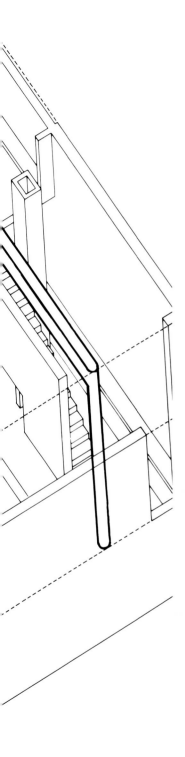

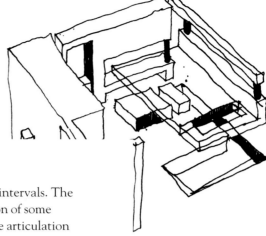

partitions, whose absence is registered by void intervals. The house is not the result of the planar organization of some gridlike skeleton of wall partitions in which the articulation of the internal volumes – the voids – is a function of the arrangement of those walls as the solids. House I, as illustrated by the axonometrics in the drawing, is a complex, often ambiguous and unresolved combination of volumes and planes seen in both their positive and negative values, as solid and void.

Eisenman's specific approach to built volume was first formulated in his Ph.D. thesis, "The Formal Basis of Modern Architecture," written in Cambridge under the supervision of Sir Leslie Martin in 1963. Here he states the difference between what he calls volume, the portion of space defined by solid, and mass, the solid itself.[15] Eisenman's Ph.D. thesis is particularly significant in this investigation, for its importance and meaning have been underestimated and largely overlooked. This is primarily because it has been superficially related to the work of both Rowe and Wittkower, flattened into a simplistic and reductive definition of either architectural structuralism or, in a more pejorative sense, architectural formalism. Such lines of thought have coalesced in the erroneous definition of an alleged "structuralist" triad formed by Wittkower, Rowe, and Eisenman, a formulation in which Eisenman, in his constant disorientation of his trackers, has himself played a part. Intentionally or not, the profound difference with, if not the radical opposition to, Rowe's position as expressed in Eisenman's thesis has remained unread or missed. To

15. The copy of Eisenman's Ph.D. thesis that I consulted is the original one kept at the office of Eisenman Architects in New York. This document is now published as a facsimile edition by Lars Müller Publishers (2006). A German translation, *Die Formale Grundlegung der Modernen Architektur*, was published in 2005 by GTA Verlag, Zurich.

GUIDO ZULIANI 327

House I, axonometric drawing.

reconsider the thesis, it is necessary to introduce into evidence a statement made in 1963, the year of Eisenman's dissertation, by an expert witness, the French philosopher Jacques Derrida, whose work later becomes particularly significant for our subject, but who in 1963 was totally unknown to him.

In his 1963 essay "Force and Signification" concerning the "questioning of the sign," Derrida writes that "the most precious and original intention of structuralism" is to preserve "the coherence and completion of each totality at its own level." Such an approach prohibits the consideration of "everything that would make the configuration appear to be a blind anticipation of, or mysterious deviation from, an orthogenesis whose own conceptual basis would be a telos or an ideal norm." Hence to be a structuralist is "to refuse to relegate every thing that is not comprehensible as an ideal type to the status of aberrational accident. The pathological itself is not the simple absence of structure, it is organized," and for structuralism "it cannot be understood as the deficiency, defect, or decomposition of a beautiful, ideal totality. It is not the simple undoing of telos."[16] To recognize the clumsiness of those who have identified Rowe's ideology with structuralism it is enough to compare Derrida's statement with the final sentence of Rowe's 1959 essay on Le Corbusier's Monastery at La Tourette: "At La Tourette [formal] precepts . . . are conspicuously breached, and breached with a sophistication so covert as to provide a new area of experience. . . . By doing so, [Le Corbusier] has been able to guarantee a visual stimulus so acute that

16. Jacques Derrida, "Force and Signification," in *Writing and Difference*, trans. Alan Bass (Chicago: The University of Chicago Press, 1978).

17. Colin Rowe, "Dominican Monastery of La Tourette, Eveux-sur Arbresle, Lyon," *Architectural Review* (1961); republished in *The Mathematics of the Ideal Villa and Other Essays*.

18. Jacques Derrida, "Force and Signification" in *Writing and Difference*.

19. The facts concerning the lockout of Rowe from the I.A.U.S. are not officially documented, but they have been related to me on many occasions by Eisenman himself.

only very retrospectively does the observer begin to be aware of the abnormal experience to which he has been subjected."[17] In his essay, Derrida provides a definition for Rowe's attitude, in which the problematic instrumentality of "structures" is turned upside down, so that the figures of arche and telos ultimately are thought to coincide as a form of "ultra-structuralism." This is, for Derrida, "a prejudice of the traditional criticism called idealist. It is not by chance that this theory flowered during the Renaissance."[18]

This idealist and essentially conservative attitude, even if, as with Rowe, the most refined analytic sensibility and methodology are applied, radically differs from the theoretical and methodological problematics common to structuralism as articulated by Derrida. While Eisenman was deeply affected by the novelty and quality of Rowe's formal analysis, he nevertheless frontally attacks Rowe in his thesis. This attack culminates in the 1968 lockout of Rowe from the Institute for Architecture and Urban Studies in New York, which Eisenman directed.[19]

While Rowe determines a set of iconographic diagrams as the ideal references for defining the architectural object from an optic, pictorial, or visually evident point of view,[20] Eisenman writes in his thesis that it is "precisely the visual, pictorial concept of form that will be argued against."[21] Eisenman critiques the iconographic definition of the architectural work, in both its symbolic and psychological manifestations, by defining a complex set of principles that articulates the elements of an interpretative or analytic code, and by structuring a set of relational conditions that

20. Colin Rowe and Robert Slutzky, "Transparency: Literal and Phenomenal." Written in 1955–56 and first published in *Perspecta* in 1963; republished in *The Mathematics of the Ideal Villa and Others Essays*.

21. Eisenman, *The Formal Basis of Modern Architecture*.

THE FORMAL BASIS OF MODERN ARCHITECTURE.

22. Eisenman, *The Formal Basis of Modern Architecture.*

understands design as a form-ordering process. While
the normative iconographic quality of Rowe's diagrams
surreptitiously reconstitutes a traditional symbolism and
semantic value for architecture, Eisenman concentrates
only on the systems of signifiers, avoiding any traditionally
diagrammatic and prescriptive configurations. He focuses
instead on a series of compositional problems concerned
with what he defines as "generic form" and their relational,
syntactic properties. For Eisenman, these generic forms, such
as the centroidal, the linear, and their development into
"specific forms," define formal properties rather than specific
iconic configurations.[22] These sets of formal properties
function as a system of relational invariants, immutable a
priori categories, which are fundamental conceptual tools
concerning forming, and which in the articulation of those
relations contain the possibility for the specific form of
the realized objects.

   Given this, it can be argued that the legendary
"structuralist triumvirate" formed by Rowe, Wittkower,
and Eisenman, so enthusiastically adopted by its future
"post-structuralist" detractors, loses its consistency. But
the ruins of its disintegration cannot be simply left alone.
On the contrary, the differences between them offer the
possibility of an alternative reconstruction, one that opens
up a different genealogy for Eisenman's work. First, it could
be productive to redirect the original alignment of Eisenman
with Rowe toward, and beyond, Wittkower. In so doing,
a series of other clues emerge, leading to a conveniently
bypassed art historian, Erwin Panofsky. Wittkower's most

PETER D. EISENMAN.   1963.

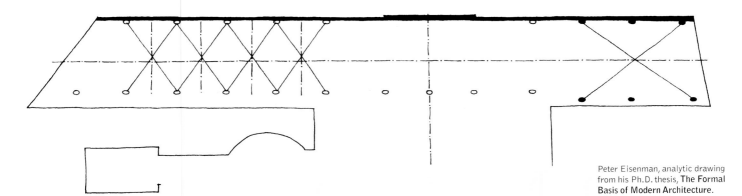

21.

TERMINATION OF LINEAR AXIS
COLUMNS IN UNDISTORTED LOCAT

Peter Eisenman, analytic drawing from his Ph.D. thesis, **The Formal Basis of Modern Architecture**. Opposite: Thesis title page.

23. Rudolf Wittkower, "Carlo Rainaldi and the Roman Architecture of the Full Baroque," *Art Bulletin* 19 (1937).

24. To my knowledge, of the essays Panofsky wrote on his theory of art during that period, only one has been translated into English. For the other essays cited here, I referred to an Italian translation published in 1961. The quotations are my translations from the Italian. Erwin Panofsky, "Das Problem des Stils in der bildenden Kunst" (The Problem of Style in the Visual Arts), *Zeitschrift für Aestetik und allgemeine Kunstwissenschaft* X (1915); "Über das Verhältnis der Kunstgeschichte zur Kunsttheorie" (On the Relationship between the History of Art and Theory of Art), *Z.A.A.K.* XVIII (1925); "Zum Problem der Beschreibung und Inhaltsbedeutung von Werken der Bildenden Kunst" (On the Problem of the Description and Interpretation of the Content of a Figurative Work of Art), *Logos* XXI (1932); "The Concept of Artistic Volition," *Critique*, Autumn 1981. The Italian translations are collected in *La Prospettiva come 'Forma Simbolica' e Altri Scritti* (Milan: Feltrinelli, 1961).

direct connection to Panofsky is via the Warburg Institute in Hamburg, where Panofsky worked under the direction of Fritz Saxl in the 1920s and early '30s, at a moment of profound transformation in the form and content of the discipline of art history in that institution. While Panofsky was at the Warburg, a radical shift occurred, thanks in part to his series of innovative, but now overlooked, essays. Scholars' interests moved from the tradition of studies that focused on iconography and iconology, or the field of the signified, to studies in the field of the signifiers. Wittkower's essays on architecture in particular, beginning with his 1937 piece on the Roman baroque and the work of Carlo Rainaldi – an architect also dear to both Rowe and Eisenman – are in debt to this shift.[23] In his work on the structures of art, Panofsky initiated a fundamental split between the Warburg's iconological tradition, which concentrated on the subject of signification, and the neo-critical tradition, which considered the study of art to be part of a more general science of the spirit.[24] Panofsky's philosophy of art history became the core of the new Warburg, the backdrop that brings him together first with Wittkower, and then with Rowe, who was Wittkower's pupil at the Warburg in the early 1940s in London. Rowe then went to Cambridge where, from 1960 to 1962, Eisenman knew him as both a colleague and mentor. There is further evidence of this connection. In Eisenman's copy of Panofsky's *Meaning in the Visual Arts*[25] there remains a Cambridge bookshop sales receipt, dated 1962, and in his thesis, Eisenman cites directly Panofsky's text on three occasions.

25. Erwin Panofsky, *Meaning in the Visual Arts* (Garden City, New York: Doubleday, 1955).

GUIDO ZULIANI 331

In reading Eisenman's thesis, we discover that its intended purpose was "at the risk of distorting the truth, to excise as far as possible iconographical and perceptual references," that is, the very possibility of an architectural "semiotic," and to consider "buildings as a structure of logical discourse." The thesis is therefore "concerned with conceptual issues, in the sense that form is considered as a problem of logical consistency, in other words, as the logical interaction of formal concepts."[26] Eisenman will continue to pursue this direction with a more articulated treatment of these ideas in his series of "Notes on Conceptual Architecture" in the 1970s.[27] In retrospect, the thesis passages seem to be a prelude to a continuing critique that Eisenman will mount against an architecture based on a metaphysics of presence and on the presupposition of the reality of a transcendental signified.

Other significant evidence supporting the hypothesis of fundamental links between Eisenman's and Panofsky's thinking is found in the latter's 1932 essay "On the Problem of the Description and the Interpretation of the Content of a Figurative Work of Art." Here Panofsky defines the essential categories for the interpretation of a work of art, denying any condition of objectivity, even in the act of description. A separation so profound as to be insurmountable is postulated between, on the one hand, the phenomenological and the semantic "strata" of the work of art, iconography being the "region of the sense of the phenomenon," and iconology the "region of the sense of meaning," and, on the other hand, the "region of the sense of essence."[28] The latter focuses on

26. Eisenman, *The Formal Basis of Modern Architecture.*

27. Peter Eisenman, "Notes on Conceptual Architecture: Towards a Definition," *Casabella* 359/360 (1971); "From Object to Relationship II: Giuseppe Terragni, Casa del Fascio," *Perspecta* 13/14 (1971); "Notes on Conceptual Architecture II A," *Environmental Design Research Association* 2 (1973); "Conceptual Architecture II: Double Deep Structure I," *A+U* 39 (1974); "Architettura Concettuale: Dal Livello Percettivo della Forma ai Suoi Significati Nascosti," *Casabella* 386 (1974).

28. This antinomy within Panofsky's theory of art was noticed by Manfredo Tafuri in his "Instrument of Criticism" in Manfredo Tafuri, *Theories and History of Architecture,* trans. Giorgio Verrecchia (New York: Harper and Row, 1980). See Erwin Panofsky, "Zum Problem der Beschreibung und Inhaltsbedeutung von Werken der Bildenden Kunst" (On the Problem of the Description and the Interpretation of the Content of a Figurative Work of Art), *Logos* XXI (1932).

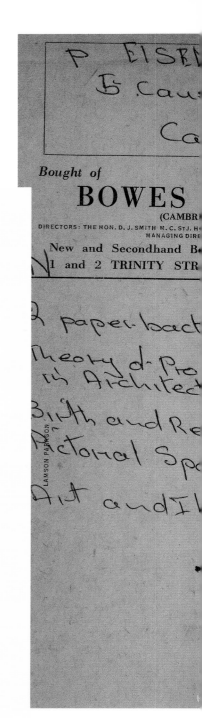

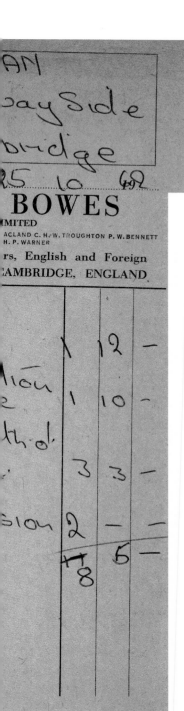

the immanent sense of a work, its formal structure. In other words, neither the perceptual sense of the phenomenon nor the iconologic sense of the meaning are, for Panofsky, of any use to a structural reading of a work of visual art.

In his 1920 essay "The Concept of Artistic Volition," Panofsky writes that "in the objects of the science of art, in the artistic phenomenon, whether in an extensive or restricted sense, an immanent sense can be retrieved. Thus there is an artistic will that is no longer psychological, but rather philosophical-transcendental."[29] Here Panofsky establishes an absolute separation between the iconic, semiologic nature of the work of art, between the work's secondariness in relation to an "external" and therefore preexisting meaning, and its intrinsic, immanent sense, a sense that requires a redefinition of its entire ontological nature. These positions outline and expand the conceptual background against which the intentions of Eisenman's thesis can be legitimately projected and thus inserted into a much larger historical and philosophical perspective, with both a tradition and a future. In 1966, approximately two years before the drawing with which we started our inquiry was made, Derrida dedicated his essay "Structure, Sign and Play in the Discourse of the Human Sciences" to the anthropologist Claude Lévi-Strauss and his critique of the logocentric tradition of the Western history of language. He writes that "as soon as one seeks to demonstrate . . . that there is no transcendental or privileged signified and that the domain or play of signification henceforth has no limit, one must reject even the concept and the word 'sign' itself, which

29. Erwin Panofsky, "The Concept of Artistic Volition," *Critique*, Autumn 1981.

30. Jacques Derrida, "Structure, Sign and Play in the Discourse of the Human Sciences," in *Writing and Difference*.

31. To support our hypothesis we could go full circle and introduce, as marginal as it may seem, the testimony of one of the fathers of structuralism, Claude Lévi-Strauss (himself investigated by Derrida), who in the early 1960s in his text "Structuralism and Criticism" writes, "In the field of art criticism . . . a work fully and totally structuralist [is] that of Erwin Panofsky" (my translation).
    Claude Lévi-Strauss in *Strutturalismo e Critica*, ed. Cesare Segre (Milan: Il Saggiatore, 1985); cited in Manfredo Tafuri, *Theories and History of Architecture*.

is precisely what cannot be done. For the signification 'sign' has always been understood and determined, in its meaning as a sign-of, a signifier referring to a signified, a signifier different from its signified. If one erases the radical difference between signifier and signified, it is the word 'signifier' itself that must be abandoned as a metaphysical concept."[30] This seems to define a possible conceptual territory within which to inscribe the unresolvable opposition presented in Eisenman's drawing. But it still leaves untouched our original question concerning the possible artful dissemination of evidences and traces. Nonetheless, based on these readings, we can credibly advance the hypothesis of a new and authentic structuralist dynamic between Panofsky, Derrida, and Eisenman that productively substitutes for the comforting but isostatic "structuralist triptych" centered on Rowe.[31] Though unstable in nature because its components articulate different developments and reach different conclusions within their specific fields of operation, despite their common set of original premises, this new triangulation reopens the possibility for a new critical reading of the last sixty years of architectural history.

The theoretical writings of Panofsky can be seen as a conceptual backdrop for Eisenman's thesis, as well as for his work to follow, to the extent that they present a series of implicit theoretical premises for an analysis of a work of art, or in Eisenman's case, a work of architecture. Derrida writes, "The passage beyond philosophy does not consist in turning the page of philosophy (which most of the time is equivalent to bad philosophizing) but in continuing to read the philosophers in a certain way."[32] If we replace the term "philosophy" with the word "architecture" (understood as a practice, the history of which has been not only sustained by but also emanates from the logocentric tradition of the metaphysics of presence), we might explain why Eisenman, the most theoretical architect of the last forty years, has not written a prescriptive treatise, like his colleagues Aldo Rossi or Robert Venturi.[33] Rather, he has based his continuous speculation, critical research, and pedagogic effort on reading "in a certain way" the work of architects: from Terragni to Palladio and Rainaldi, from Brunelleschi and Bramante to Piranesi, to Le Corbusier and Mies, Stirling and the Smithsons, Rossi and Hejduk, his most recent efforts concentrating on the work of late Le Corbusier, Kahn, Moretti, Venturi, Gehry, and Koolhaas.[34] Moreover, in the objectification of those works, as predicated by Panofsky, Eisenman not only considers them outside of a particular time and place but also separates them from the psychological investment of their producers. Likewise, in his critical work, Eisenman rereads even his own architecture in a continuous process of auto-analysis.[35] Most importantly, Eisenman shares with Panofsky a conceptual structure based on an idea that a work of art is a "solution" to a set of "a priori 'fundamental problems,'" themselves the expression of pairs of concepts ordered according to the form of an antithetical structure, which Panofsky assumed to be "the fundamental concepts of a theory of art." Among the pairs that Panofsky proposes (which range from a general antithesis in the ontological sphere – the two polarities being

GUIDO ZULIANI 335

32. Jacques Derrida,"Structure, Sign and Play in the Discourse of the Human Sciences" in *Writing and Difference*.

33. Aldo Rossi, *L'Architettura della Città* (Padua: Marsiglio, 1966); Robert Venturi, *Complexity and Contradiction in Architecture* (New York: The Museum of Modern Art Papers on Architecture, 1966).

34. Lévi-Strauss states that Panofsky is a great structuralist, first because he is a great historian, and because history offers him an unrivaled source of information, a combinatory field in which the truth of interpretation can be tested in many ways. (Lévi-Strauss in *Strutturalismo e Critica*.) Panofsky is explicit with regard to the necessity of a dialogue with history. In his essay "On the Relationship Between the History of Art and the Theory of Art," he says the reciprocal dependencies between the "fundamental concepts of a theory of art" are the tools of a structuralist approach to the immanent sense of an artistic product and the history of art: "The concepts that must be elaborated by a theory of art could become instruments of a properly scientific knowledge only if their verification starts from an intuitive observation of the material offered by art history. Conversely, the evidence that weighs upon art history could become the contents of a properly scientific knowledge only if those contents refer to artistic problems formulated by a theory of art; the final task of a science of art, that is, the definition of an 'artistic volition,' can only be done through a collaboration between historical and theoretical research." The former is interested in empirical-real phenomena, and the latter in conceptual and nonsensible speculation. Such a synthesis, which Panofsky defines as the "history of art as a science of interpretation," has the specific task to acknowledge "artistic volition." It would be the articulation of an understanding of the work of art as either being conditioned by the historical nexus of cause and effect or by an absoluteness, extracted from the nexus of cause and effect, that is beyond historical relativity, as a solution outside of time and place. Panofsky, "Über das Verhältnis der Kunstgeschichte zur Kunsttheorie" (On the Relationship between the History of Art and the Theory of Art).

35. See, for example, Peter Eisenman, *Diagrams Diaries* (New York: Universe, 1999).

plenum and form – to one in a methodological sphere – time and space) is a "longitudinal tendency" and a "tendency to centralization," which corresponds to Eisenman's a priori "linear" and "centroidal" formations. These are absolute in their nature and used to define the characteristics of a "generic form." Eisenman will articulate other antithetical pairs specific to his focus on architecture, such as "volume and mass," "mass and plane," "column and wall."[36] This last one also appears in Panofsky as a pair of "specific artistic concepts." It is perhaps a short distance from here to the magazine published by Eisenman's Institute for Architecture and Urban Studies, significantly titled *Oppositions*, in which the historian Michael Hays recently recognized the ideologically antinomic relation between autonomy and history, the opposition "between architecture's autonomy – its self-organization into a body of formal elements and operations that separate it from any particular place and time – and its contingency on, even determination by, historical forces beyond its control."[37]

Having now constructed a genealogical thread significantly different from the conventional wisdom that has dominated architectural discourse for the last twenty years, let us return to the two primary questions with which we began, and look at them in a different way.

Consider the unsettling feeling raised by the sensation of the presence of something carefully and systematically disguised under a layer of what we have defined as "a willful dissemination of evidence," a particular form of disguise, one that seems to presuppose the presence of something beyond

336 TRACING EISENMAN

36. In order not to repeat the common misreading of Panofsky's and Eisenman's theoretical positions, caused by a reductivist understanding of structuralism that partisans of post-structuralism tend to espouse, I will repeat here that the antithetical pair of science and art perform for both Panofsky and Eisenman the function of designating a polarity between these values, but are beyond the world of artistic phenomena; two values that in works of art meet in the most different forms. To merit their use as the idea of fundamental concepts, they must not be reduced to a formula as a way in which artistic problems are to be resolved; instead they are the way in which problems are posed. Panofsky says that fundamental concepts do not pretend to be a fundamental grammar to classify artistic phenomena. Rather, their task is to make phenomena speak. They may be reduced to a formula, but it is not the solution to artistic problems. Therefore, these fundamental concepts are only useful in determining the questions that we must put to objects, but not the always unpredictable answers. Panofsky, "Über das Verhältnis der Kunstgeschichte zur Kunsttheorie" (On the Relationship between the History of Art and Theory of Art); Eisenman, *The Formal Basis of Modern Architecture*.

37. K. Michael Hays, ed., *Oppositions Reader* (New York: Princeton Architectural Press, 1998).

A Journal for Ideas and
Criticism in Architecture

Fall 1976/6

Published for The Institute
for Architecture and Urban Studies

By The MIT Press

OSI

a simple case of cause and effect. If our reconstruction is correct, that Panofsky's theoretical apparatus also made Eisenman's possible, we must consider the premises articulated by the German philosopher Ernst Cassirer in his seminal work *The Philosophy of Symbolic Forms* and Conrad Fiedler's seminal 1876 essay "On Judging Works of Visual Art".[38] In Panofsky's thinking, among language, myth, ritual, and art – the autonomous structures that are the subject of Cassirer's philosophical inquiry – works of art have a privileged position because they are the "formative act directed to determine the content of reality," therefore the ontological nature of a work of art must be seen as a construction rather than a particular form of representation. Panofsky said, "The artist does not represent the Spirit of the Time, he builds it."[39] Fiedler's essay is a direct precursor of Panofsky's 1932 essay "On the Problem of the Description and the Interpretation of the Content of a Figurative Work of Art" and articulates the fundamental premises, critical tropes, and implications of the tradition initiated with neo-criticism and later developed in formalism, structuralism, and now deconstruction. It is here that the work of Eisenman, with all its original intuitions, is, consciously or not, inscribed. It is also here, with Fiedler's essay, that this detective's retracing and construction of a different genealogy for Eisenman's ideology can provisionally rest and some conclusions begin to be drawn.

Fiedler's primary intent is to demonstrate the fundamental autonomy of the content of the work of art from any preexisting, preconceived referent external to the

38. Ernst Cassirer, *The Philosophy of Symbolic Forms*, trans. Ralph Mannheim (New Haven: Yale University Press, 1955); Conrad Fiedler, "On Judging Works of Visual Art" (University of California Press, 1949).

39. Erwin Panofsky, "The Concept of Artistic Volition."

GUIDO ZULIANI 337

Peter Eisenman, Maison
Dom-ino analytic drawings.

work of art itself. He sustains this assertion by demonstrating the absolute otherness of "artistic judgment" from any other possible reading of a work of art based on categories and instrumentalities external to the work. These externalities include the esthetic, iconographic, scientific, historical, socio-cultural, and the philosophical within which artistic production would be subsumed according to the rules of a general semiotic. For Fiedler, like Panofsky after him, the artistic content of a work of art is immanent to the work itself and coincides with its immanent formal structure. The "imaginary thinking" specific to a work of art is counterposed in the form of a radical and insurmountable difference to a "conceptual thinking" specific to every language, and by its very nature, based on a logic of the signified over the signifier. "Imaginary thinking" is an autonomous cognitive approach toward the world, an approach based not on the necessary presupposition of an anteriority of a transcendental signified and a defined form of a metaphysics of presence, but rather based on a condition of presentness; that is, the being of the world in the form of its coming forward, not its representation; its appearing in an artistic intuition.[40] This makes possible the privilege Panofsky attributes to art within Cassirer's field of symbolic forms. Fiedler's position constitutes the work of art as a very particular object juxtaposed to, but coexisting with, the products of conceptual knowledge, an object the nature of which is ultimately both impossible and Utopian. But in such an object a short circuit takes place: the difference, both spatial and temporal, between signifier and signified collapses, and

40. Fiedler's arguments are seen in this inquiry in terms of a general ontology of a work of art, beyond the multiple phenomenologies that constitute the history of art. Moreover, only on these bases can there be any well-founded consideration of the autonomy of an artistic work that will not succumb to the conceptually irrelevant and ultimately simplistic attitude that is today labeled the postcritical.

41. Peter Eisenman, "Aspects of Modernism: Maison Dom-ino and the Self-referential Sign," *Oppositions* 15/16 (1980).

Peter Eisenman essay from
Oppositions 15/16, 1980.

Aspects of Modernism:
Maison Dom-ino and the Self-Referential Sign

Peter Eisenman

The modes and identit
down with their own
express the order of bei
Michel Foucault.

It can be argued that
some manner be traced
the most tangible cha
brought about by adval
opment of new conditi
nificance of certain ritı
ance. Thus, it would se
of the architectural obj
in man's consciousness
fifteenth century and tl
centric to an anthropoc

Such changes in archite
in spatial manipulations
the physical manifesta
gies made possible by
representation. While
are easily grafted onto
changes in elevation ar
in plan and section; pla
development of orthog
the animating principl
classical Western sense
devices that reflect be
meaning and the tec
changes. One has only
6) to one of Bramante
12) to one of Palladio,
external expression of 1
a platonic square or re
complete dissolution, ¢
anthropocentric society

consequently an object of art becomes irreducible to any semiotic condition.

A connection between Fiedler's positions and essential elements of Eisenman's architectural ideology is found in many forms of Eisenman's work, from his Ph.D. thesis to the drawing of House I [32], to his interest in a definition of a "conceptual architecture," as well as his idea of a "textual architecture" and his more recent concern with the "becoming unmotivated of the architectural sign," a preoccupation that appears in the title of his 1980 essay "Aspects of Modernism: Maison Dom-ino and the Self-referential Sign."[41] It is due to Fiedler's explicit juxtaposition of the work of art and the products of all other forms of languages that what is implicit in the autonomy of the former becomes explicit. If, as Eisenman articulates, autonomy can only define the artistic product as self-referential, this in turn implies a condition of otherness, or exteriority, in relation to a semiotic regime. This constitutes an absence, each time a work of art is understood as autonomous, an absence of that difference between signifier and signified, of that "imperfection" intrinsic to language, which allows language itself to be, to communicate and at the same time to be the object of a critique. It is that difference which opens out to the very possibility of sense.

In the removal of the work of art from the semiotic nature of language, the concept of autonomy contains a Utopian desire for a condition of pure presentness; it also illustrates its impossibility. As Derrida writes, "As soon as one seeks to demonstrate . . . that there is no transcendental

GUIDO ZULIANI 339

buildings like Charles
Le Corbusier's Maison
ferent use and signifi-
e witnesses an altera-
to announce historical
plaid grid of the opera
o, possibly one of the
e continuous cycle of
ive cultural phenome-
ility that is to parallel
rn thought.

scribes the change that
enth century in man's
and its artifacts—aes-
philosophical, and sci-
ritique of the formerly
, which viewed man as
the center of his phys-

where Modernism has
irly easy to distinguish
which can be labeled
idition is characterized
to be self-referential.
non-narrative prose or
reflects in its historical
ı of the relation of man
ere the writer or com-
terposed between the
Man is seen to be in
lativistic condition vis-
of rather than the de-
prose and music incor-
ı of the object/maker,
that is, how the object

The record of the later history of Western architecture, from the early nineteenth century to the present, also documents the changes which have occurred in man's conception of his object-world as they come to be reflected in his architecture. For example, if one examines the differ- reveals its condition of being and its manner of coming into being, how these are recorded and the inherent condition of such notations. Since the object of prose, music, painting, and sculpture is no longer merely a narrative record and mimetic representation of man's condition, it becomes more fundamentally concerned with its own ob-

or privileged signified and that the domain or play of signification henceforth has no limit, one must reject even the concept and the word "sign" itself – which is precisely what cannot be done."[42]

This is an obvious problem for any kind of expression, and particularly for architecture. Both Fiedler and Eisenman are explicit about this. "In works of architecture, it is more difficult than in other objects of art to distinguish which of their parts are based upon artistic achievement and which parts owe their existence to other nonartistic demands," Fiedler writes. The "history of architecture . . . does not distinguish between building construction and architecture as art, but on the contrary offers a history of the forms of buildings and does not offer a history of the artistic qualities of architectural form."[43] Thus the drawing with which we started this inquiry now takes on a specific meaning: it explicitly presents the same irreducibly double nature, that is, the semiotic and the artistic polarities, of a work of architecture as implicit in Fiedler's text, later articulated by Derrida, that Eisenman, carrying on that tradition and opening it up to new questions, will put at the core of his architectural work.

The programmatic nature of that manifesto seems to delineate the development of an architecture that Eisenman considered to be framed both by the desire to find architecture's true nature, its specific interiority, liberated from a metaphysics of presence, and by the impossibility of such a liberation. The irreducibility of the opposition meaning/form presents as inevitable the coexistence of both

42. Jacques Derrida, "Structure, Sign and Play in the Discourse of the Human Sciences" in *Writing and Difference*.

43. The definition of the architectural qualities of such forms has been the ideological center animating Eisenman's entire production, beginning with his thesis and his work on Terragni. His continuous rereading of architecture can be seen as an attempt precisely to define the evolution of architectural qualities within architectural form. See Fiedler, "On Judging Works of Visual Art" and Peter Eisenman, *Giuseppe Terragni: Transformations, Decompositions, Critiques* (New York: Monacelli Press, 2004).

terms, which constantly and reciprocally undermine each other. Eisenman preempts both the possible dominance of one over the other and, at the same time, the possibility of a dialectic synthesis, or a mediating third element. In his project, these two conditions are simultaneously present, one inscribed within the other in a form that could be defined, for lack of a better term, as a "suspended dialectic."

The pursuit of this instability, of an undecidability intrinsic to the work itself, as the constituent moment of the work, and its readability, must be seen as the spark that initially elicited our curiosity about Eisenman's attempt to "disseminate evidence," a tendency that has been, throughout his work, subsumed by his constant attention to issues such as "trace," "index," "virtuality," and in particular, the concept of an "architectural text."

Eisenman's preoccupation with "autonomy," in Fiedler's sense, as the condition for an authentic architecture's language, and at the same time the recognition that the very possibility of that language is founded on its disappearance as language, is at the base of what I called a "suspended dialectic."[44] Such a "suspended dialectic" has forced Eisenman to face a dramatic predicament, the disappearance within the concept of autonomy itself of the necessary gap on which the semantic nature of every language is inexorably built. Eisenman must face the paradox of the disappearance of an absence, of that lacuna internal to language that also makes language possible. Thus for an autonomous architecture the supplemental nature of its signs is missing, and with it the traces that language naturally

44. In light of these considerations of Eisenman's work, today's pursuit of an asemantic status for architecture, which the promoters of "smoothness" and the "postcritical" are seeking – an architecture defined, both physically and ideologically, as a surface from which every trace, every index is removed – then takes on a specific connotation. They speak of the dream of a realized Utopia, as consolatory and regressive as any realized Utopia is, aimed at installing a pure, autonomous, and in fact impossible language within reality, thereby "resolving" its own history, its ideal, uncontradictory fullness. This neutralization of the multiple into a monistic unity can only be achieved by the radical repression of all contradictions contained in language itself, a repression obtained by adopting a truly self-referential mathematic language and its applications.

GUIDO ZULIANI 341

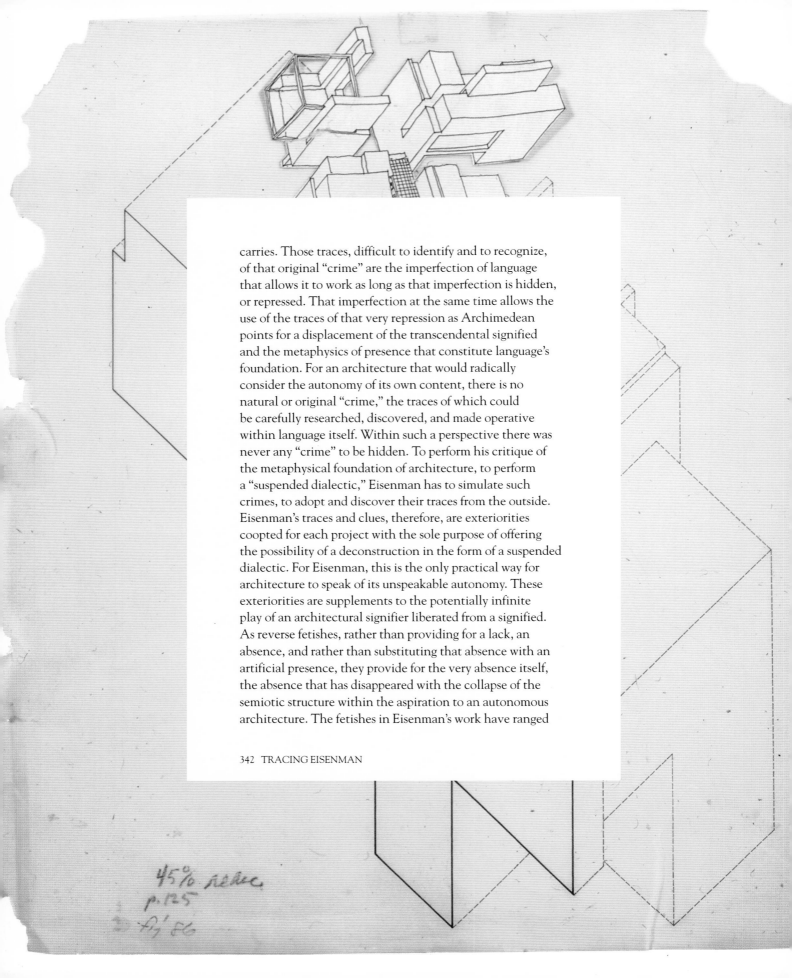

carries. Those traces, difficult to identify and to recognize, of that original "crime" are the imperfection of language that allows it to work as long as that imperfection is hidden, or repressed. That imperfection at the same time allows the use of the traces of that very repression as Archimedean points for a displacement of the transcendental signified and the metaphysics of presence that constitute language's foundation. For an architecture that would radically consider the autonomy of its own content, there is no natural or original "crime," the traces of which could be carefully researched, discovered, and made operative within language itself. Within such a perspective there was never any "crime" to be hidden. To perform his critique of the metaphysical foundation of architecture, to perform a "suspended dialectic," Eisenman has to simulate such crimes, to adopt and discover their traces from the outside. Eisenman's traces and clues, therefore, are exteriorities coopted for each project with the sole purpose of offering the possibility of a deconstruction in the form of a suspended dialectic. For Eisenman, this is the only practical way for architecture to speak of its unspeakable autonomy. These exteriorities are supplements to the potentially infinite play of an architectural signifier liberated from a signified. As reverse fetishes, rather than providing for a lack, an absence, and rather than substituting that absence with an artificial presence, they provide for the very absence itself, the absence that has disappeared with the collapse of the semiotic structure within the aspiration to an autonomous architecture. The fetishes in Eisenman's work have ranged

45% reduc
p.125
fig 86

from the linguistic to the philosophic, to geography, biology, literature, structuralism, deconstruction, topology, fractals, and genetics; to figures as diverse as Chomsky and Derrida, Leibniz and Deleuze, Proust, Pynchon, Blanchot; to the abstract and figural, smooth and striated, curvilinear and orthogonal, wavy and Cartesian, and so forth. These are all socialized discourses, in spite of their specific content, and for Eisenman they are all a succession of adopted paradigms that work as a simulated ground sustaining the sophisticated exercises of a unique dialectic. Only through their radical criticism, the "deconstruction" of their logo-centric bases – and here lies the profound resonance of the work of Eisenman with the work of Derrida – does the possibility of an autonomous architecture emerge. The use of provisional, but historically determined paradigms, the constant moving from one to the next as one way to articulate something that can never be fully made present, has allowed Eisenman to be a critical and radical presence in the field of architecture and culture in general for the last forty years.

But a close reading of the sequence of his "critical" projects reveals two objects as radically different from all the others, so different that it is quite difficult, if not impossible, explicitly to articulate their nature. One is what Eisenman calls the "el-form," first formulated in House X and then, in a purer, more radical way, in House 11a; the other is the project for the Memorial to the Murdered Jews of Europe in Berlin [290].[45]

To articulate a reading of these two exceptions and their quality within Eisenman's body of work, it is necessary to go

45. Peter Eisenman, *House X* (New York: Rizzoli International, 1982); "Sandboxes: House 11a," *A+U* 112 (1980); also *Fin d'Ou T Hou S* (London: Architectural Association, 1985); *Holocaust Memorial Berlin* (Baden: Lars Müller Publishers, 2005).

GUIDO ZULIANI 343

House 11a study diagrams.

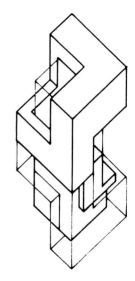

back to one of Panofsky's central concepts of his theory of art. Panofsky says the work of art is the specific solution to a set of fundamental problems in art, which in turn are framed and defined by what he calls the fundamental concepts of the science of art. These are articulated in the form of polarities that can never be actualized as a pure condition in the work of art itself. As an example, Panofsky cites two values that form a specific and fundamental problem that a work of art must resolve: the optic value and the haptic value, which he simplifies as open space and bodies. These two values could never purely exist in a work of art, which itself consists in the resolution of their encounter. Hence it will never be possible to have a purely optical work of art because it will correspond to a "luminous, completely amorphous phenomenon," nor a purely haptic work, which would result in an "abstract geometric figure."[46] The Panofskian trope of antinomies is wholly innate to Eisenman's ideology of architecture, to the degree that it informs its ontological structure and the invention of his meta-methodology, his "suspended dialectic." In his thesis, as well as in his book on Giuseppe Terragni and his essays on House I and House II, one of Eisenman's primary contributions to the development of the work of architecture as autonomous is the definition of a fundamental antinomy specific to architecture: the polarity of volume, that is, the "particularized, defined and contained" assumption of space, and mass, the traditional volumetric, solid nature of the architectural object.[47] For Eisenman, like Panofsky, every work of architecture, its specificity, its immanent sense, consists in the specific

46. Panofsky, "Über das Verhältnis der Kunstgeschichte zur Kunsttheorie" (On the Relationship between the History of Art and Theory of Art).

47. Eisenman, *The Formal Basis of Modern Architecture; Giuseppe Terragni: Transformations, Decompositions, Critiques*; "Cardboard Architecture: House I" and "Cardboard Architecture: House II" in *Five Architects*.

formalization of the resolution of their relation. The two poles can never be actualized alone, for pure volume would result in the pure extension of an unqualified space, and pure mass would result in a monolithic geometric solid. It is obvious how these two values could be related to Panofsky's optic value (open space) and haptic value (body). But the el-form, in its purest version, transcends the customary solution of the problem of the relation between mass and volume. In its formal definition, also ironically illustrated by the short animation "HOUSE 11a: A documentary in which le void meets el solid," puts these two polarities into a direct unmediated confrontation.[48]

With the excavation of the void cube into the solid one, with the volume being one-eighth of the mass, the point that would constitute the stable center of the overall geometric cubic figure finds itself located in a provisional position capable of virtually moving along a diagonal axis that connects the opposite apices of the void and the solid respectively, the volume and the mass. The movement of that point along that diagonal axis changes the ratio between the pure value of volume and that of mass, and, at the extremities, the object, dominated neither by the value of volume nor by that of solid, will transform either into pure space or into a solid cubic figure.

There is a direct correspondence between the formal content of the el-form and the very functioning of the antithetical structure of solid-void, which in Eisenman's theory constitute the essential nature of every architectural phenomenon. Its embodiment, without any of the

48. Peggy Well, "HOUSE 11a: A documentary in which le void meets el solid." Animation, date unknown.

GUIDO ZULIANI 345

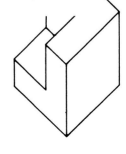
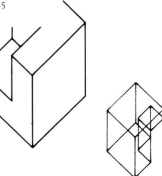

traditional, iconic, programmatic, and architectural connotations places this el-form, and the related projects, outside the traditional phenomenology of architecture outside, also, of Eisenman's suspended dialectic. The el-form may then be understood as a pure manifestation of Eisenman's theory, its most original contribution to the tradition to which that theory belongs. It may also be identified with that elusive entity that would be a self-referential architecture. An entity that by its very nature is impossible to name but can only be described as simply and radically "other" from all those that have names.

The project for the Memorial to the Murdered Jews of Europe [290] goes further, or perhaps deeper, in a direction that reaches the more archetypal, primal attributes of architecture as an autonomous work of art. The antithesis actualized by Eisenman's el-form is located inside what Panofsky calls the "sphere of the phenomenon." All artistic problems are "implicitly contained within one unique large original problem that is itself in the form of an antithesis, and it presents itself as a priori," Panofsky writes. For Panofsky, the terms of the antithesis that temporally and logically precede those in the sphere of the phenomenon can be defined as plenum and form. Plenum and form frame the problem of the original relation between the continuous flux of sensations and their organization into some sort of order, a relation that constitutes, for Panofsky, the original form of being in the world. Therefore, their relation constitutes the a priori possibility-in-itself for every subsequent artistic problem. For Panofsky the values of plenum and form

49. - Panofsky's fundamental concepts of the science of art (my translation):

General antithesis in the sphere of ontology	Specific oppositions within the phenomenal sphere, in this case visual			General antithesis in the sphere of methodology
	1. opposition of elemental values	2. opposition of figural values	3. opposition of compositional values	
plenum is juxtaposed to *form*	*optical* values (open space) juxtaposed to *haptic* values (bodies)	*values of depth* juxtaposed to *values of surface*	values of interpenetration (fusion) juxtaposed to *values of contiguity* (subdivision)	*time* is juxtaposed to *space*

Memorial to the Murdered Jews
of Europe, Berlin, Germany,
map of stone heights.

constitute the poles of a fundamental opposition, and he
considers them the two distinct elements of the "general
antithesis in an ontological sphere."[49]

Eisenman's project in Berlin, and to a lesser extent
his project for The City of Culture in Spain [308],[50] seem
directly to confront the terms of this opposition in the
manner demonstrated in the el form. In Santiago, the
surface of the artificial topography is engraved by a series
of Cartesian grids; the confrontation of plenum and form
takes the configuration of a superposition, of the reciprocal
inscription of one element onto the other. The technique
of superposition holds this project within the condition
of a suspended dialectic. For that superposition to take
place, two elements, the undulating artificial topography
and the Cartesian grid, are reconstructed in terms of their
objecthood, that is, as figurative elements endowed with an
iconic and rhetorical significance. Their confrontation, or
superposition, is a mutual act of erasure that introduces a
critique of language as a locus of the metaphysics of presence.

In Berlin the opposite strategy is used; the trope of
superposition is now one of separation. Here, in a way, no
preexisting object is de facto necessary for the actualization
of such a unique moment of encounter, no figurative
element exists before its emergence, hence the embodiments
of the Panofskian antithesis at the ontological level
– plenum and form – can appear from the absolute silence
of the neutral surface of the urban site. The indissoluble
relation of the interdependency of two conditions is
presented literally and yet absolutely abstracted, without

50. Peter Eisenman,
CodeX: The City of Culture
of Galicia (New York:
Monacelli Press, 2005).

GUIDO ZULIANI 347

Memorial to the Murdered Jews
of Europe, Berlin, Germany, 2005.

any iconic referent, as a pure state of the indistinct fullness of plenum and a pure state of the separateness that sustains the *principio individuationis* that allows for the recognition of individual beings.

As such, the Berlin memorial reaches down to the most primordial condition necessary for an artistic expression to take place, and fulfills the deepest, most conceptual meaning of Eisenman's work, bringing to its inexorable conclusion that body of tradition within which his work has been inscribed. The memorial has the courage simply to be, in a state of pure presentness, and to be the petrification of that state, of a moment, a most primordial one, which is the real kingdom of the artist, absolute and mute. It is a state that precedes yet makes possible the attribution of names that Martin Heidegger, and later Maurice Blanchot, defined as the moment of "the struggle between the Earth and the World," the moment in which the Earth *becomes* the World.[51]

And that can happen only once.

51. The subject of the work of art as a "struggle between the Earth and the World" as pertinent to both Martin Heidegger and Maurice Blanchot has been raised by Stefano Zampieri in his "L'Arte, l'Opera, l'Origine. M. Blanchot," *Verifiche* (January–June, 1995).

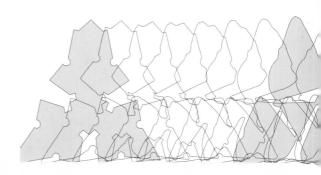

Spree Dreieck Tower
2000
Berlin, Germany

The challenge given to Eisenman Architects was to create "an Eisenman building haunted by the spirit of Mies." If Mies van der Rohe could propose a 100-meter-tall skyscraper for Berlin in 1922, a 200-meter-tall tower could be proposed for 2002. The Spree Dreieck triangle site is filled with history, including the history of Mies's two famous but unbuilt tower projects: the edgy, triangular Friedrichstrasse Office Building project of 1921, and the more organic, curved Glass Skyscraper project of 1922.

The 48-story Spree Dreieck Tower is proposed to stand 795 feet above the ground, providing 883,000 square feet of space for office and commercial use. The concept for the tower is derived from the footprints of Mies's two proposals. The design begins with the base plans of Mies's two towers superimposed on one another. Then the top plan is rotated off of the base plan to produce a new, flowing vertical surface that combines the rationality of Mies with the fluidity of today. The undulating form of the new glass-clad tower causes the interior floor plates to vary slightly in dimension, thus offering unique layouts and views throughout the project.

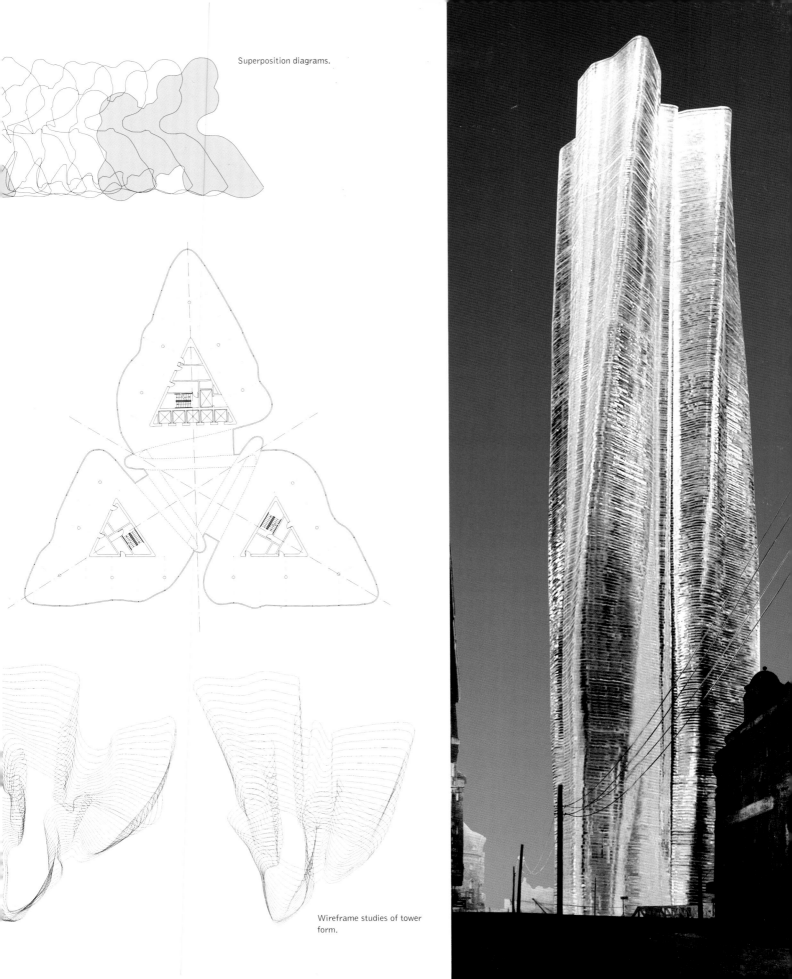

Superposition diagrams.

Wireframe studies of tower
form.

Eindhoven Railroad Station 2000+ Project

1999–2000
Eindhoven, The Netherlands

In the 1990s, the Philips Company, the industrial backbone of Eindhoven, began turning the scope of its work toward research and sales management, vacating half of its two million square feet of built space. To keep the city from becoming a postindustrial wasteland of abandoned buildings, Philips commissioned a master plan for redevelopment. Our approach focused on defining the role of the train in a city whose character has shifted from the industrial to the technological. No other place in the city is more open to the flow of information than the railroad, an infrastructural node between several urban dynamics: the inner city, the office and commercial districts, the university, and the green area along the Dommel River.

To enhance the east-west connections, the station is redesigned along the diagonal connecting the university campus to the inner city. The improvement of the north-south axis is achieved by developing a tunnel connection between the business district to the north of the tracks and the inner city shopping district to the south. The new "station-mall" acts as a central node that connects all infrastructural flows and needs. The huge transfer hall becomes an accelerator, catalyst, and dispatcher of flows of information, people, goods, and events.

The design process evolved through a series of superposed grids (the inner city grid superposed on the university grid) rotated along the railroad. The rotation angle was determined by the difference between the axial directions of the grids. The rotation and thus the blurring of the grids on the station area results in an animated series of surface foldings, which induce the volumetric forms of the proposed station-mall and the diagonal cuts. The building, passage, and plaza patterns result from a diagrammatic reading/writing of the blurred grids.

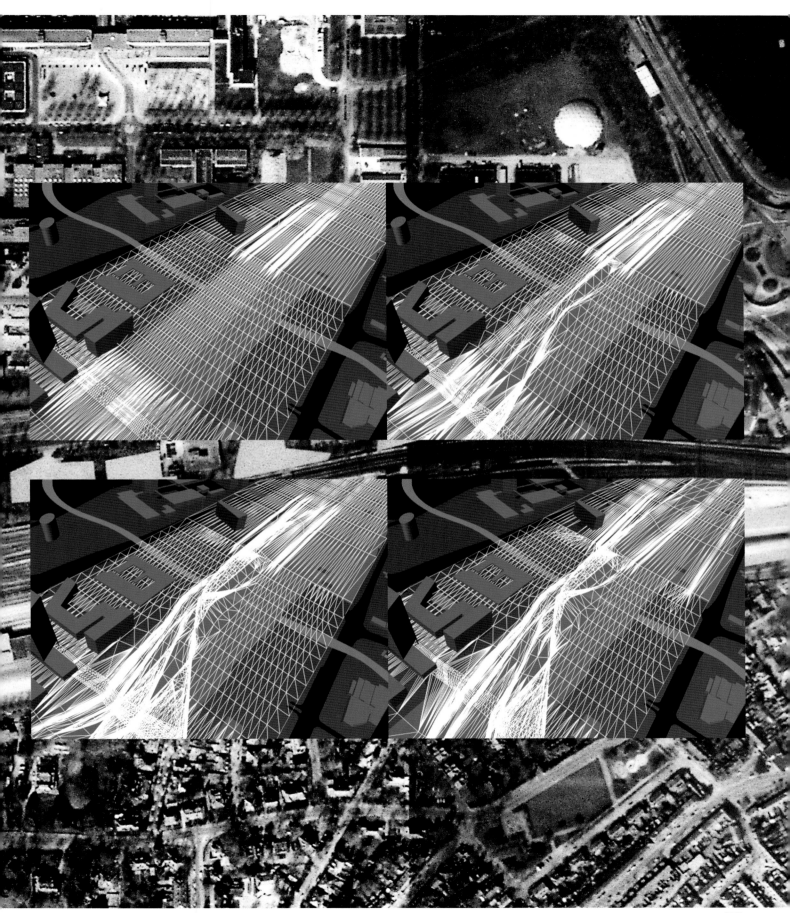

Previous page: Concept diagrams.
Below and right: Models.
Bottom: Plans.

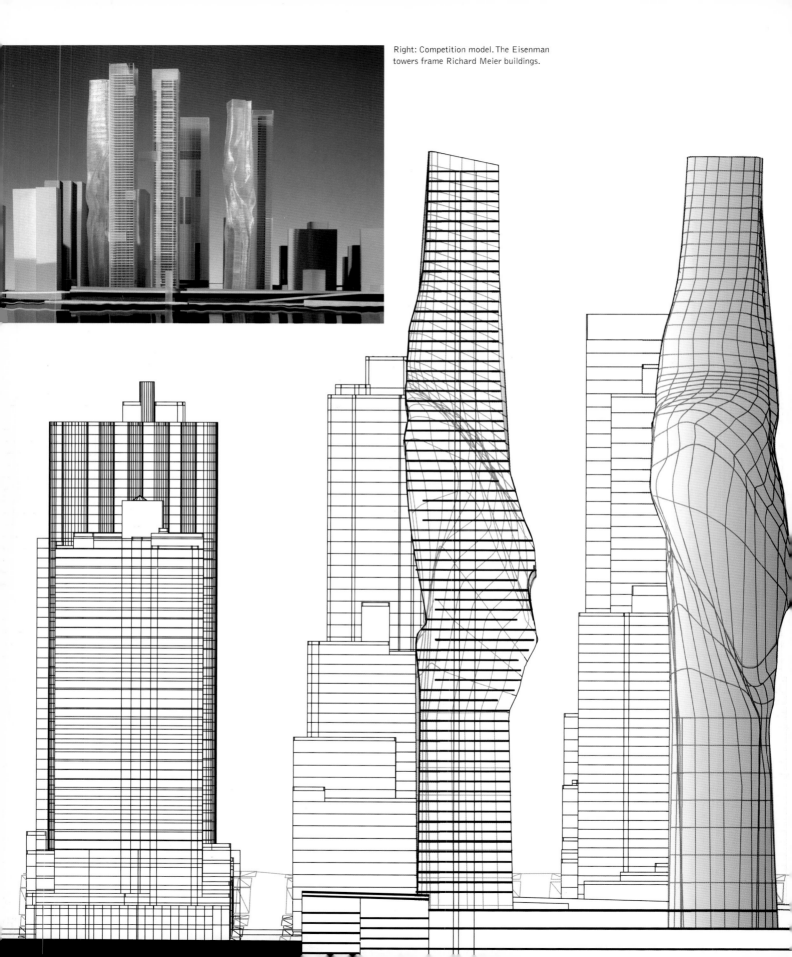

Right: Competition model. The Eisenman
towers frame Richard Meier buildings.

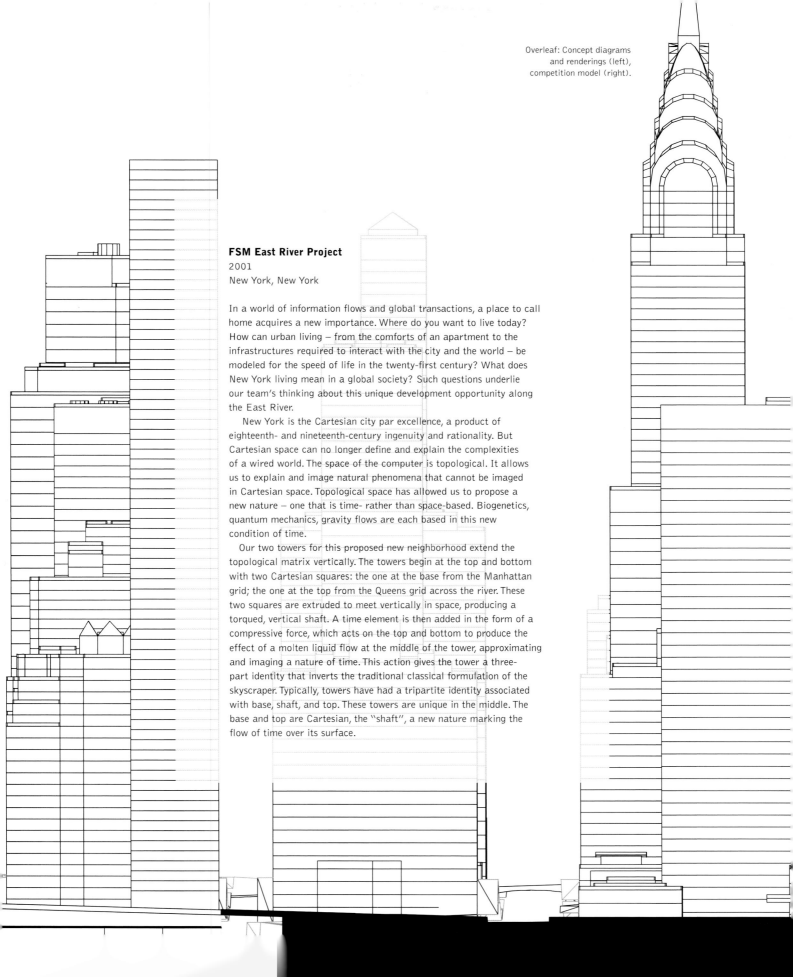

Overleaf: Concept diagrams
and renderings (left),
competition model (right).

FSM East River Project
2001
New York, New York

In a world of information flows and global transactions, a place to call
home acquires a new importance. Where do you want to live today?
How can urban living – from the comforts of an apartment to the
infrastructures required to interact with the city and the world – be
modeled for the speed of life in the twenty-first century? What does
New York living mean in a global society? Such questions underlie
our team's thinking about this unique development opportunity along
the East River.

New York is the Cartesian city par excellence, a product of
eighteenth- and nineteenth-century ingenuity and rationality. But
Cartesian space can no longer define and explain the complexities
of a wired world. The space of the computer is topological. It allows
us to explain and image natural phenomena that cannot be imaged
in Cartesian space. Topological space has allowed us to propose a
new nature – one that is time- rather than space-based. Biogenetics,
quantum mechanics, gravity flows are each based in this new
condition of time.

Our two towers for this proposed new neighborhood extend the
topological matrix vertically. The towers begin at the top and bottom
with two Cartesian squares: the one at the base from the Manhattan
grid; the one at the top from the Queens grid across the river. These
two squares are extruded to meet vertically in space, producing a
torqued, vertical shaft. A time element is then added in the form of a
compressive force, which acts on the top and bottom to produce the
effect of a molten liquid flow at the middle of the tower, approximating
and imaging a nature of time. This action gives the tower a three-
part identity that inverts the traditional classical formulation of the
skyscraper. Typically, towers have had a tripartite identity associated
with base, shaft, and top. These towers are unique in the middle. The
base and top are Cartesian, the "shaft", a new nature marking the
flow of time over its surface.

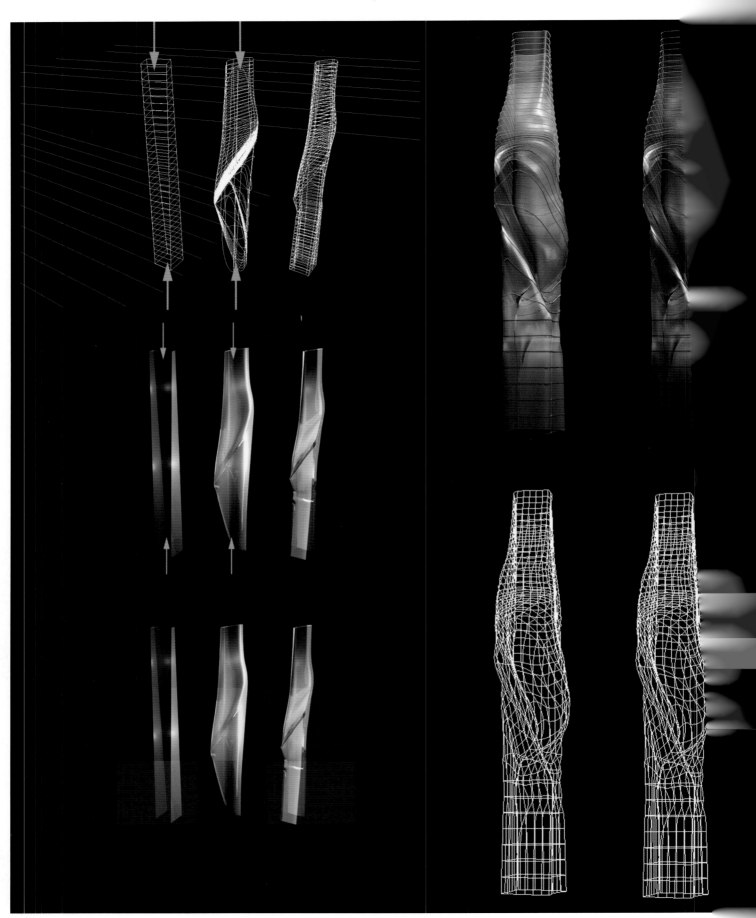

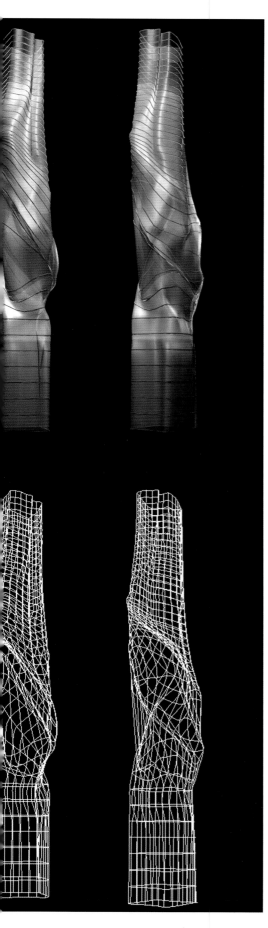

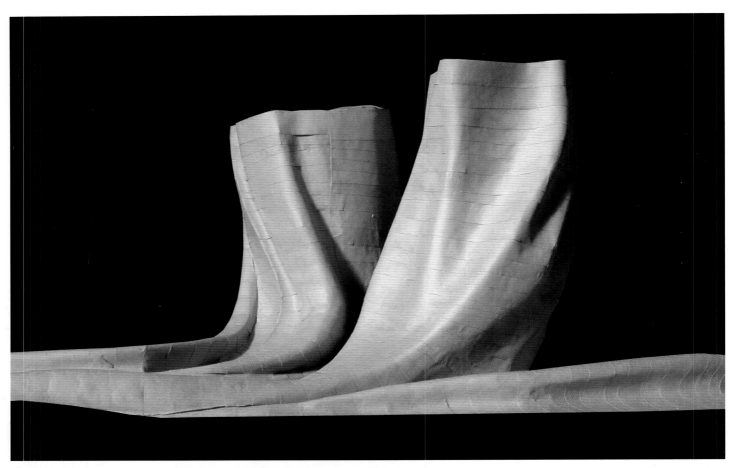

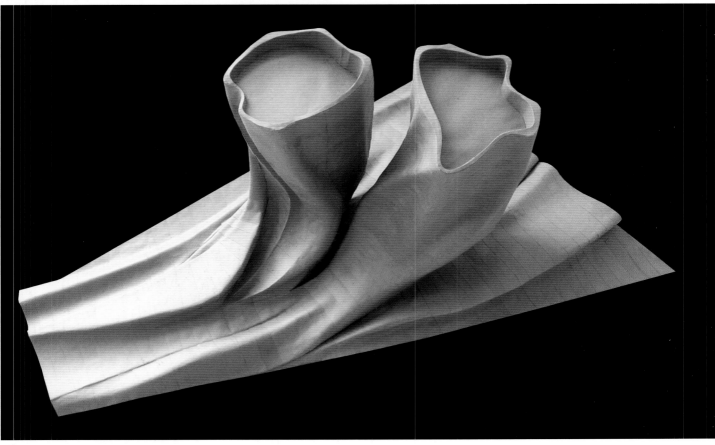

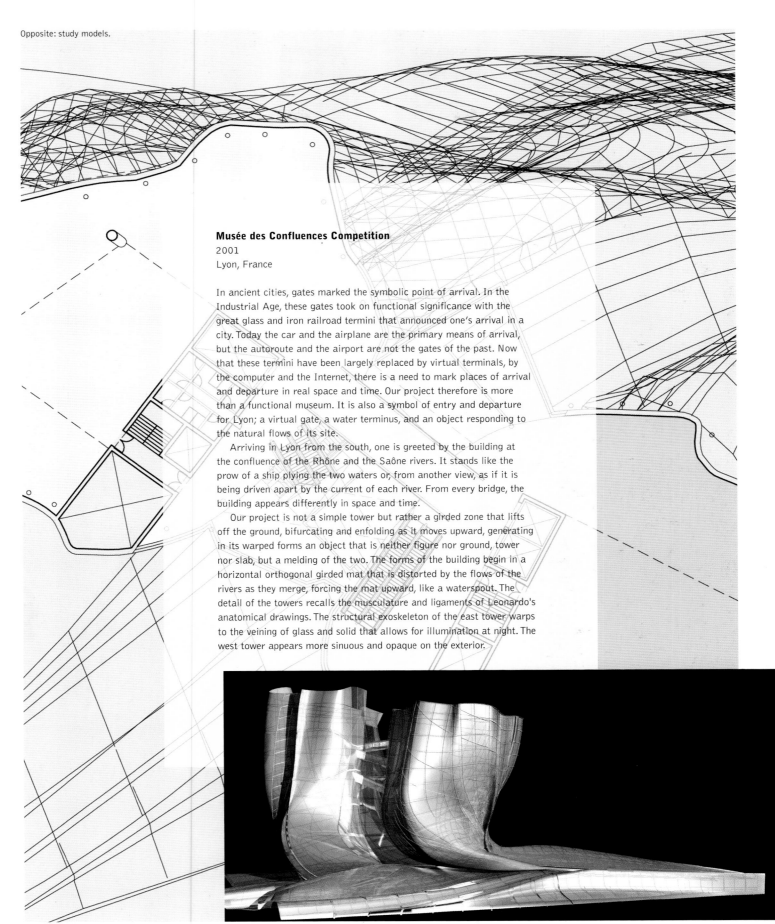

Musée des Confluences Competition
2001
Lyon, France

In ancient cities, gates marked the symbolic point of arrival. In the Industrial Age, these gates took on functional significance with the great glass and iron railroad termini that announced one's arrival in a city. Today the car and the airplane are the primary means of arrival, but the autoroute and the airport are not the gates of the past. Now that these termini have been largely replaced by virtual terminals, by the computer and the Internet, there is a need to mark places of arrival and departure in real space and time. Our project therefore is more than a functional museum. It is also a symbol of entry and departure for Lyon; a virtual gate, a water terminus, and an object responding to the natural flows of its site.

Arriving in Lyon from the south, one is greeted by the building at the confluence of the Rhône and the Saône rivers. It stands like the prow of a ship plying the two waters or, from another view, as if it is being driven apart by the current of each river. From every bridge, the building appears differently in space and time.

Our project is not a simple tower but rather a girded zone that lifts off the ground, bifurcating and enfolding as it moves upward, generating in its warped forms an object that is neither figure nor ground, tower nor slab, but a melding of the two. The forms of the building begin in a horizontal orthogonal girded mat that is distorted by the flows of the rivers as they merge, forcing the mat upward, like a waterspout. The detail of the towers recalls the musculature and ligaments of Leonardo's anatomical drawings. The structural exoskeleton of the east tower warps to the veining of glass and solid that allows for illumination at night. The west tower appears more sinuous and opaque on the exterior.

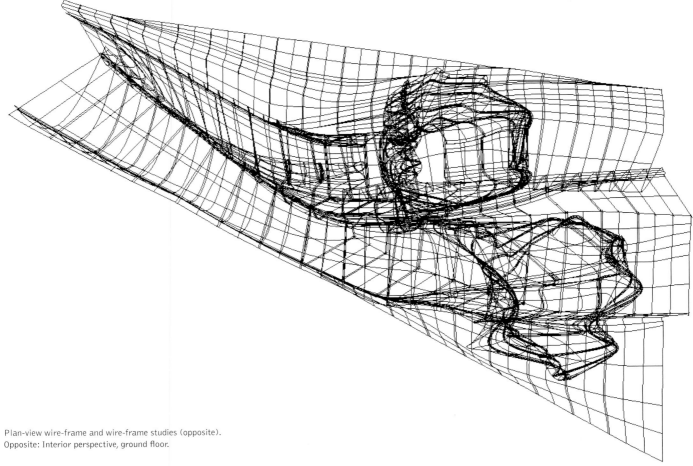

Plan-view wire-frame and wire-frame studies (opposite).
Opposite: Interior perspective, ground floor.

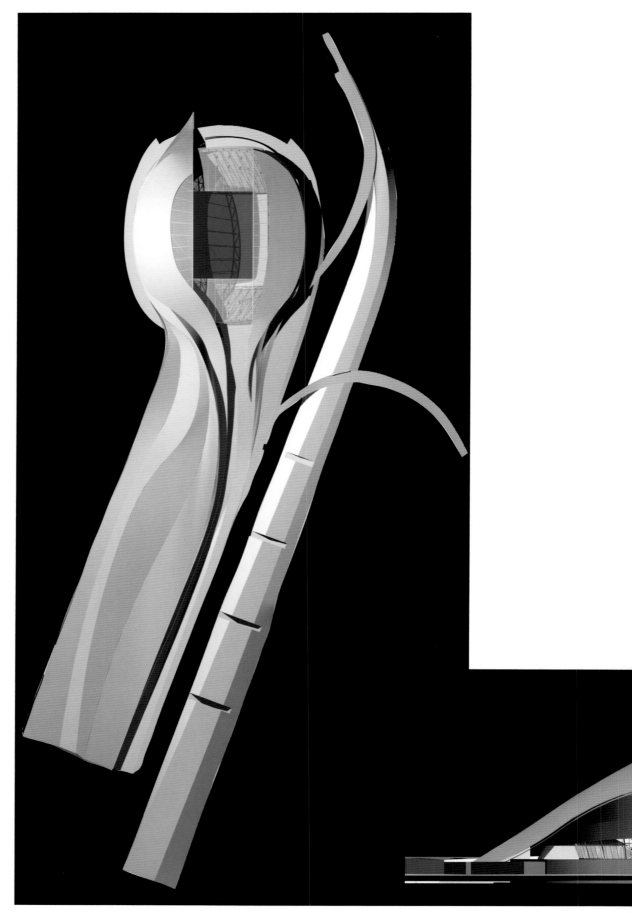

Bayern Munich Stadium

2001
Munich, Germany

Symbolism in architecture has never been literal. It has always required the imagination of the viewer to decide what an object symbolized. In public buildings, which have traditionally attempted to express through form the differences between sacred and profane, public and private, this meant producing an image of something recognizable to the general public. To provide these images with value, historical precedents were often used to relate the present-day viewer with some absolute truths of the past. This was particularly true for the stadium. In the early twentieth century, when stadiums were located in dense urban contexts, they needed some kind of iconic distinction, usually in the form of classical colonnades reminiscent of the Colosseum in Rome. The colonnade gave the sense of a public building. As cities and their suburbs expanded after World War II, stadiums moved to remote areas. Surrounded by vast parking lots, the stadium became a stand-alone object. When stadiums began to adapt to modern structural and functional requirements, the symbolic became located in the spectacle of structure, yet still stood alone in a sea of parking.

What kind of stadium is a symbol of Munich today? The symbolism of static, hierarchic forms is no longer valid. Rather, the forms of the stadium need a symbolism that is plastic, flowing, and organic; an image of mobility and movement. Starting with the great arched roof, we attempt to distance the symbol of the stadium as a centralized form of power to become one of environmental and ecological responsiveness. This proposal reconsiders not only the experience of the game but also the expectancy that builds along the approach to the stadium. This promenade allows for fans' activities not only on game days, but every day, melding the stadium into a natural flow of space and time.

Opposite: Site plan without context.
Below: Elevation drawing.

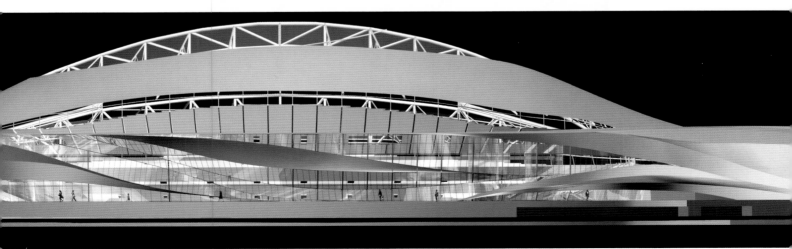

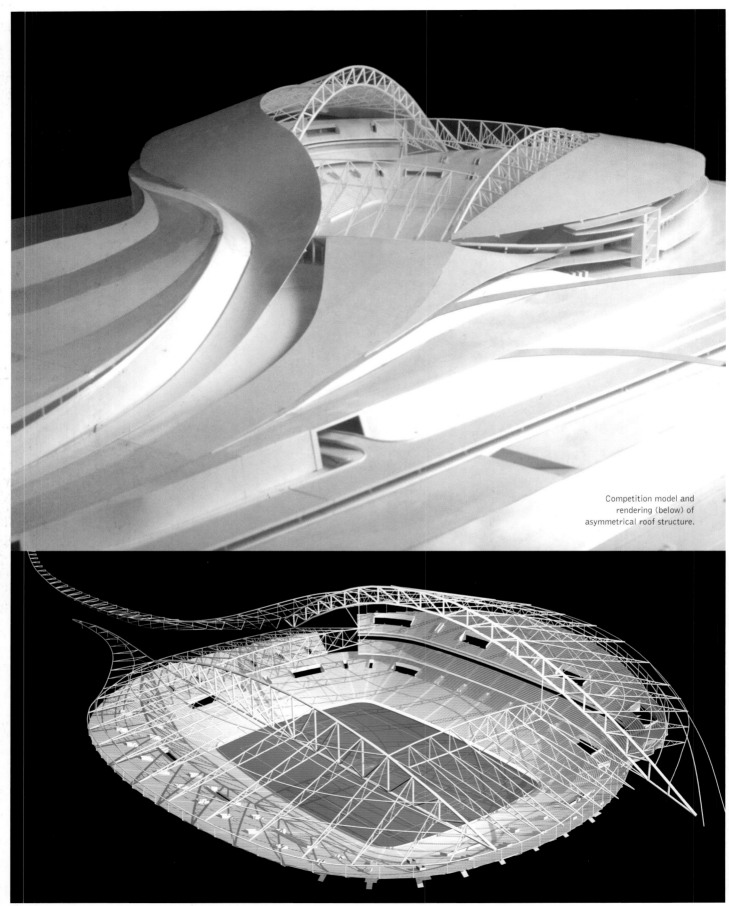

Competition model and
rendering (below) of
asymmetrical roof structure.

Site plan.

Section drawing.

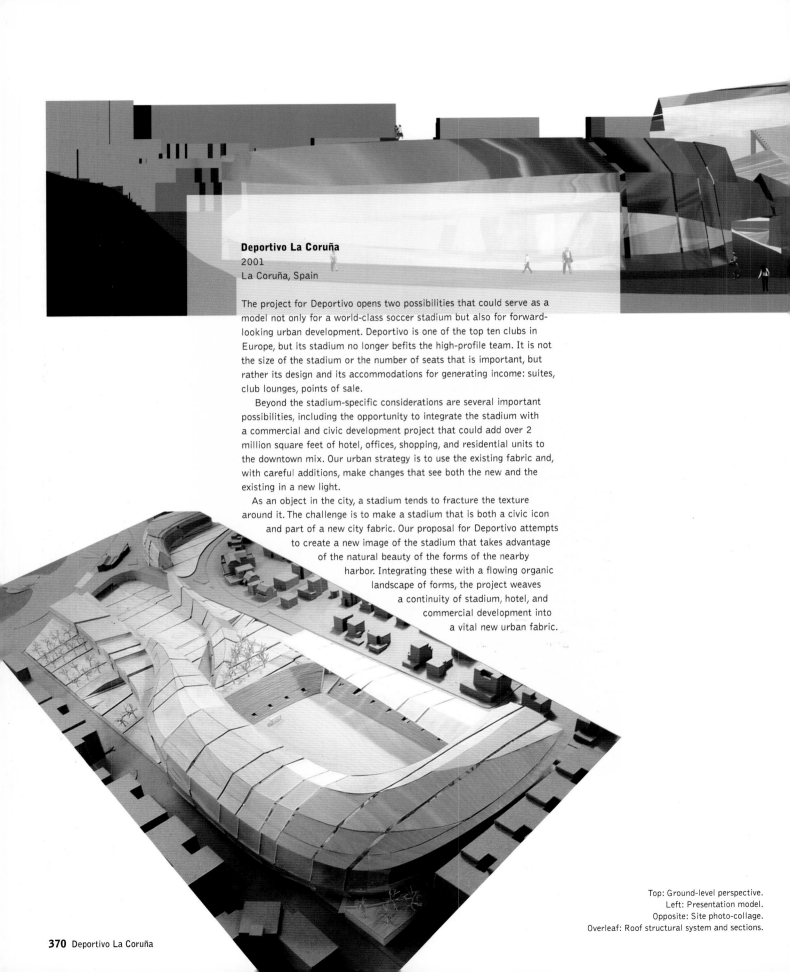

Deportivo La Coruña
2001
La Coruña, Spain

The project for Deportivo opens two possibilities that could serve as a model not only for a world-class soccer stadium but also for forward-looking urban development. Deportivo is one of the top ten clubs in Europe, but its stadium no longer befits the high-profile team. It is not the size of the stadium or the number of seats that is important, but rather its design and its accommodations for generating income: suites, club lounges, points of sale.

Beyond the stadium-specific considerations are several important possibilities, including the opportunity to integrate the stadium with a commercial and civic development project that could add over 2 million square feet of hotel, offices, shopping, and residential units to the downtown mix. Our urban strategy is to use the existing fabric and, with careful additions, make changes that see both the new and the existing in a new light.

As an object in the city, a stadium tends to fracture the texture around it. The challenge is to make a stadium that is both a civic icon and part of a new city fabric. Our proposal for Deportivo attempts to create a new image of the stadium that takes advantage of the natural beauty of the forms of the nearby harbor. Integrating these with a flowing organic landscape of forms, the project weaves a continuity of stadium, hotel, and commercial development into a vital new urban fabric.

Top: Ground-level perspective.
Left: Presentation model.
Opposite: Site photo-collage.
Overleaf: Roof structural system and sections.

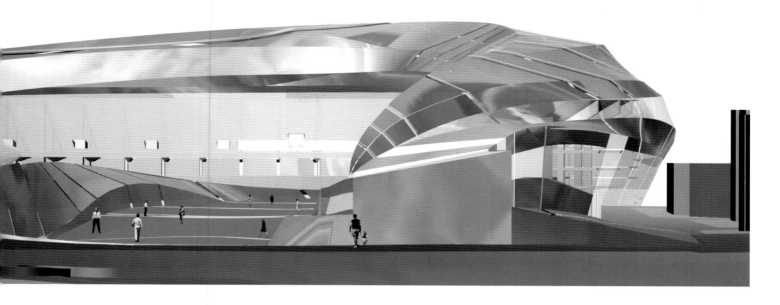

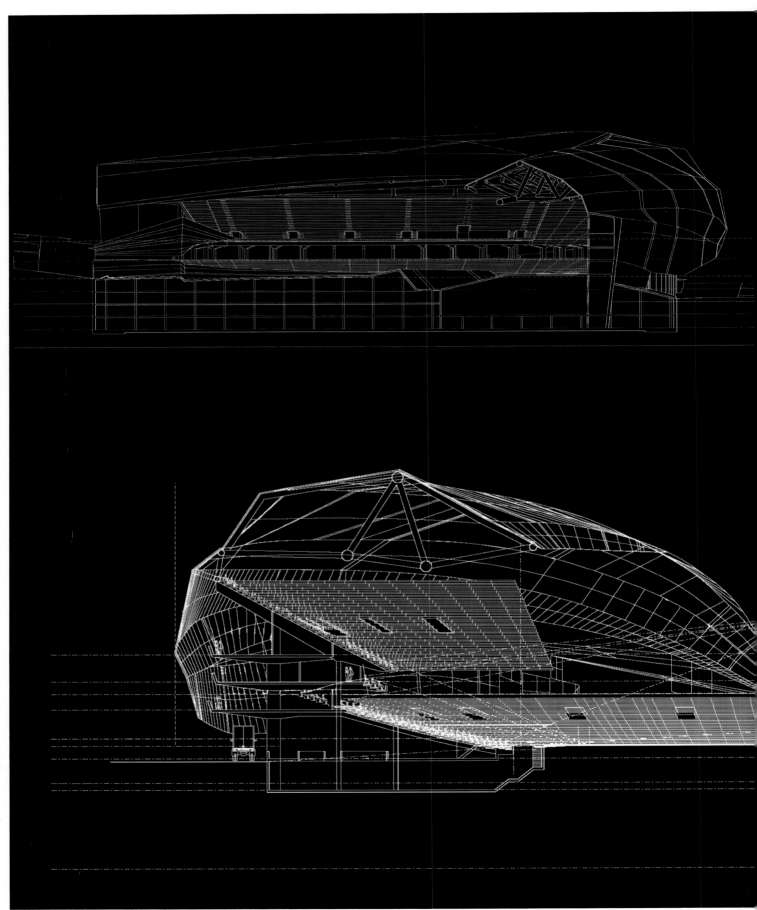

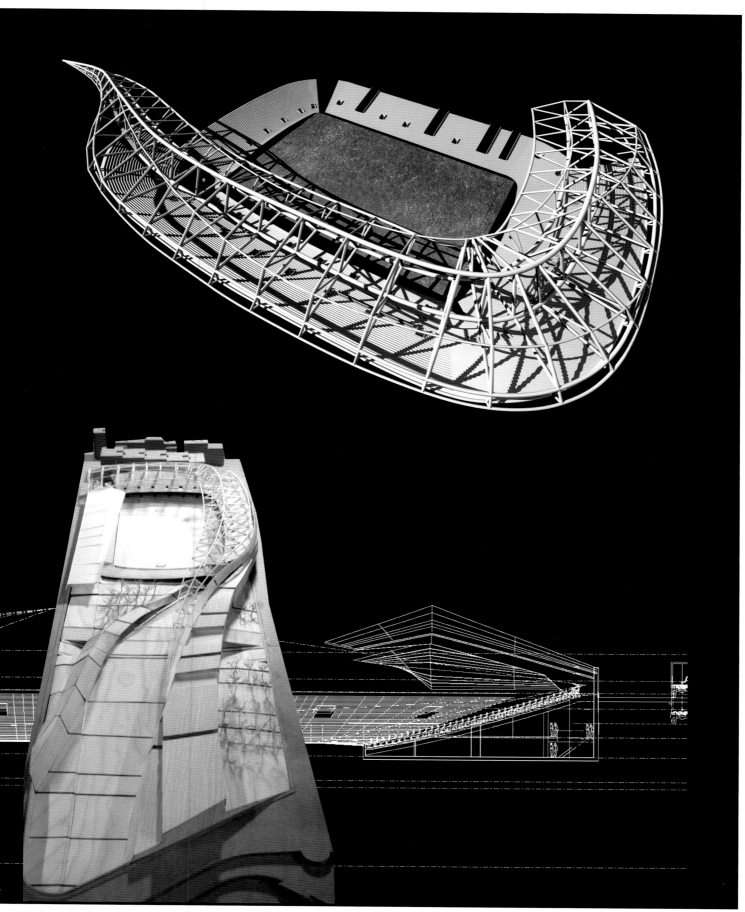

World Trade Center Innovative Design Proposal
2002
New York, New York

In the tradition of Rockefeller Center and Union Square, Peter Eisenman, Charles Gwathmey, Steven Holl, and Richard Meier proposed a great public space for New York City at the World Trade Center site. Called Memorial Square, this space is both contained and extended, symbolizing its connections to the community, the city, and the world.

The ideas of presence and absence, containment and extension, are conveyed across every element of the design proposal. The site is extended into the surrounding streets through a plan that contains a series of "fingers," reminders that the magnitude of what happened here was felt far beyond the immediate site. At the same time, the fingers facilitate pedestrian connections between Memorial Square, the Hudson River, the proposed Transit Center, and Lower Manhattan.

The granite-paved fingers orient pedestrians and enable them to enter the site above and below grade. Pedestrians from the north pass through a ceremonial gateway into Memorial Square and can then enter the Transit Center or take a stairway down to the retail concourse under the square, which also leads to commuter and subway trains.

The most visible sign of the site's renewal is the proposed hybrid buildings, which rise 1,111 feet to restore the New York skyline with geometric clarity and an image of dignity and calm. Composed of five vertical sections and interconnecting horizontal bars, each three floors deep, the two mixed-use buildings represent a new typology in skyscraper design. At grade, their forms become ceremonial gateways into the site. In their abstraction of solids and voids, the buildings seem like screens, suggesting both presence and absence, and inspiring reflection and imagination. Their cantilevered ends extend outward, like the fingers of the ground plan, reaching toward the city and each other. Nearly touching at the northeast corner of the site, they resemble the interlaced fingers of protective hands.

World Trade Center design proposal, looking southeast.

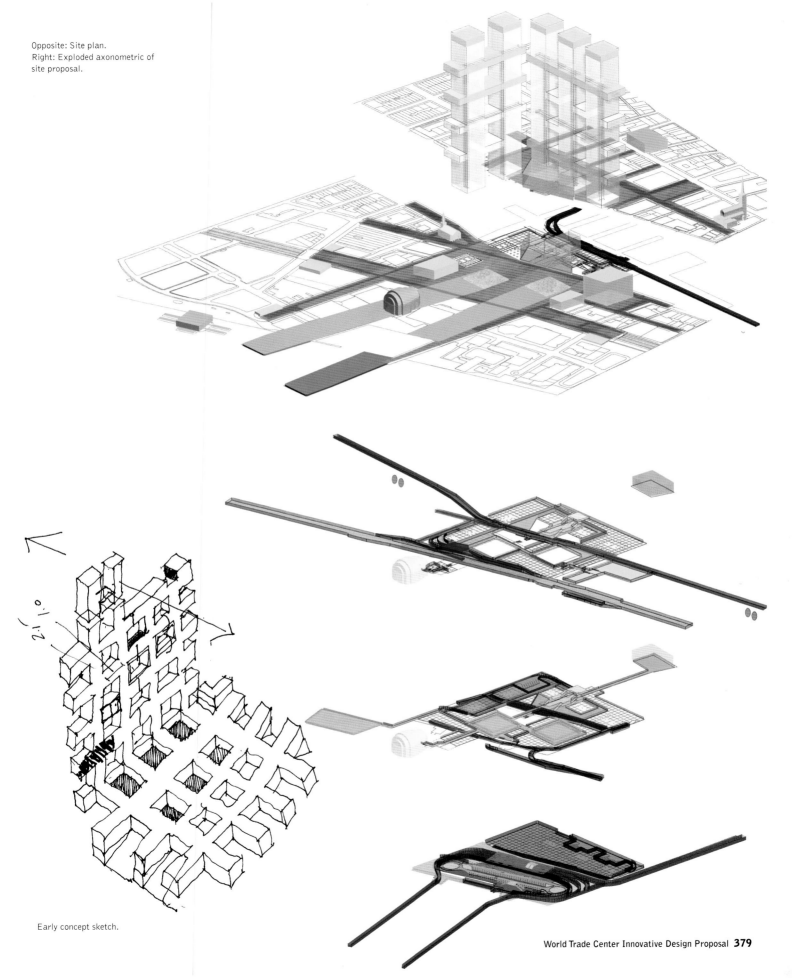

Opposite: Site plan.
Right: Exploded axonometric of
site proposal.

Early concept sketch.

Rendering of west façades. Opposite: View from Brooklyn of east elevations.

Model viewed from southwest.

Leipzig 2012 Olympic Stadium
2002
Leipzig, Germany

Our proposal for the Leipzig 2012 Olympic Games site features both a bold constructional idea for a stadium and a way to use the Elsterbecken Canal as a major design opportunity. While the canal divides the site in two, our design overcomes any apparent circulation problems and unifies the appearance of the site. Rather than design a single, signature bridge, we propose to design a lattice of bridges that creates a new central axis running north-south along either side of the canal and east-west across the waterway. This makes the canal a unique and integral figure in the massive circulation requirements for the Games. The two east-west bridges connecting the new stadium with the soccer stadium, basketball arena, and swimming venue will remain after the Olympic stadium has been returned to its 20,000-seat legacy mode. The long axis of the waterway bridge will be terminated at the northern end with a water feature.

The Leipzig Olympic Stadium is designed with sixteen temporary stadium pods, each holding 4,000 seats. These temporary stands are covered with distinctive roof structures and are economical to erect and disassemble. Circulation throughout the site is contained and controlled by functional and decorative landscaped earthworks. These extend from the soccer stadium berm to the tram station, crossing over and under the east-west connections to the swimming and basketball venues. The entire site plan forms a single unique image that could symbolize the Olympics in Leipzig: a city of bridges, a bridge between nations.

Study model.

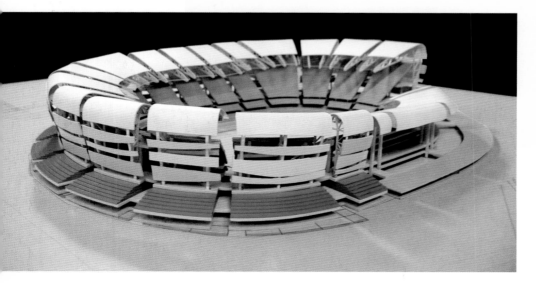

Opposite and below: Site plan and Olympic stadium plans.

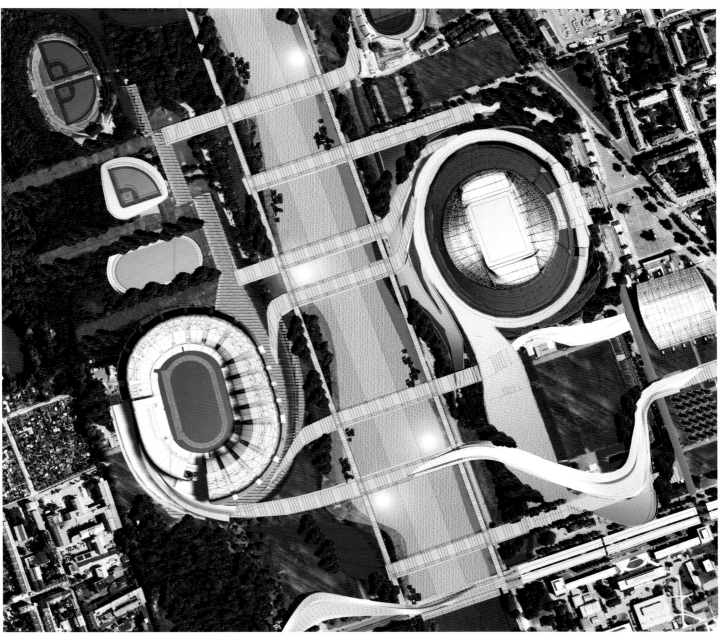

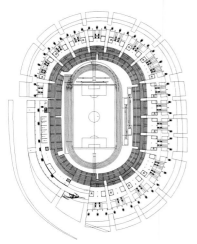

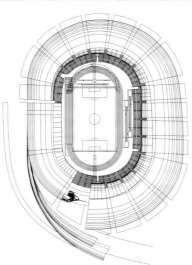

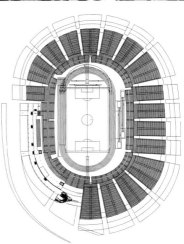

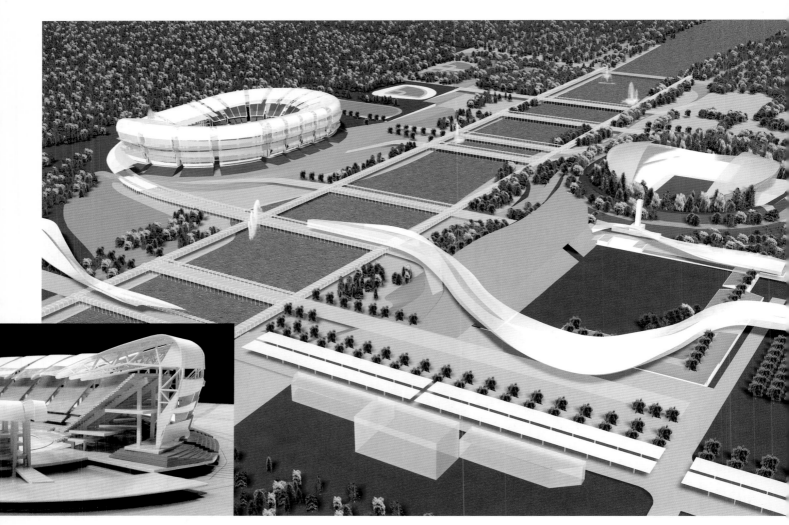

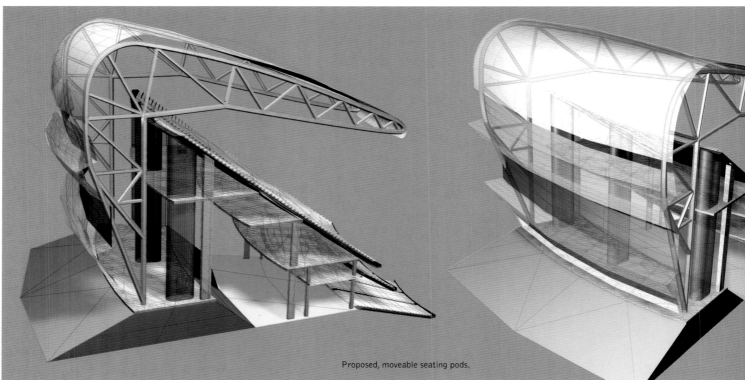

Proposed, moveable seating pods.

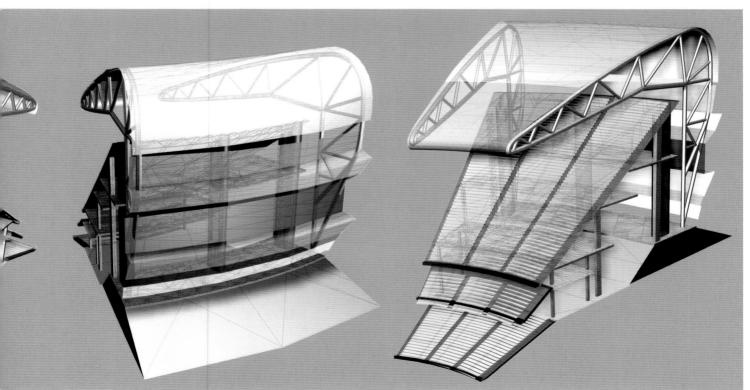

Giuseppe Sanmartino, **Veiled Christ** (detail) at Sansevero Chapel, Naples.

Naples Railway Station Competition
2003
Afragola, Italy

What distinguishes our project for the Nuova Stazione AV Napoli Afragola from other contemporary rail terminals, even distinguishes it from our own previous work, and what makes it distinctly Neapolitan is its sensuous lyricism. Our project combines structural invention and functional precision to produce a contemporary organicism that is an integral condition of both its symbolic form and its successful operation. Our objective is to produce a station that will symbolize not only the technology and speed of the railroad but also the Naples of history and the Naples of tomorrow in all its manifest complexity.

The sculptor Giuseppe Sanmartino captured in the Sansevero Chapel a spirit that was and is Naples. His **Veiled Christ** sculpture captures a sensibility that is distinctly Neapolitan, the veil simultaneously covering and revealing, thus becoming a subtle, ambiguous diaphragm. We attempt to capture this ambiguity and translucency, suspended between reality and a mysterious feeling of the sacred, in our project. As with Sanmartino's layered work in marble, the project embodies the familiar and the unfamiliar. There are aspects of structure, space, and form, which one knows from existing and past railroad stations, as well as new, unexpected, and original elements.

The station erupts from the flat Pianura Campana, seemingly heaving back the fields and orchards of the valley. The surrounding fields at times form unusual relationships to the roads and buildings. The structure is rational and fluid. Trains and automobiles glide between and under the system of great tubes, which frames a commanding view of Vesuvius. A unique, recognizable image on the landscape, the station both mirrors and complements the linear nature of the high-speed train.

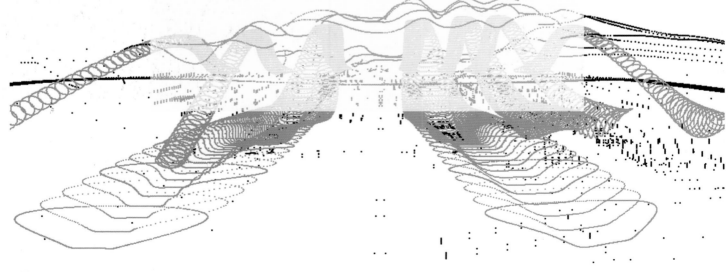

Competition model and landscape proposal.

Model detail.
Rendering of station with platforms and trains.

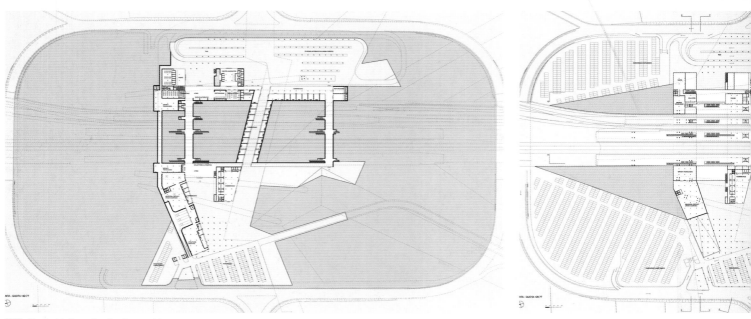

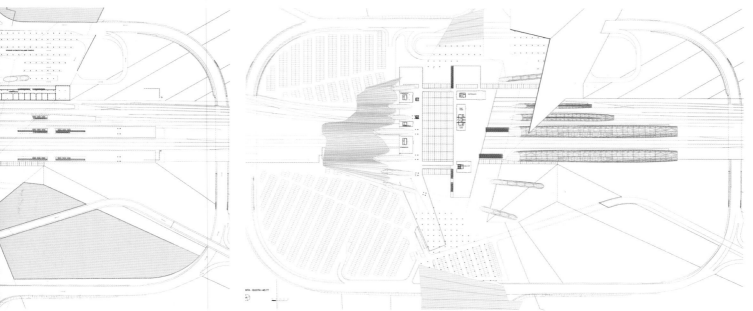

View out of station toward Vesuvius.

Longitudinal section.

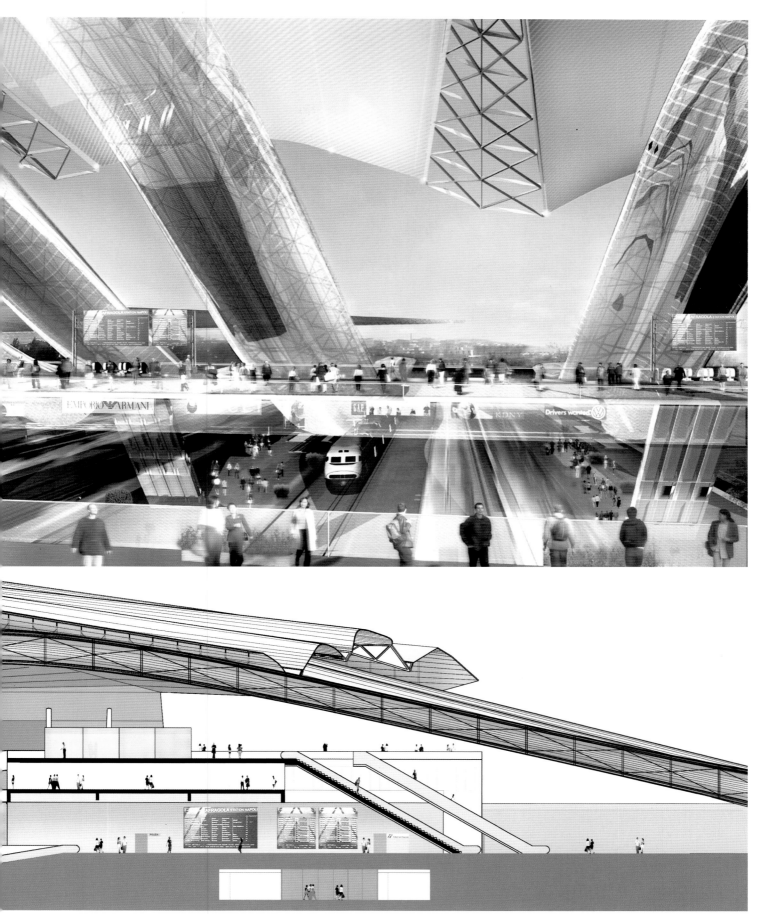

Il Giardino dei Passi Perduti
2004–2005
Verona, Italy

When considering ways to have a dialogue with the work of Carlo Scarpa at Castelvecchio, we chose to demonstrate that the struggle over seemingly disparate paths also represents a search for an internal disciplinary logic for architecture. This reflection would be an amalgam of projects and their critical reflections, an excessive "hypertext," as it were, combining text and objects beyond the limits of their former textuality. It would attempt to reinvent the project as a metacritical one, an idea that is more problematic, but also more realizable, because it must address the fragmentary and the poetic aspects of Scarpa's work.

The exhibition itself is a project located as a didactic work in the garden and as a fragmentary work in the galleries. Scarpa placed striated concrete floors in the five interior exhibition rooms. These five squares are replaced in the garden as five "excavated" pads, located on an axis parallel to the internal sequence of rooms. A second, Eisenman axis moves diagonally across the garden, intersecting with and crossing over Scarpa's pads. It keys off the rotated room at the end of Scarpa's sequence of spaces, suggesting that the skewed axis preexisted. The concrete pads are revealed as one moves from Scarpa's corner bridge toward the museum entry. The pads crack open to reveal an amalgam of Eisenman projects – Cannaregio [76], IBA Social Housing [80], the Wexner Center for the Arts [112], the Musée du Quai Branly [304], and The City of Culture of Galicia [308] – which erupt out of the ground with a Proustian quality of "time regained."

Inside, the fragmentary nature of the project pieces confronts Scarpa and his thematics. These fragments of the "excavated" grid of Berlin and the Cartesian grid of Santiago, painted red, appear as a series of poetic residues in the interstices between Scarpa's floors and the walls of the castle. Here, as in the garden, time becomes part of a network of crossing paths to a past and future place. The work is no longer a museum exhibition (an exhibition in a museum) but rather a transformation of the nature of the museum itself.

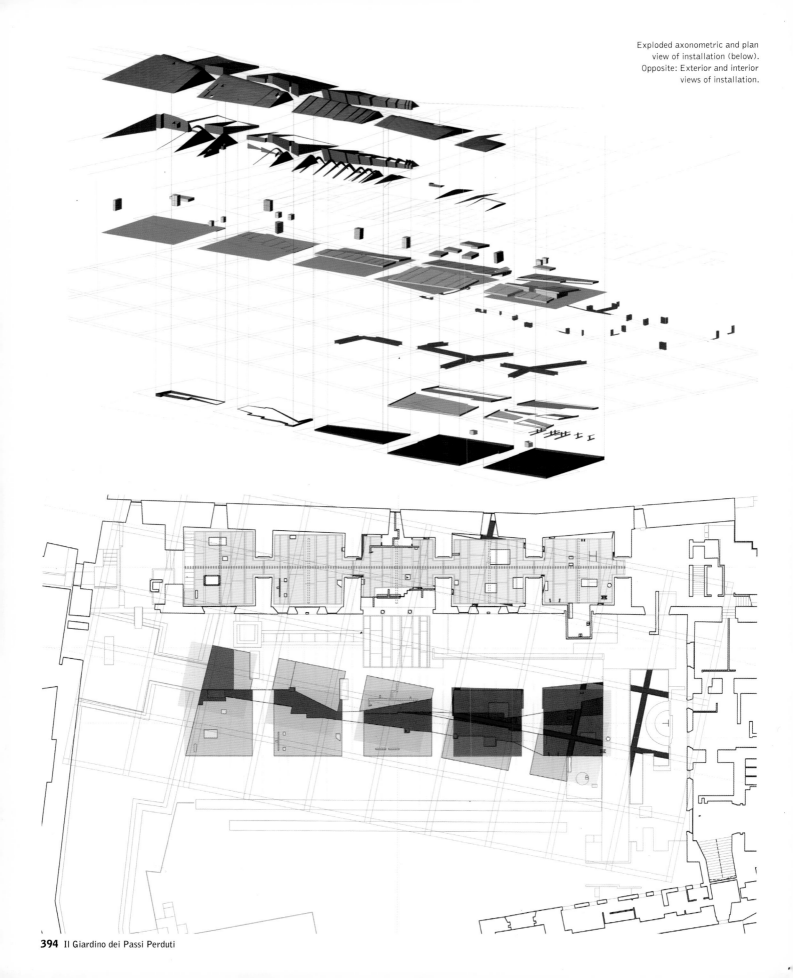

Exploded axonometric and plan
view of installation (below).
Opposite: Exterior and interior
views of installation.

Complete Projects List

* denotes built work

<u>Peter Eisenman, Architect</u>

Liverpool Cathedral
Competition
1960
Liverpool, England

Boston City Hall
Competition
1961
Boston, Massachusetts
(with Anthony Eardley)

Boston Architectural Center
Competition
1963
Boston, Massachusetts
(with Michael Graves)

The American Institute of
Architects Headquarters
Competition
1964
Washington, D.C.
(with Michael Graves)

Jersey Corridor Project:
A Case Study of a Linear
City in the Jersey Corridor
between New York and
Philadelphia 1964–1966
(with Anthony Eardley and
Michael Graves)

Arts Center Competition
1965
University of California
(with Michael Graves)

Manhattan Waterfront
Project
1966
New York, New York
Museum of Modern Art
(with Michael Graves)

* House I
1967–1968
Princeton, New Jersey
Mr. and Mrs. Bernard
M. Barenholz

Townhouse Project
1968
Princeton, New Jersey

* House II
1969–1970
Hardwick, Vermont
Mr. and Mrs. Richard Falk

* House III
1969–1971
Lakeville, Connecticut
Mr. and Mrs. Robert Miller

House IV
1971
Falls Village, Connecticut

House V
1972

* House VI
1972–1975
Cornwall, Connecticut
Mr. and Mrs. Richard Frank

Low-Rise High-Density
Housing
1973
Staten Island, New York
New York State Urban
Development Corporation

House VIII
1973

House X
1975
Bloomfield Hills, Michigan
Mr. and Mrs. Arnold
Aronoff

House 11a
1978
Palo Alto, California
Mr. and Mrs. Forster

Cannaregio Town Square
1978
Venice, Italy
Municipal Government
of Venice

House El even Odd
1980

<u>Eisenman Robertson
Architects</u>

Pioneer Courthouse Square
Competition
1980
Portland, Oregon

* Madison Components
Plant
1981–1982
Madison, Indiana
Cummins Engine Company

* New Brunswick
Theological Seminary
1981–1982
New Brunswick, New Jersey
New Brunswick Theological
Seminary

* IBA Social Housing
1981–1985
Berlin, West Germany
Hauert Noack, GmbH &
Company

Beverly Hills Civic Center
1982
Beverly Hills. California

* Travelers Financial Center
1983–1986
Hempstead, New York
Fair Oaks Development and

Schottenstein Properties
(with Trott & Bean
Architects, Columbus, Ohio)

* Firehouse for Engine
Company 233 and Ladder
Company 176
1983–1985
Brooklyn, New York
The City of New York

Fin d'Ou T Hou S
1983

* Wexner Center for the
Visual Arts and Fine Arts
Library
1983–1989
Columbus, Ohio
The Ohio State University

Moving Arrows, Eros, and
Other Errors
Romeo + Juliet
1985
Verona, Italy

Tokyo Opera House
Competition
1985
Tokyo, Japan

Cite Unseen II
1985
Milan, Italy
XV Triennale di Milano

* Tableware
1986
Swid Powell

* Hardware
1986
Franz Schneider Brakel
Gmbh & Co.

* Jewelry
1986
Cleto Munari

Biocentrum
1987
Frankfurt am Main, West
Germany
J. W. Goethe University

* Fuller Toms Loft
1987
New York, New York
Ms. Fuller/Mr. Toms

La Villette
1987
Paris, France
Etablissement Public du
Parc de la Vilette

EuroDisney Hotel
1987
Paris, France
Disney Development
Company

University Art Museum
1986
Long Beach, California
California State University
at Long Beach

Progressive Corporation
Office Building
1986
Cleveland, Ohio
Progressive Corporation

Museum of Futurism
1986
Rovereto, Italy

House
1986
Palm Beach, Florida
Mr. Leslie Wexner

<u>Eisenman Architects</u>

Technology Center Master
Plan
1987–1988
Pittsburgh, Pennsylvania
Carnegie Mellon University/
University of Pittsburgh

Carnegie Mellon Research
Institute
1987–1989
Pittsburgh, Pennsylvania
Carnegie Mellon University

Oxford Office Building
1987–1989
Pittsburgh, Pennsylvania
Oxford Development
Corporation

Guardiola House
1988
Cadiz, Spain
D. Javier Guardiola

* Aronoff Center for Design
and Art
1988–1996
Cincinnati, Ohio
University of Cincinnati

* Koizumi Sangyo
Corporation Headquarters
Building
1988–1990
Tokyo, Japan
Koizumi Sangyo
Corporation

Monte Paschi Bank
Competition
1988
Siena, Italy
Siena Chamber of
Commerce

Residential Building
1988
The Hague, The Netherlands
200,000th Home Housing
Festival

Banyoles Olympic Hotel
1989
Banyoles, Spain
Consorci Pel
Desenvolupament De La Vila
Olimpica

The Cooper Union Student
Housing
1989
New York, New York
The Cooper Union

Zoetermeer Houses
1989
The Netherlands
Geerlings Vastgoed B.V.,
J.G.A. Geerlings

* Groningen Music-Video
Pavilion
1990
Groningen, the Netherlands
Groningen City Festival

* Nunotani Corporation
Headquarters Building
1990–1992
Tokyo, Japan
Nunotani Corporation

* Greater Columbus
Convention Center
1990–1993
Columbus, Ohio
Greater Columbus
Convention Center Authority

Atocha 123 Hotel
1990–1993
Madrid, Spain
Sociedad Belga de Los
Pinares De el Paular

Rebstockpark Master Plan
1990–1991
Frankfurt, Germany
City of Frankfurt, Dieter
Bock, and Buropark an der
Frankfurter Messe GdR

* Knoll Textiles
1990
The Knoll Group

Alteka Office Building
1991
Tokyo, Japan
Alteka Corporation

Center for the Arts
1991
Atlanta, Georgia
Emory University

The Max Reinhardt Haus
1992
Berlin, Germany
Advanta Management AG,
Dieter Bock OSTINVEST,
Klaus-Peter Junge and
Dieter Klaus

Nördliches Derendorf
Master Plan Competition
1992
Düsseldorf, Germany
City of Düsseldorf Planning
Department

Advanta Haus
1992
Berlin, Germany
Advanta Management AG,
Dieter Bock

Zurich Insurance
Headquarters Study
1992
Frankfurt, Germany
Buropark an der Frankfurter
Messe

Friedrichstrasse Competition
1992–1993
Berlin, Germany
Advanta Management AG
and Ostinvest

Magdeburg, Damaschkeplatz
II
1993
Magdeburg, Germany
Hauert and Noack GMBH
& Co.

Haus Immendorff
1993
Düsseldorf, Germany
Professor Jörg Immendorff

* Cities of Artificial
Excavation
1993–1994
Montreal, Canada
Canadian Centre for
Architecture

* Cities of Artificial
Excavation
1995
Madrid, Spain

Tours Regional Music
Conservatory and
Contemporary Arts Center
Competition
1993–1994
Tours, France
City of Tours
(With Jean Yves Barrier
Architect)

Celebration Fire Station
1995
Orlando, Florida
Disney Development
Company

Celebration Day Care Center
1995
Orlando, Florida
Disney Development
Company

The New National Museum
of Korea
1995
Seoul, Korea

Place des Nations Master
Plan
1995
Geneva, Switzerland

* Architecture of Display
1995
New York, New York
Comme des Garçons, The
Architectural League

Klingelhöfer-Dreieck
Housing
1995
Berlin, Germany

Monument and Memorial
Site Dedicated
to the Jewish Victims of
the Nazi Regime in Austria
1938–1945
1995–1996
Vienna, Austria

La Triennale di Milano
1995–1996
Milan, Italy

Church of the Year 2000
1996
Rome, Italy

BFL Software, Ltd.
Headquarters Building
1996
Bangalore, India
BFL Software, Ltd.

The Jewish Museum of San
Francisco
1996
San Francisco, California

Bibliothèque de L'IHUEI
1996–1997
Geneva, Switzerland
L'Etat de Genève

J C Decaux Bus Shelter
1996
Aachen, Germany
J C Decaux

Virtual House Competition
1997
Berlin, Germany
FSB Corporation

Student Center Competition
1997–1998
Chicago, Illinois
Illinois Institute of
Technology

Staten Island Institute for
Arts and Sciences
1997–2001 (canceled after
9/11/01 for lack of funding)

Staten Island, New York
Staten Island Institute for
Arts and Sciences

TSA/Cardinals Multipurpose
Stadium
1997–present
Tempe, Arizona
Arizona Cardinals

Hockey Arena
1998
Long Island, New York
Huber, Hunt & Nichols

Rutgers University
Basketball Arena
New Brunswick, New Jersey
1998

Memorial to the Murdered
Jews of Europe
1998–2005
Berlin, Germany
Federal Republic of
Germany

Bruges Concert Hall
Competition
1998–1999
Bruges, Belgium
City of Bruges

Razorback Stadium
Expansion
1998–1999
Fayetteville, Arkansas
University of Arkansas

* Columbus Convention
Center Expansion
1998–2000
Columbus, OH
Greater Columbus
Convention Center Authority

IFCCA Prize Competition
for the Design of Cities
1999
New York, New York
Canadian Centre for
Architecture

Cidade da Cultura de Galicia
1999–present
Santiago de Compostela,
Spain
Xunta de Galicia

Musée du Quai Branly
1999
Paris, France
La Ville de Paris

Museum of Arts and Digital
Arts
Hsinchu, Taiwan
1999

Spree Dreieck Tower
2000–present
Berlin, Germany

Carnegie Science Center
2000
Pittsburgh, PA
Carnegie Science Center

Parramatta Rail Link
(With DesignInc 2000)
2000
Parramatta, Australia
State of New South Wales

Eindhoven
2000–present
Eindhoven, The Netherlands
City of Eindhoven

FSM East River Project
2001
New York, New York
FSM East River Associates
LLC

Musée des Confluences
2001
Lyon, France
Counseil Général du Rhône

Neues Fussball Stadion in
München
(with HOK Sport)
2001
Munich, Germany

Deportivo at La Coruña
2001–present
La Coruña, Spain
Deportivo

Memorial Square
World Trade Center
Innovative Design Proposal
2002
New York, New York
Lower Manhattan
Development Corporation

Leipzig Olympic Park 2012
(with HOK Sport + Venue +
Event, London)
2002
Leipzig, Germany
Leipzig, Freistaat Sachsen
und Partnerstädte GmbH

Multipurpose Sport Complex
Manzanares Park
Madrid, Spain
2002

Napoli TAV Station
2003
Napoli, Italy

Perth Amboy High School
2003–4
Perth Amboy, New Jersey

Guangdong Museum (New)
2003–4
Guangzhou, China

Se-Woon District #4 Urban
Redevelopment

Seoul, South Korea
2004

Il Giardino dei Passi Perduti
Museo di Castelvecchio
Verona, Italy
26 June 2004 – May 2005

Bibliography

The Formal Basis of
Modern Architecture.
Ph.D. diss., University of
Cambridge, 1963.

Five Architects: Eisenman,
Graves, Gwathmey, Hejduk,
Meier. New York: Oxford
University Press, 1975.
Peter Eisenman et al.

The Wexner Center for
the Visual Arts: Ohio
State University. New
York: Rizzoli, 1989. Peter
Eisenman, with Anthony
Vidler and Rafael Moneo.

Peter Eisenman & Frank
Gehry. New York: Rizzoli,
1991. Catalog for the Fifth
International Exhibition of
Architecture at the 1991
Venice Biennale.

Re:Working Eisenman.
London: Academy Editions/
Ernst & Sohn, 1993.
Andrew Benjamin, ed.

Peter Eisenman: Opere e
progetti. Serie Documenti
di Architettura, No. 71,
Milan: Electa, 1993. Pippo
Ciorra, ed.

Cities of Artificial
Excavation: The Work of
Peter Eisenman, 1978–
1988. New York: Rizzoli
International, Ltd., and
Montréal: Centre Canadien
d'Architecture, 1994. Jean-
François Bedard, ed.

Eisenman Architects:
Selected and Current Works.
Master Architect Series.
Mulgrave, Australia: Images
Publishing, 1995. Stephen
Dobney, ed.

M Emory Games: Emory
Center for the Arts. New
York: Rizzoli, 1995. Peter
Eisenman, ed.

Eleven Authors in Search
of a Building: The Aronoff
Center for Design and Art at
The University of Cincinnati.
New York: Monacelli Press,
1996. Cynthia Davidson, ed.

Chora L Works: Jacques
Derrida and Peter
Eisenman. New York:
Monacelli Press, 1997.
Jeffrey Kipnis and Thomas
Leeser, eds.

Diagram Diaries.
Peter Eisenman, with
introduction by R.E. Somol.
New York: Universe and
London: Thames & Hudson,
1999.

Eisenman Digitale. Digital
Eisenman: An Office
of The Electronic Era.
Basel; Boston: Birkhauser-
Publishers for Architecture,
1999. Luca Galofaro.

Blurred Zones:
Investigations of the
Interstitial: Eisenman
Architects 1988–1998. New
York: Monacelli Press, 2003.
Cynthia Davidson, ed.

Giuseppe Terragni:
Transformations,
Decompositions, Critiques.
New York: Monacelli Press,
2003.

Eisenman Inside Out:
Selected Writings,
1963–1988. New Haven:
Yale University Press, 2004.
Mark Rakatansky, ed.

Die Formale Grundlage
der Modernen Architektur.
Berlin: Gebr. Mann, 2004.
Peter Eisenman, with
introduction by Werner
Oechslin.

Peter Eisenman: Barefoot
on White-Hot Walls. Vienna:
Hatje Cantz, 2005. Peter
Noever, ed.

The Formal Basis of
Modern Architecture.
Baden: Lars Müller
Publishers, 2006.

Contributors

Emily Abruzzo
Francesca Acerboni
Gianluca Adami
Barbera Aderbeauer
Yota Adilenidou
Karina Aicher
James Alexander Jr.
Franco Alloca
Jean-Paul Amato
Tobias Amme
Sam Anderson
Michelle Andrew
Susumu Arasaki
Ted Arleo
Arcand Arnold
Tracy Aronoff
Diego Arraigada
Alper Aytac
Philip Babb
Larissa Babij
Lars Bachmann
Joseph M. Bailey
Arthur Baker
Agustin Balangione
Charles Barclay
Donna Barry
Andrew Bartle
David Beers
Hans-Georg Berndsen
Markus Beuerlein
Federico Beulcke
Neeraj Bhatia
David Biagi
Hervé Biele
Armand Biglari
Rony Bitan
Francois Blanciak
Andres Blanco
Jasmijn Bleijerveld
Lawrence Blough
Walter Wulf Boettger
Volker Bollig
Pornchai Boonsom
Karolina Boruch
Massimiliano Bosio
Joachim Bothe
Sylvain Boulanger
Sergio Bregante
Marc Breitler
Sam Britton
Andrea Brown
James Brown
Anja Brueggemann
Mick Fischer Brunkow
Andrew Buchsbaum
David Buege
Frederico Buelcke
Michael Burkey
Andrew Burmeister
Harvey Burns
Francine Cadogan
Matteo Cainer
Gustavo Calazans
Marta Caldeira
Yolanda do Campo
Kristina Cantwell

Frederico Cappellina
Edward Carroll
Arturo Carulla
Jeremy Carvalho
Michael Casey
Ronald Castellano
Francisco Ceballos
Juliette Cezzar
Christopher Chan
Hui-Min Chan
Chi Yi Chang
Christine Chang
Pu Chen
Danny Chiang
Frank Chirico
Robert Choeff
Jean Choi
Julia Suna Choi
Stephanie Choi
Michal Cieszewski
David Clark
Adriana Cobo
Donna Cohen
Rosa-Maria Colina
Catherine Colla
Stefano Colombo
Sarah Connoly
Julia Conradi
Libby Cooper
Vincent Costa
Lise Anne Couture
Wendy Cox
Edgar Cozzio
Charles Crawford
Nestor Crubellati
John Curran
Yvonne Dahl
Christophe Dahm
Cynthia Davidson
Jean-Cédric de Foy
Jasón Deboer
Nina Delius
Michael Denkel
Larry Dennedy
Hernan Diaz Alonso
Constantin Doehler
Cees Donkers
Stanislas Dorin
Ken Doyno
Winka Dubbeldam
Daniel Dubowitz
Michael Duncan
Ellen Dunham
John Durschinger
Arthur Dyess
Michael Eastwood
Hayley Eber
Mats Edlund
David Efaw
Guillaume Ehrman
David Eisenmann
Alexa Eissfeldt
Erkan Emre
Rajip Erdem
Manou Ernster
Andrea Etspueler
Sergio S. Falatiski
Christiane Fashek

Sabine Feil
Abigail Feinerman
Ralf Feldmeier
Simon Fellmeth
Martin Felsen
Elena Fernandez
Scott Ferris
Karsten Fiebiger
Lars Filmann
Gunter Filz
Gunther Filz-Di
Andrea Fischer
Juliane Fischer
Jerome Flynn
Mathew Ford
Bobby Fogel
Jean-Pierre Fontanot
Tom Frantzen
David Fratianne
Brenden Frederick
Reid Freeman
Jason Frontera
Minoru Fuji
Chieko Furukawa
Sophie Lamort de
  Gail
Marco Galofaro
Carolina Garcia
Chris Garcia
Luis Garcia
John Garra
Sigrid Geerlings
Judy Geib
Andri Gerber
Claudia Gerhäusser
Lihi Gerstner
James Gettinger
Fabio Ghersi
Diana Giambiagi
Benjamin Gianni
Brad Gildea
Daisy Ginsberg
Jorg Gleiter
Joseph Godlewski
Monika Goebel
Eric Goldemberg
Nazli Gonensay
Mercedes Gonzalez
Jakimovska Gordana
Lilach Safran Gorfung
David Goth
Mara Graham
Shany Granek
Susanne Grau
Stephen Griek
Felipe Guardiola
John Gulliford
Christian Guttack
Nicholas Haagensen
Judith Haase
Daniel Hale
Jan-Henrik Hansen
Jim Harrell
Jan Hartman
John Peter Hartman
Helena Van gen
  Hassend
Silke Haupt

Sandra Hemingway
Claudia Hirsemann
Jean Paul Hitiipeuw
Julia Hochgesand
Bart Hollanders
Matthias Hollwich
Tina Holmboe
Robert Holten
Norbert Holthausen
Nadine Homann
Jethro Hon
Amber Hong
Kelly Hopkin
Martin Houston
Kimberley Hoyt
Chien-Ho Hsu
Frances Hsu
Simon Hubacher
Lloyd Huber
Peter Hufer
Joanne Humphries
Richard Hunt
Thomas Hut
Timothy Hyde
Claire Hyland
Diana Ibrahim
Ricardo Gardenas
  Infante
Thomas Ingledue
Kazuhiro Isimaru
Antoinette Jackson
Lewis Jacobsen
Gordana Jakimovska
Nikola Jarosch
Matthias Javernik
Zheng Ji
Sang-Wook Jin
Rasmus Joergensen
Mathew Jogan
David Johnson
Jeffrey Johnson
Brian Jones
Wes Jones
Philippe Jouanneault
Ena Jung
Jan Jurgens
John Juryj
Annette Kahler
Keelan Kaiser
Rudolph Kammeri
Rachel Kaplan
Sofia Karim
Orit Kaufman
Patrick Keane
James Keen
May Kellner
Therese Kelly
Gwendolyn
  Kerschbaumer
Inka Kersting
George Kewin
Bradley Khouri
Marina Kieser
Jörg Kiesow
Andre Kikoski
Kojiro Kitayama
Christopher Kitterman
Rebecca Klapper

Jan Kleihues
Holger Kleine
Tom Kleinman
Susan Knauer
Tanya Koch
Selim Koder
Christian Kohl
Yuhang Kong
Hyunah Kook
David Koons
Erin Korff
Justin Korhammer
Bernard Kormoss
Rolando Kraeher
Kenneth Kraus
Miroslaw Krawczynski
Shirley Kressel
Tilman Kriesel
Hiroyuki Kubodera
Szymon Kuczinsky
Lucas Kueng
Richard Labonte
Lorenzina Laera
Abhijeet Lakhia
Oliver Lang
Christian Lange
Thomas Lanzelotti
Bernadette Latour
Joseph Lau
Maria Laurent
Jakob Ohm Laursen
Vincent Le Feuvre
Dirk LeBlanc
Joseph Lechowicz
Helen J. Lee
Jeanne Lee
John Leeper
Thomas Leeser
Fabian Lemmel
David Lessard
Jorg Lesser
Luc Levesque
Frédéric Levrat
Andrew Liang
Stephano Libardi
Alexandra Ligotti
Jim Linke
Ingel Liou
Jung Kue Liou
Peter Lopez
Pablo Lorenzo-Eiroa
Philip Loskant
Yanni Loukissas
Gregory Luhan
James Luhur
N G Yat Lun
Claudine Lutolf
Greg Lynn
Yangsong Ma
George Mahnke
Jake Malis
Jon Malis
Dean Maltz
David Mancino
Vera Marjanovic
Marisabel Marratt
Lucia Martinez
Ceu Martinez

Hiroshi Maruyama
Jonathan Marvel
Anne Marx
Paola Marzatico
Mark Mascheroni
Nuno Mateus
Audrey Matlock
Dominik Mayer
Madelaine Mayer
John Maze
Heidi McCahan
Mark McCarthy
James McCrery
Michael McDonald
Megan McFarland
Michael McInturf
Mary Jane McRory
Carolin Mees
Maria Menrique
Gregory Merryweather
Kathleen Meyer
Steven Meyer
Will Meyer
Magdalena Miladovski
Gianluca Milesi
Kevin Miller
Benedicte Mioli
Edward Mitchell
Joseph Mitlo
Sebastian
    Mittendorfer
Itaru Miyakawa
Milisani Mniki
Julian Monfort
David Moore
Ivan Morales
Graeme Morland
Richard Morris
Michael Morrow
Alexis Moser
Michel Mossessian
Tamihiro Motozawa
Jacobo Muelas
Philipp Muessigmann
Matthias Muffert
Jennifer Mujat-Kearns
Max Muller
Michael Muroff
David Murphee
Maureen Murphy-
    Ochsner
Matias Musacchio
Karim Musfy
Elizabeth Muske
Corrine Nacinovic
Murali Nallamothu
John Nambu
Kristi Nelson
Jean-Gabriel
    Neukomn
Yasmin Nicoucar
Raphael Niogret
Fabio Nonis
Marlin Nowbakht
Jean Nukomn
Alex Nussbaumer
Patrick O'Brien
Joan Ockman

Yayoi Ogo
Doug Oliver
Sheri O'Oreilly
Elisa Rosana Orlanski
Antonio di Oronzo
Joseph Ostrafi
Olivier Ottevaere
Elizabeth Pacot
Katherina Panagiotou
Debbie Park
Sojin Park
Celine Parmentier
Boris Paschotta
Maria-Rita Perbellini
Daniel Perez
Ivan Pazos Perez
Tony Pergola
Matteo Pericoli
Raleigh Perkins
Astrid Perlbinder
Anne Peters
Kai Peterson
Emmanuel Petit
Damian Petrescu
Sven Pfeiffer
Bernd Pflumm
Angela Phillips
Maria Florencia Pita
Anna Pla
Karen Pollock
Christian Pongratz
Tom Popoff
Silke Potting
Justine Poy
Paul Preissner
Christi Raber
Carlene Ramus
Axel Rauenbusch
Rachel Ravitz
Ali Reza Razavi
Jurgen Reimann
Mirko Reinecke
Sasha Reinking
Wolfgang Rettenmaier
David Richardson
Jeremy Ricketts
David Ricon
Jens Riehl
Tilo Ries
Stefania Rinaldi
Giovanni Rivolta
Miranda Robbins
Heather Roberge
Nicholas Robertson
Peter Robson
Ingeborg Rocker
Richard Roediger
Luis Rofriguez
Christian Rogner
Luis Rojo
Joseph Rosa
Louise Rosa
Richard Rosson
Shari Rotella
Lindy Roy
Michael Rubin
David Ruzicka
Leslie Ryan

Claire Sà
Patrick Salomon
Ashraf Sami Abdala
James Samuelson
Inigo Rodriguez San
    Pedro
Antonio Sanmartin
Mario Santin
Andy Saunders
David Schatzle
Mark Schendal
Nicholaus Scheper
Florian Scheytt
Dagmar Schimkus
Nicole Schindler
Michael Schmidt
Olaf Schmidt
Wiebke Schneider
Stephan Schoeller
Rainer Scholz
Joe Schott
James Schriefer
Oliver Schütte
Michael Schuyler
Nina Schweiger
Chiara Scortecci
Jerome Scott
Mark Searls
Raquel Sendra
John Seppanen
QS Serafijn
Setu Shah
Wei Wei Shannon
Begona Fernandez
    Shaw
Jody Sheldon
Kuo-Chien Shen
Tadao Shimitzu
David Shultis
Julie Shurtz
Scott Sickeler
Stefan Siebrecht
Maria Sieira
Adam Silver
Marcin Skolimowski
Tod Slaboden
Jeff Smith
Leslie Smith
Barry Smyth
Sergio Socolovsky
Massimo Sodini
Giovanni Soleti
Angelika Solleder
Paul Sorum
Lucy Sosa
Emanuel Sousa
Michael Speaks
Madison Spencer
Theodor Spyropoulos
Cordula Stach
Barry Stedman
Lucas Steiner
Ted Steinmann
Jon Stephens
Andrea Stipa
Urban Stirnberg
Bettina Stolting
Marc Stotzer

Stephanie Streich
Susanne Sturm
Michael Su
Matthias Suchert
Kathleen Sullivan
Yakob Sutanto
Masahiro Suzuki
David Swanson
Jane Tai
Kylene Tan
Minako Tanaka
Joseph Tanney
Kim Tanzer
Ilka Tarkkanen
Mati Teiblum
Onur Teke
Peter Thaler
Anne Theismeinn
Sabine Thiel
Thor Thors
Lucien Tinga
Alyssa Tomasi
Lisa Toms
H.K. Tran
David Trautman
Wolf von Trotha
Richard Trott
Wolfgang Tschapeller
Martin Ulliana
Hakan Buke Uras
Henry Urbach
Weiland Vajen
Magdalena Vaksanovic
Erin Vali
Federica Vannucchi
Raquel Vasallo
Nicholas Vaucher
Pascal Vauclair
Nicolas Vernoux
Irina Verona
Florencia Vetcher
Maximo Victoria
Andres Viditz-Ward
Mauricio Virgens
Selim Vural
Benjamin Wade
Marcus Wallner
Joseph Walter
Mark Wamble
Janine Washington
Khalid Watson
Benjamin Wayne
Karen Weber
Lois Weinthal
Ian Weisse
Robert Wetzels
Matthew White
Sarah Whiting
Alexander Wiedemann
Jim Wilson
Markus Wings
Brad Winkeljohn
Jason Winstanley
Marcus Witta
Colby Wong
Susan Wong
Chia Fang Wu
Corinna Wydler

Yujiro Yamasaki
Evan Yassy
Faruk Yorgancioglu
Gilly Youner
Leslie Young
David Youse
Harry Zernike
Tao Zhu
Katinka Zlonicky
Oliver Zorn
Guido Zuliani
Martina Zurmuehle